MEDICAL GROUP MANAGEMENT

Strategies for Enhancing Performance

MEDICAL GROUP
MANAGEMENT
Strategies for Enhancing
Performance

Steven T. Valentine, MPA
Laura P. Jacobs, MPH
The Camden Group

Vienna, Virginia

ʍ
MANAGEMENTCONCEPTS

8230 Leesburg Pike, Suite 800
Vienna, VA 22182
(703) 790-9595
Fax: (703) 790-1371
www.managementconcepts.com

Printed in the United States of America

Library of Congress Cataloging-in-Publication Data

Valentine, Steven T.
  Medical group management : strategies for enhancing performance / Steven T. Valenetine, Laura P. Jacobs.
      p. cm
  Includes bibliographical references and index.
  ISBN 1-56726-102-7 (hbk.)
    1. Group medical practice--United States. 2. Group medical practice --United States--Management. I. Jacobs, Laura P., 1956- II. Title.

  R729.5G6 V35 2001
  610'.65--dc21

                                                                2001030776

TABLE OF CONTENTS

CHAPTER 5
Designing an Effective Compensation Plan 101
Laura P. Jacobs, MPH

CHAPTER 6
Improving Provider Productivity 135
Mary J. Witt, MSW

CHAPTER 7
Managing Costs in Today's Environment 151
Mary J. Witt, MSW

CHAPTER 8
Keeping a Focus on Quality and Service 171
Karen E. Dunbar, MBA, MHS
Benjamin S. Snyder, MPA, FACMPE

CHAPTER 9
Effective Staffing: What Does It Take?

Karen E. Dunbar, MBA, MHS
Benjamin S. Snyder, MPA, FACMPE

CHAPTER 10
Accounts Receivable Management

Robin G. Wallace
Karen E. Dunbar, MBA, MHS

CHAPTER 11
Managed Care and Capitation: Strategies for Success

Michael E. Harris, MS
Laura P. Jacobs, MPH

CHAPTER 12
Enhancing and Finding New Sources of Revenue

Benjamin S. Snyder, MPA, FACMPE

FOREWORD

Medical Group Management: Strategies for Enhancing Performance is a book that should be read and understood by physicians and administrators dedicated to creating successful health care delivery systems. Today we find ourselves at a significant juncture in medical practice, when optimal business practices will determine the winners and losers among medical groups. Preserving the enduring and critical relationship between doctors and their patients now depends more than ever on careful strategic planning and execution by medical management.

It has been estimated that approximately 80 percent of medical groups in California, and a majority of groups nationwide, are currently experiencing severe financial challenges. Premium decreases, combined with the constraints of Medicare reimbursement dictated by the Balanced Budget Act of 1997 and health plans, have outpaced productivity and performance gains and led to a crisis in medical group stability never experienced before by medical group management. As the Chief Executive Officer of HealthCare Partners Medical Group, one of the largest medical groups, independent practice associations (IPAs), and management services organizations in California, I strongly support the disciplined approach outlined in *Medical Group Management*. Important and timely, this critical "how-to" book is a useful guide in these uncertain times.

HealthCare Partners has succeeded by designing efficient practice management systems. Combining effective management processes with effective medical leadership, performance measurement, and feedback—all focused on a singular mission of high-quality, high-satisfaction, value-driven care—takes effort and commitment. But the payoff is measured in healthier patients, solvent organizations, and enthusiastic, committed physicians and staff.

Medical Group Management: Strategies for Enhancing Performance describes many of the difficulties that HealthCare Partners Medical Group has experienced over the past four years and many of the techniques that we used to reinforce our medical group practice and IPAs. This book is organized to lead your thinking through the various elements of a performance improvement process that describe the importance of developing rigorous strategic plans. It tackles the basic challenge: How do you set workable revenue and cost projections in a fee-for-service or capitated practice environment where declining premiums and cuts to Medicare and Medicaid hold down revenue, while rapidly escalating outside vendor costs, new technology, and patient expectations raise expenses? Those of us who have been through a performance improvement process recognize that the delivery of medical services is a business requiring disciplined management techniques. Good intentions are not enough.

Physician practices are not capable of managing real growth until their operational systems and processes are well defined, understood, and expandable. Additionally, overall cost structures must be able to flex with decreasing revenues. Many groups have tried to expand rapidly, under the illusion that growth by mergers and acquisitions could protect them from rising costs during a period of constrained revenue. Several physician practices and medical management groups have engaged in unplanned growth, spelling the end of their businesses. The lessons we should learn from these failures are that (1) size does not compensate for ineffective management systems, and (2) an organizational culture must embrace a disciplined approach.

I recommend this book to you. It contains a straightforward explanation of what it takes to make it in the rough-and-tumble business of medical group practice today. *Medical Group Management: Strategies for Enhancing Performance* is in a class by itself, a powerful combination of "how-to" and "why" that speaks the hard truth about the business of medical group management. Ultimately, the survival of medical groups and IPAs is critical if we are to preserve an accountable system of health care delivery. The accountability for high-quality, value-driven care belongs at the doctor/patient level. Only through systems of care successfully run by a team of physicians and administrators within an organized medical group practice can we hope to obtain the vision of quality, affordable care, and improved population health.

Robert Margolis, MD, CEO
HealthCare Partners Medical Group

PREFACE

Medical groups have perhaps never before faced such daunting challenges as they do today. The uncertainty of the future, combined with the economic pressures of the present, creates an atmosphere that is difficult for medical group administrators and physicians alike. This book provides a practical guide for dealing with the full range of issues—from strategic planning to staffing—faced by medical group leaders. It is intended to support performance improvement activities for medical groups, regardless of their current position: It can be used to turn around groups in crisis, or just to sharpen performance. Medical group CEOs, board members, department managers, and physicians, as well as leaders in integrated delivery systems, will benefit from the practical approach this book takes.

This book was compiled by individuals with many years of hands-on experience in physician organizations throughout the United States. As a result, it is full of specific examples and "take away" tools intended to be put to use in medical practices. Whether it's planning for the future, designing physician compensation formulas, increasing productivity and efficiency, improving reimbursement, selecting information systems, or enhancing quality and patient service, *Medical Group Manaagement: Strategies for Enhancing Performance* provides useful information for experienced and new medical group leaders alike.

Steven T. Valentine, MPA
Laura P. Jacobs, MPH

1

LOOKING TO THE FUTURE

Developing Strategic Direction

Laura P. Jacobs, MPH

"What road should I take?" asked Alice.
"Where do you want to go?" asked the cat.
"I don't know," replied Alice.
"Then it won't matter what road you take," answered the cat.
— Lewis Carroll, Alice in Wonderland

In light of the daily challenges they face, it is not surprising that medical group leaders often maintain a short-term focus. This focus is dictated largely by necessity, but unless short-term actions are based within a context of a common vision and strategy, costly missteps can occur. Moreover, focusing on the short term can cloud the organization's sense of long-term commitment. So while it may seem to be a distraction to review strategic direction as part of a performance improvement process, it ultimately may be one of the most important steps a medical group can take to ensure a successful result.

Strategic planning is particularly important in medical groups today: Many of the environmental factors that caused medical groups to pursue various strategies in the past (for example, hospital and physician acquisition, physician practice management—PPM—involvement, geographic expansion, and capitation) may be very different in the current climate. One of the most difficult challenges that medical groups struggle with is the uncertainty of future trends. It is not clear what economic structure will emerge as the dominant reimbursement mechanism within the next five to ten years. However, it is critical that physician organizations clarify their expectations of the future and their role in the local health care delivery system before embarking on a formal performance improvement effort. Doing so sets the stage for all operational and financial decisions to follow, not to mention pursuit of business development opportunities.

This chapter will review a process for medical group leaders to use in determining and developing strategic direction while ensuring widespread organizational commitment to that strategy. Further, it will provide some tools for analyzing the various strategic alternatives that medical groups often consider.

THE STRATEGIC PLANNING PROCESS

In its purest sense, the strategic planning process is fairly straightforward. Figure 1-1 illustrates the essential steps.

Some review of the strategic position of the organization should be performed annually, particularly given the rapid changes in the health care industry today. However, it may not be necessary to complete an in-depth analysis every year. Many organizations will update the strategic plan annually but perform a rigorous review every three years.

Typically, the leadership of the organization drives the strategic planning process. For most medical groups, this means that the board of directors in larger groups or the physicians in smaller groups—in conjunction with administrative leadership—lead this process. During certain phases, particularly the situation assessment and later in the development of action plans, it will be useful to involve others throughout the organization to provide insight into current issues facing the group. The external assessment will probably require interviews with some of the group's outside constituents as well.

Figure 1-1. Strategic Planning Process

```
┌─────────────────────────────────┐
│                                 │
│     Situation Assessment        │
│                                 │
└─────────────────────────────────┘
                 │
                 ▼
┌─────────────────────────────────┐
│                                 │
│   Mission, Vision, and Values   │
│                                 │
└─────────────────────────────────┘
                 │
                 ▼
┌─────────────────────────────────┐
│                                 │
│      Goals and Strategies       │
│                                 │
└─────────────────────────────────┘
                 │
                 ▼
┌─────────────────────────────────┐
│                                 │
│          Action Plan            │
│                                 │
└─────────────────────────────────┘
```

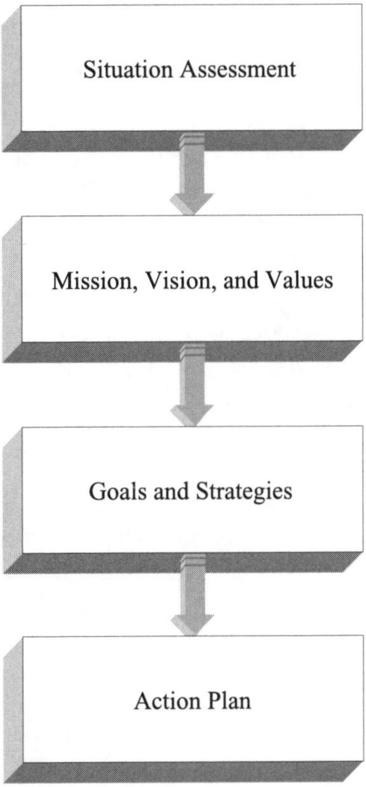

The discussion and determination of the organization's goals and strategies, however, must come from its leadership. This process requires that the governing body and its administrative leadership agree on the future course of the enterprise. It will be an educational process, as well as a clear opportunity for leaders to debate the priorities of the organization. Often this requires at least one or two days in a "retreat" setting to allow full discussion of the issues, and to minimize operational distractions. Once completed, however, uniform acceptance and endorsement of the strategies set forth will be critical. For this reason, while the situation assessment can be completed with internal resources, facilitation of the process often requires outside assistance. This will enable all leaders to participate equally in the debate as well as ensure that the discussions are facilitated objectively.

Situation Assessment

The situation assessment requires the organization to look objectively at its position from both an internal and an external perspective. It can be performed as part of the assessment phase, which begins the improvement process outlined in Chapter 2. As part of a strategic planning process, the external review is emphasized more than it might be under an operational assessment. Figure 1-2 illustrates the components of the situation assessment.

Internal Assessment
As outlined in Chapter 2, an objective review of the internal strengths and weaknesses of the organization is an important first step in determining management's focus. Information will be gathered from a variety of sources, including financial and operational data and interviews

Figure 1-2. Situation Assessment

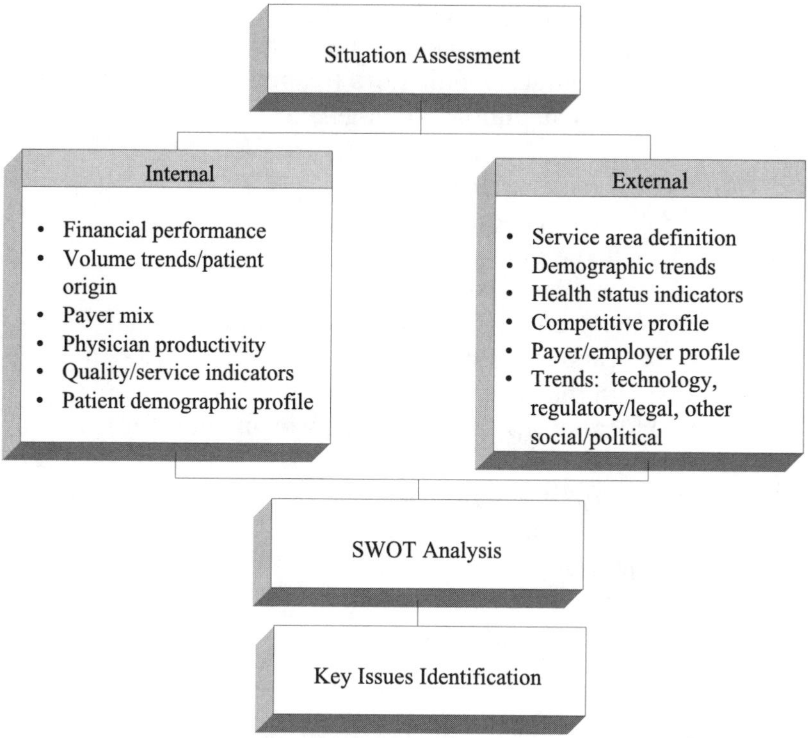

```
                    ┌─────────────────────────────┐
                    │   Situation Assessment      │
                    └─────────────────────────────┘
          ┌──────────────────────┴──────────────────────┐
┌──────────────────────┐              ┌──────────────────────────────┐
│      Internal        │              │          External            │
├──────────────────────┤              ├──────────────────────────────┤
│ • Financial          │              │ • Service area definition    │
│   performance        │              │ • Demographic trends         │
│ • Volume trends/     │              │ • Health status indicators   │
│   patient origin     │              │ • Competitive profile        │
│ • Payer mix          │              │ • Payer/employer profile     │
│ • Physician          │              │ • Trends: technology,        │
│   productivity       │              │   regulatory/legal, other    │
│ • Quality/service    │              │   social/political           │
│   indicators         │              │                              │
│ • Patient            │              │                              │
│   demographic        │              │                              │
│   profile            │              │                              │
└──────────────────────┘              └──────────────────────────────┘
          └──────────────────────┬──────────────────────┘
                    ┌─────────────────────────────┐
                    │      SWOT Analysis          │
                    └─────────────────────────────┘
                    ┌─────────────────────────────┐
                    │  Key Issues Identification   │
                    └─────────────────────────────┘
```

with physicians and managers. A thorough internal assessment will include a review of the following:

Financial performance
- Revenues and expenses in total, as well by department and per unit (per visit, per managed care enrollee)
- Payer mix (HMO, capitated, fee-for-service), PPO, private, workers' compensation, self-pay)
- Cash flow
- Balance sheet analysis and ratios

Operating indicators
- Volume by department/service line
- Staffing ratios
- Physician productivity
- Accounts receivable management performance
- Other operating indicators (claims volume, patient no-shows, scheduling backlogs, etc.)

Quality/service measures
- Patient satisfaction surveys
- Employee/physician surveys
- Disenrollment rates
- Grievance/patient complaint reports
- Malpractice claims experience
- HEDIS measures
- Clinical protocols/quality improvement efforts

Patient demographic profile
- Age/sex/ethnicity
- Patient origin
- Payer mix
- Diagnosis or treatment

Managed care
- Contract status: enrollment, rates, payment types (full capitation vs. primary care capitation, case rates, fee-for-service, etc.)
- Profitability by plan

Marketing/business development initiatives
- Service area definition/patient origin studies
- Surveys performed (awareness/preference)
- Marketing plans by market segment/niche
- Service line expansion plans (procedures, facilities, programs).

This analysis can be performed internally, but it is imperative to analyze and present the data objectively. It is also best if the data can be trended over time, usually three to five years.

External Assessment

Many medical groups do not take the time to assess realistically their position in the marketplace. Depending on the size of the group, this exercise can be fairly simple, or it can be a more rigorous review of the environment. For small groups (10 or fewer physicians), much of the information required may be available through the local medical society or hospital. Hospital planning departments often are excellent sources for demographic, competitor activity, market share, and local market data.

Larger groups may need to compile more primary data to reflect the specific service area and population served by the physician organization. This may include interviews with local insurance brokers, major employers, city/county health or planning officials, and payers in the market. Understanding the plans of local hospitals will also be an important consideration for groups of any size. Table 1-1 provides a list of possible data sources for the external assessment.

An important step before beginning the external assessment is to agree on a clear definition of the medical group's service area. This could be defined by zip codes, or in the case of some specialty services, by larger areas, such as counties or states. Typically, the service area should comprise the location in which at least 75 percent of the patients reside. Once this is determined, information can then be gathered regarding this region. Some of the information to be considered in the external assessment will include:

Demographic profile/trends
- Population size and growth rates by age/sex
- Population density by geographic region
- Ethnicity, age, gender, income, and education
- Physician/population ratio for relevant specialties

Table 1-1
Information Sources for Strategic Planning

Internet
- Brochures, publications, annual reports of hospitals, other local providers
- Government sources
- State, city, county health departments
- District health authorities
- City, county planning departments

Hospital planning departments
- Population, demographics, and mapping databases
- Dow Jones, other publication search services
- Blind telephone calls (pricing information, accepting new patients, services provided)

Trade associations
- American Medical Association
- Medical Group Management Association
- American Medical Group Association
- National, state, and local hospital associations
- National, state, and local health plan/insurance associations
- Business/purchasing coalitions

Health status
- Prevalence and incidence of disease
- Public health initiatives
- Payer initiatives (disease management)
- Community benefit studies (hospitals, United Way, Chamber of Commerce)

Payer profile
- Health plan enrollment and growth by plan type (HMO, POS, PPO, etc.)
- New product introductions planned
- Internet strategies (provider and patient links)
- Broker influence, selection criteria
- Provider contracting strategy (direct contracting, network, capitation, fee-for-service)
- IPA/PHO trends in the market

Competitor profile
- Competing groups within the service area (size, composition, services offered, hours, facilities)
- Competing groups in adjacent service areas
- Map with locations of competing groups
- Hospital, PPM, MSO trends
- Internet strategies

Government trends
- Federal regulations (antitrust, Health Insurance Portability and Accountability Act—HIPAA, fraud, patient bill of rights, Stark) and reimbursement expectations (Medicare)
- State regulations (Medicaid, HMOs, patient bill of rights, State Children's Health Insurance Program—SCHIP) and other licensing trends (mid-level providers, complementary medicine providers, facility licensing, telemedicine, etc.)
- Local (county) actions (indigent, public health initiatives)

External trends
- Technology (biomedical, telemedicine, teleradiology, Internet, pharmaceutical) changes affecting specialties within the group
- Technology changes affecting potential referral sources to the group
- Public opinion/consumer activism regarding health care.

Strengths, Weaknesses, Opportunities, and Threats (SWOT) Analysis

In the process of gathering and analyzing as much available internal and external data as possible, the medical group leadership will have an opportunity to take a critical, yet constructive, review of the organization in light of its mission, vision, and goals. Management or whoever compiled the data can present a summary of the internal and external assessment. This is best accomplished as part of a one- or two-day "retreat," where the governing body and management have ample time to review the data and discuss the findings.

SWOT analysis is a common tool to help participants in the planning process synthesize all of the analysis presented. It is simply a summary of the strengths, weaknesses, opportunities, and threats that will affect the medical group over the next three to five years. Figure 1-3 illustrates a SWOT grid.

Figure 1-3. SWOT Analysis

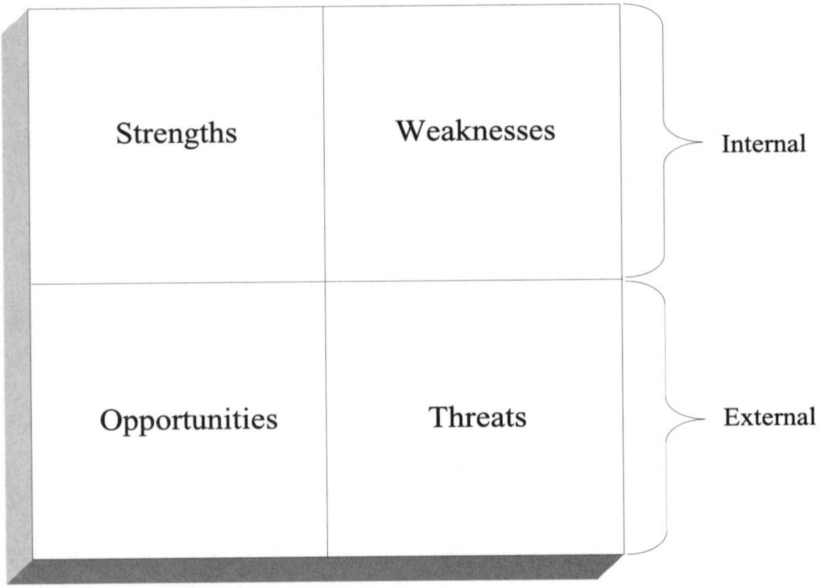

Strengths	Weaknesses	Internal
Opportunities	Threats	External

The most effective way to use this grid is through discussion during the planning retreat. Participants will provide their assessment of each of these components based on what has been presented in the situation assessment. Strengths and weaknesses should be focused on internal factors, while threats are more likely to be from external sources. Opportunities can represent either internal or external factors. After the initial brainstorming session, identify specific strengths and weaknesses that are competitive advantages or disadvantages.

It may be helpful to use the data presented, as compared to "critical success factors," for your organization. For example, the following are some critical success factors for medical groups in the early 21st century:

- Clear authority of the governing body
- Strong internal culture that is unique to the group
- Strong leadership with an efficient decision-making process
- Partnership between management and physicians; authority delegated appropriately
- Clear and consistent communication throughout the organization
- Adaptable organization that embraces change
- Realistic perspective of the group's role in the market
- Financial performance that allows reinvestment in the group
- Commitment to quality and superior service throughout the organization.

This can be an excellent opportunity for participants to voice opinions about the medical group's market position. The situation assessment should provide a basis for most of the opinions. However, be prepared for emotional factors to be raised during this discussion, particularly if it is the first opportunity the leadership has had to identify issues in a group setting. The facilitator must use careful judgment about including emotional or anecdotal input at this stage. Typically, it should be minimized, using the facts presented in the situation assessment to drive the discussion vis-á-vis the mission, vision, and goals.

Key Issues Identification

The SWOT analysis allows the leadership to synthesize information into a relatively concise summary of the issues. However, it is still often a long list of factors that is difficult to respond to in a focused way. Therefore, the next step in the situation assessment review is to force the retreat participants to identify the most important issues identified in the SWOT analysis.

This can be accomplished by first listing 10-15 important issues, which should be driven by the SWOT analysis, with an emphasis on the group's competitive position. From this list, the participants should then be asked to prioritize those issues again. Conjoint analysis (forced ranking by comparing each issue to all other issues) or having all participants list their top three choices can achieve this prioritization. Another option is to use computerized systems, such as the OptionFinder™, which allow participants to vote anonymously, producing a visual display of the results in real time. Through this exercise, the participants will have synthesized a vast array of data into the most critical issues for the medical group to address in the development of goals and strategies.

Mission, Vision, and Values

Much is written about the importance of establishing a clear mission and vision for the organization. In most medical groups, the mission is often unstated but assumed to be on the order of "to improve the health of our patients through compassion and the science of medicine." Or, if it is stated, it is a long-winded, multi-sentence elaboration on this theme that is difficult to comprehend, let alone remember. Further, there is often confusion between the mission and the vision.

The *mission* statement is a concise definition of the primary purpose for which the organization exists. This should be long-lasting and able to withstand the ups and downs of health care trends and outside influences. It may change over time, and it should be reviewed as part of the strategic planning process; however, it is more likely to be relatively constant. It should be a fairly broad statement identifying the essential "business" of the organization. The best mission statements are those that are short, concise, and easily repeated by employees. Posting the mission statement throughout the group's facility can serve as a reminder to all.

The *vision* statement should provide more direction and describe the kind of organization the medical group wants to be now and in the future. It is a "visual" statement of an overarching goal for the enterprise. The following is a vision statement for HealthCare Partners, a large multi-specialty medical group in Southern California:

HealthCare Partners is dedicated to the well-being and the respectful compassionate healing of our patients and our communities. As a physician-led organization, we will achieve this vision by:

- *Partnering with our patients to excel in the healing arts*
- *Partnering with our staff to continually improve our systems and services and to build a work environment grounded in dignity, trust, accountability, and collaborative teamwork*

> • *Partnering with our clients and customers to provide the best value in health care and to be a recognized leader in our industry*
> • *Partnering with our community to work for the common good.*[1]

This statement actually incorporates the medical group's mission: "...dedicated to the well-being and the respectful compassionate healing of our patients and our communities." It also incorporates some of the values of the organization through its focus on partnering.

Values are seldom articulated by medical groups but are a fundamental aspect of the culture of the group and the way it operates. A discussion of the organization's values can be a healthy part of a strategic planning retreat. It will provide the leaders with an opportunity to express what they want the values to be, as opposed to what may be exhibited at the present time. Table 1-2 presents a tool for engaging leaders in a healthy discussion. It is also a useful exercise during a merger or joint venture discussion, forcing participants to voice expectations or feelings that they may not otherwise state. The ensuing discussion could help to avoid a future "culture clash."

[1] HealthCare Partners Medical Group. *Strategic Plan 2000-2002*, n.d.

Table 1-2
Shared Values Tradeoffs

Assessing and determining the core values of an organization is a fundamental part of developing a strategic vision. The purpose of the following exercise is to measure your personal perceptions regarding the organization's core values. For each category below, please mark an "X" at the point that best describes our group culture and values between the two styles listed. Mark with an "O" where you would *like* it to be:

Group Decision-making		
Long-term focus	1 2 3 4 5 6 7	Short-term focus
Measured	1 2 3 4 5 6 7	Spontaneous
Democratic	1 2 3 4 5 6 7	Autocratic
Analytical	1 2 3 4 5 6 7	Intuitive

Group Operating Style		
Uniform policies	1 2 3 4 5 6 7	Individualized policies
Patient convenience	1 2 3 4 5 6 7	Physician convenience
Personalized care	1 2 3 4 5 6 7	Efficient care
Department/location focused	1 2 3 4 5 6 7	Group focused
Reward performance	1 2 3 4 5 6 7	Reward tenure

Strategic Planning		
Growth	1 2 3 4 5 6 7	Stability
Integration	1 2 3 4 5 6 7	Independence
Proactive	1 2 3 4 5 6 7	Opportunistic/Reactive
Short-term financial gain	1 2 3 4 5 6 7	Long-term value
Innovative	1 2 3 4 5 6 7	Conservative

Business Development		
Expand geographic presence	1 2 3 4 5 6 7	Expand range of services
Maximize fees	1 2 3 4 5 6 7	Maximize volume
Add services	1 2 3 4 5 6 7	Reduce costs
Add physicians	1 2 3 4 5 6 7	Maximize productivity
Pursue managed care	1 2 3 4 5 6 7	Avoid managed care

Goals and Strategies

The goals and strategies are the core of the strategic plan and will typically chart the course of the organization for the next two to three years. The goals will be created from the key issues articulated during the situation assessment. Through the prioritization process, no more than five key issues should have been identified that can be restated into goals for the organization. For example, HealthCare Partners identified the following four key areas in which to establish goals:[2]

- **Clinical performance:** Provide superior patient care and service
- **Financial performance:** Diversify and increase profitable revenue streams
- **Market development:** Grow patient base
- **Business and clinical systems:** Reduce variability in utilization and expenses by applying best practices and process improvement.

In each of these areas, measurable objectives should be established to help guide management actions and provide milestones for achievement. To the extent possible, they should be quantifiable and exhibit a "stretch" for the organization to achieve over a two-to-three-year period.

The strategies will provide the mechanisms to achieve the goals. In other words, what initiatives will the organization pursue to achieve the goals and the objectives as outlined? During a retreat process, it is most helpful to allow the participants to brainstorm. If a more structured discussion is desired, a framework of discussion questions can be provided. Table 1-3 provides a sample discussion guide for this purpose.

[2] HealthCare Partners Medical Group. *Strategic Plan 2000-2002*, n.d.

Table 1-3
Medical Group Development
Strategic Direction
Discussion Guide

Group Development

1. Discuss the group's priorities now (Year 1) and in future years (Years 2–5) with respect to methods and strategies for increasing group size.

Aggressive growth (quantify)	Measured growth (quantify)
Growth by recruitment	Growth by absorption
Primary care	Specialty services
New sites	Existing sites

Business Development

2. How will the group expand its patient base?

Pursue managed care	Focus on fee-for-service market
Utilize existing IPA	Contract directly with payers
Cooperative marketing with payers	Direct marketing to patients
High touch (service)	Aggressive promotion
Focus on internal retention and referral	External focus/new markets

3. What pricing strategies will be utilized?

Charge whatever market will bear (low fees, high volume)	Competitive pricing (high fees, low volume)
Standardized fees	Fees dependent on location

4. Consider the following operational issues that affect patient convenience and operating costs.

Extended hours:
      Schedule by office   Centralize urgent care

Ancillary services:
      Basic services at most sites Centralize all ancillary services

      Outsource all ancillary services   Develop group (centralized) services

Once the governing body identifies the strategies, management and physician leadership can then review the ideas and analyze their feasibility, which the governing body can review at a later date. Once the strategies are defined, they form the basis for management and department leaders to develop their action plans.

Action Plan

Developing specific action plans and smaller, focused task forces to take on some of the strategies may often be useful in larger groups. This will allow more participants throughout the organization to develop a sense of "ownership" in the strategic plan. It will also ensure that the strategic plan is a "living" document—one that truly works as a management tool, converting board direction to implementation. Action plans will likely be more short-term in nature, providing annual objectives for managers throughout the medical group.

EVALUATING STRATEGIC ALTERNATIVES

During a financial crisis, medical groups may wish to consider options other than an internal improvement effort. That is, a financial crisis or changes in the external marketplace may precipitate consideration of other options for the group. This could include practice sale, merger, joint venture, or other affiliation arrangements. When considering these alternatives, the governing body should review the following questions frankly:

1. *Do we have the necessary resources and the stamina to produce the necessary results?* As described throughout this book, an improvement process requires an enormous commitment by the leaders of the organization to make the difficult decisions required to reverse negative financial trends. Because it may take 12-18 months to achieve consistently positive financial results, the organization must assess its

cash flow and ability to sustain itself in the short-term. Depending on the gravity of the situation, the answers to these questions may dictate more drastic action, including sale or bankruptcy protection.

2. *Are there organizations with which we would consider partnering to facilitate the medical group's improved performance?* This could include other medical groups in the community that may have strong management capabilities or other strengths that complement the group's strengths and weaknesses. This is a time for the group to be brutally honest with itself regarding its own strengths and weaknesses. If there is a vacuum of leadership or management capabilities, it may be necessary to obtain them externally. If a relationship with another medical group isn't an option, firms that provide interim management or other management services may be considered.

3. *What role might a hospital or other health care entity play?* Many groups today are living through transitions from hospital or PPM ownership or management. However, there continue to be integrated delivery systems that seek to strengthen their relationships with medical groups. This may not mean acquisition but could include other joint venture relationships or the provision of certain management services. While many of the multi-specialty PPM companies have fragmented or gone out of business, there remain certain specialty-focused PPMs that may provide the needed capital resources to effect the required improvement in financial performance. This may be particularly true in capital-intensive specialties such as orthopedics and oncology. Given the experience of many medical groups with these options, however, the impact on the group's culture and sense of commitment that this type of relationship may have should be carefully and thoroughly assessed. It should be recognized that whatever operational problems exist will not vanish simply because someone else takes on management responsibilities.

4. *Can we access additional sources of revenue through a joint venture arrangement?* Many medical groups are reconsidering joint venture arrangements (surgery centers, imaging centers, or complementary medicine) as an option to obtain new sources of revenue while sharing the risk and financial investment required. These can be viable initiatives, but the following considerations must be addressed:

- Do we share the same business goals with our prospective partners?
- Who has the proven capabilities to operate the venture? Will the other party cede enough operating control to ensure success?
- How will major decisions be made (additional investment, merger, sale, or expansion)?
- How does this joint venture relate to the medical group's core business? Is it complementary, or is it merely a distraction?
- What does the business plan call for in terms of investment, and what are the expected returns? What are the risks of the returns not being realized? What is the group's sensitivity and ability to handle risk?

5. *Short of dissolution or bankruptcy, is the sale of the practice the only option?* The preference of most groups is to try to stay together, even if an internal turnaround doesn't appear likely. This may mean that a sale is the only option. In the event of a potential sale, the following, at a minimum, should be considered:

- How will the group be valued? What will the group's consideration be for its value: equity, cash, debt, or a combination?
- What is the operating style and culture of the acquiring company? How will it mesh with that of the medical group's?

- What are the acquirer's expectations of the purchase? Be sure that the acquirer's goals are compatible with those of the group.
- Are the group's expectations of the sale realistic? Remember that there is no panacea for a medical group with significant financial and/or operational problems. Any major improvement effort, whether or not it is internally solved, is a difficult process that will involve a certain amount of pain.

AVOIDING THE TRAPS

The strategic planning process is a positive exercise to engage the entire organization toward a successful future. To be effective, however, the process must be grounded in fact. There is a difference between creating a vision for the organization and a fantasy of what it might be. Particularly when faced with today's challenges, there is a heightened need for facing up to the harsh reality of the weaknesses that must be overcome. At the same time, it is also an opportunity to recognize the strengths that can be used to carry the organization forward.

The following are seven traps of strategic planning:[3]

1. Failing to recognize and understand events and changing conditions in your environment
2. Basing conclusions and strategic direction on a flawed set of assumptions
3. Pursuing a strategic direction that fails to create or sustain a long-term competitive advantage
4. Diversifying for all the wrong reasons
5. Failing to structure and implement mechanisms to ensure the coordination of processes and key functions across organizational boundaries
6. Setting arbitrary and inflexible goals and implementing a system of controls that fails to achieve a balance among culture, rewards, and boundaries

[3] Adapted from Joseph C. Picken and Gregory G. Dess. *INC,* November 1996.

7. Failing to provide leadership essential to the successful implementation of strategic change.

Strategic thinking is an important aspect of the improvement process and is often necessary to change the medical group's strategic direction before focusing on internal issues that may be affecting its financial position. A thorough strategic planning process will ensure that all aspects of the group's performance, both internal and external, are being considered. Furthermore, it identifies long-term direction that will still be applicable when financial performance improves. As a fundamental management function, strategic planning is paramount in ensuring a long-lasting, positive result.

2

IMPROVING OPERATIONAL PERFORMANCE
A Process That Works
Mary J. Witt, MSW

While it is easy to know when a medical group is in trouble, it is not always clear what dynamics created the situation or what the solution is. Thus, it is crucial that a thorough assessment of the practice be conducted before any improvement effort begins. This chapter describes the process of developing and implementing a successful performance improvement plan. We also review the challenges and identify strategies for achieving success.

MEDICAL GROUP SUCCESS FACTORS

Before examining the assessment process, it is important to remember the critical requirements of a successful medical group because they also drive the analysis of the practice. Figure 2-1 shows these all-important building blocks for success.

Figure 2-1. Medical Group Building Blocks For Success

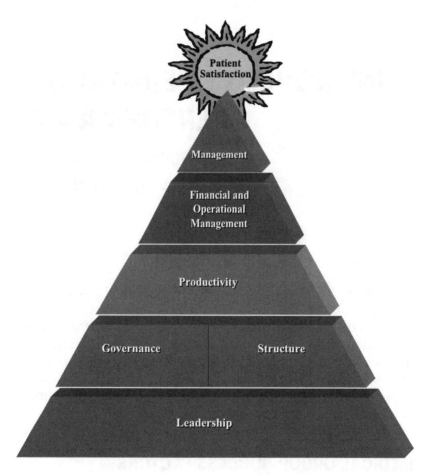

The foundation of a sound medical group starts with strong medical and lay leadership. These leaders must have a vision and be able to inspire that vision in others. At the same time, they must have the foresight to develop an effective organizational and governance structure.

Physician productivity creates the revenue stream to support the group, and the compensation plan should create incentives for and reward productivity. Strong operational and financial management provides the environment in which to be successful. Effective care management ensures quality patient care, and the ultimate success is satisfied patients. Generally, when a medical group is working to improve performance, each of these areas will require attention. The degree to which specific areas receive focus depends on the organization and its particular situation.

THE PERFORMANCE IMPROVEMENT PROCESS

The process of improving performance consists of three distinct phases: assessment, planning, and implementation. Put another way, the phases can be characterized as "Ready, Set, Go," as shown in Figure 2-2.

Figure 2-2. Performance Improvement Process

Each step must be carefully completed to ensure that performance improves. Often the impulse is to assume that the problems are well known and that, therefore, the first phase is not necessary. However, a hastily developed recovery plan can often lead to missed opportunities. Steps 1 and 2 not only confirm understanding of the issues but are also critical to achieving buy-in from all important constituencies. Also, it is not unusual to identify additional issues that can significantly affect the success of the process during this step. Step 2 is necessary because it identifies the goals for the improvement effort and, thus, drives development of the performance improvement plan itself.

Step 1: Collect Data

This step requires intensive review of data, multiple interviews, observation, and analysis. It may require outside assistance to ensure objectivity (see Figure 2-3).

Figure 2-3. Data Collection

Data
- Provider mix
- Staffing
- Operational performance
- Financial performance
- Competition
- Payer mix
- Patient satisfaction

Interviews
- Organizational capabilities
- Leadership
- Communication/reporting
- Group culture
- Sense of involvement/morale

Observations
- Work flow processes
- Policies and procedures
- Efficiency and effectiveness
- Decentralized vs. centralized

This first step requires key data elements for analysis. Data requirements are based on the critical drivers of medical group success and come from the success factors identified in Figure 2-1. Data are collected from all facets of the organization and cover all major processes.

Table 2-1 lists critical items that must be gathered for analysis. While various reports will provide much of the information, the interviews and observation will provide a context in which to understand and validate the numbers.

Table 2-1. Key Data Elements

Category	Data Element
Providers	• Composition • Location • Productivity • Compensation • Governance/leadership • Turnover
Staffing	• Number • Skill mix • Expense • Turnover
Operations	• Clinic hours • MIS • Policies/procedures • Processes • Efficiency • Performance standards by department
Management	• Organizational structure • Capabilities • Communication/reporting • Accountability • Leadership
Financial Performance	• Revenue/expenses (detail/trends) • Accounts receivable • Materials management
Care Management	• Medical records • Quality review • Resource management • Medical costs
Patient Satisfaction	• Surveys • Complaints

It is possible that some information requested may not be readily available. In these cases, the analysis should proceed without the data, recognizing that this may create gaps in the analysis. The fact that certain key elements are unavailable could be a factor contributing to the poor performance of the group and can be addressed in the implementation plan.

However, numbers alone cannot provide the complete picture because they do not describe human interactions and reactions, nor do they detail the processes that drive the numbers. Therefore, personal interviews with physicians, mid-level providers, management, and staff are another critical component of the assessment process. They can identify leadership, organizational, and procedural issues affecting performance. They also provide an opportunity for participants to share their insights and, more importantly, facilitate their involvement in the search for solutions. Starting with an inclusive approach in the data-gathering stage facilitates buy-in by all key parties for the performance improvement action plan. This can also be accomplished through staff, physician, and patient focus groups.

At the same time, however, it is important to avoid old or anecdotal information that interviewees may provide. While old information is useful in the context that it has become part of group lore and influences the behavior of many in the group, anecdotal information is generally not helpful unless there is a pattern of similar examples that are validated by multiple parties.

On-site observation provides the opportunity to validate findings from data analysis and interviews. It also assists in assessing the effectiveness of work flow processes and existing procedures and policies. It can identify organizational roadblocks to efficiency and effectiveness.

Step 2: Analyze and Identify Performance Targets

Analysis can begin as soon as information is available. In fact, it is important that analysis of the numbers precede interviews and observation so that interviews and observation time can be focused appropriately. The analysis involves comparison or benchmarking of group performance to internal goals and objectives as well as industry standards. (For a thorough discussion of the benchmarking process and setting of performance targets, see Chapter 4.)
The analysis process is critical to the performance improvement process because it provides the foundation for development of the implementation plan. Identifying the negative variances makes it possible to set new targets that will turn the group around. Targets will focus on leadership, governance and organizational structure, productivity, and financial/operational/care management. Table 2-2 identifies potential target areas.

When establishing targets, it is important to consider both industry benchmarks and the group's history. If there are significant variances from industry benchmarks, creating short-term (3 month), intermediate (6 month), and long-term (12-18 month) targets might be necessary to reach industry standards. Not only does this help make the long-term goal appear achievable, but it creates opportunities for success along the way.

To achieve long-term success, it is crucial that all key constituencies be involved in the development of performance targets. Industry standards and the group's performance as compared to those standards should be shared with both staff and physicians. They can see how others are performing and understand what it takes to survive in today's environment. As performance targets are developed, they should be shared with key physicians and staff to test feasibility and gain support for them.

Table 2-2. Potential Target Areas

Category	Target
Providers	• Visits, relative value units (RVUs), dollars • Accessibility/scheduling • Citizenship/performance standards • Governance/leadership
Staffing	• Salary/benefit expense • Full-time equivalents (FTEs)/provider • Hours worked/unit of service
Operations	• Call abandonment rate/hold times • Time spent by patient at visit • Staff and provider performance standards • Patient complaints
Management	• Strategic vision/goals • Organizational structure • Communication • Data availability (reports)
Financial Performance	• Profit/loss for organization and by site/department • Collection rate • Days in accounts receivable (A/R) • A/R over 90 days • Managed care contracts and rates
Care Management	• Patient complaints • Risk management indicators • Quality measures • Medical costs • Health plan audit results

Step 3: Create the Performance Improvement Plan

Performance issues are generally related to the following:

- Lack of clearly defined goals, objectives, and performance standards
- Lack of leadership

- Physician productivity/accessibility
- Poor accounts receivable management and financial processes
- Inefficient work flow processes and procedures
- Lack of staff knowledge and skill sets.

These issues affect all facets of the organization. Therefore, improvement efforts will likely affect everyone in the medical group. As in the first phase, physicians and staff should be involved in development of the action plan; if they already agree with the targets, it will be much easier for them to help identify what must be done to achieve them.

Given the issues, action plans generally focus on the following areas: physician leadership/compensation, organizational structure/accountabilities, and operational/financial management. The action plan must be specific so that everyone understands what steps need to be accomplished. In addition, it should include time frames and responsibilities, as well as set priorities. It cannot avoid the difficult decisions. Trying to do so impairs the credibility of the plan. Therefore, the tough actions should be undertaken at the beginning to demonstrate the organization's seriousness and commitment to the change process.

The action plan also should include the identification of milestone events—those that result in accomplishing a critical task or target. These milestone events then become opportunities to celebrate. Turning an organization around is a challenging process that is stressful for everyone. The opportunities to celebrate and feel successful reinforce the momentum required to make it to the top.

The initial action plan does not need to include how each step will be accomplished because it is important that staff and physicians be involved in defining the "how." They are the ones, in the end, who must accomplish the task. This means that authority should be appropriately delegated. Staff may already know what and how something should be changed. However, it is unrealistic to expect that all solutions will be self-evident, especially if lack of skill or knowledge is contributing to the poor performance. Therefore, it is critical that resources be available to assist them. It can be helpful to have others review the procedures, even if physicians and staff are certain about their approach. Review by others can ensure that the impact on the organization as a whole is considered so that there are no negative ramifications elsewhere.

In some cases, a reengineering process will be required, and it must involve an interdisciplinary team to identify the solutions. Process improvement/quality improvement methodologies are helpful here to guide the process.

Once the action plan is finalized, it should be presented to all members of the organization so they know what will be required of everyone to achieve success. The presentation should paint the vision of a successful organization and then focus on what needs to be done, why it needs to be done, and who should do it. When reviewing the plan, it is important for leaders to appear confident that it can be accomplished and enthusiastic about the changes that will be required. Implementation should begin immediately after these presentations occur so that momentum is not lost.

Step 4: Project the Financial Impact

As a crucial part of the planning process, it is necessary to understand the financial impact of the plan both from an implementation cost standpoint, as well as in terms of the immediate and long-term financial performance of the group. It obviously makes little sense to begin a reorganization if the group still loses money in the end. The implementation plan should identify the financial impact of the action. This may include:

- Expense reduction (staff, facilities, supplies, services)
- Revenue enhancement (collection improvements, managed care contracts, new services, increased productivity, retail business-cash not tied to insurance)
- Resources required (capital, outside assistance, space, staff, etc.).

To summarize these impacts, it is useful to prepare a financial table like that in Table 2-3 to demonstrate the overall financial results.

Table 2-3. Financial Impact

INCOME STATEMENT DATA	FYE 1998	Budget 1999	Plan Estimated Impact	Revised 1999 [1]	FYE 1998	Budget 1999	Revised 1999 [1]
Revenue:							
Net Revenue	$6,920,660	$8,950,099	$170,700	$9,120,799	100.0%	100.0%	100.0%
Operating Expenses:							
Provider Compensation	4,358,315	5,724,085	0	5,724,085	63.0%	64.0%	62.8%
Employee Salary	1,777,417	1,906,487	(105,900)	1,800,587	25.7%	21.3%	19.7%
Employee Benefits	290,210	366,763	0	366,763	4.2%	4.1%	4.0%
Building Rent	217,731	232,967	(102,000)	130,967	3.1%	2.6%	1.4%
Other Professional Expenses	23,162	20,149	0	20,149	0.3%	0.2%	0.2%
Legal and Accounting	12,584	10,000	0	10,000	0.2%	0.1%	0.1%
Leased Equipment	172,205	175,714	0	175,714	2.5%	2.0%	1.9%
Facility Costs	190,182	188,417	0	188,417	2.7%	2.1%	2.1%
General and Administrative	408,646	450,171	0	450,171	5.9%	5.0%	4.9%
Total Operating Expenses	7,450,452	9,074,753	(207,900)	8,866,853	107.7%	101.4%	97.2%
Earnings Before Depreciation, Interest, Taxes and Amortization	(529,792)	(124,653)	378,600	253,947	-7.7%	-1.4%	2.8%
Other Expenses							
Interest (Income)	0	0	0	0	0.0%	0.0%	0.0%
Interest Expense	109,726	126,875	0	126,875	1.6%	1.4%	1.4%
Depreciation	105,435	111,572	0	111,572	1.5%	1.2%	1.2%
Total Other Expenses	215,161	238,447	-	238,447	3.1%	2.7%	2.6%
Earnings before Taxes	($744,953)	($363,100)	$378,600	$15,500	-10.8%	-4.1%	0.2%

[1] Includes implementation plan cost savings assumptions

Source: The Camden Group

Table 2-3 compares previous revenue and expenses, current budget, and the estimated impact on current budget. It is a simple way of documenting targeted changes in revenue and expenses. By incorporating the estimated change column on monthly financial reports, tracking progress toward the projected targets for expenses and revenue becomes easy.

In this example, an assessment of Top Quality Medical Group identified two areas requiring changes. Because of poor controls, the group was not capturing all charges related to services and supplies provided by nursing staff. By implementing a number of process changes, it was estimated that an additional $170,000 in net revenue could be generated, as shown in the column titled "Plan Estimated Impact." At the same time, it was identified that the in-office laboratory was losing money. Through reorganization of lab staff and renegotiating the amount of space leased, it was estimated that $207,900 could be saved.

Step 5: Implement the Plan

Once the goals are established and the action plan is in place, it is time to implement the plan.

After implementation begins, progress must continue to be monitored. This creates accountability and provides the opportunity to respond quickly if problems occur with implementation or if performance targets require modification.

It also is important that staff and physicians are updated regularly about progress in achieving the identified goals. If there is no feedback, staff and physicians may perceive that the crisis is over or that the performance improvement plan lacks importance in the day-to-day world. It also is difficult to maintain momentum or enthusiasm for the monumental changes generally required if people cannot see that progress is being made. Last, there is no opportunity to celebrate those milestone events if results are not being tracked or reported.

LEADING THE PROCESS: WHO SHOULD DO IT?

The performance improvement process is a complex, labor-intensive effort. While many organizations feel they possess the expertise to complete the assessment process, it often makes sense to use external resources to perform the assessment or at least to validate the analysis. The decision to use an outside resource is dependent on the problems, politics, capabilities, staff availability, and skill sets within the group. In addition, the speed with which progress must occur will influence the need for outside resources. If any of the following conditions exist, it is likely that use of outside resources to perform the assessment will be more effective:

1. There is disagreement about the group's vision, whether problems exist, reasons for the problems, or potential solutions.

2. There are concerns about the capabilities of the physician or management leadership.

3. There is skepticism and mistrust of the physician leaders or management.

4. Having multiple factions among the physicians has led to physician conflict.

5. It is likely that the performance improvement plan will require painful action, which could potentially impair the long-term effectiveness of physician leadership and management.

6. Management and staff are so busy with day-to-day operations that they cannot complete the assessment and planning process in a timely manner.

7. The skill sets and knowledge necessary to perform the tasks do not exist within the group.

Thus, external resources are best used when there is a lack of credibility in leadership, the potential for conflict exists, internal resources are unavailable, or difficult decisions need to be made.

If the decision is made to use an outside resource or consultants, they must possess certain qualities for the assessment to be effective. Therefore, you will want to evaluate potential consultants on the following:

1. Do they have strong medical group management experience, and do they understand the operational challenges of running a medical group in today's environment?

2. Do they have a successful track record in medical group performance improvement?

3. What is their process for assessing the organization, and what do their performance improvement plans include? What components of the organization do they review?

4. What is their timetable for the project, and who will perform it?

Using outside consultants can be an effective tool for completing a successful operations improvement process. They can provide external validation for change and are often better able to deal with internal politics because they will not be there permanently. However, their use does not eliminate the need for the group to manage this process. Someone from the group should serve as a liaison with the consultant. The collection of data needs to be coordinated internally, as do consultant contacts with physicians and staff. Project time frames need to be monitored, and the project budget must be managed. As the assessment is completed, review of and feedback on draft findings must occur.

CHALLENGES TO AN EFFECTIVE PROCESS

Regardless of who or how the improvement process is initiated, a number of challenges must be resolved to succeed:

1. There must be a common understanding of the problems and agreement among all key constituencies as to their root causes.

2. A change in culture and leadership style is often required to maintain any initial success. Changes in management and physician leadership are often required.

3. Physicians and staff must buy in to both the targets and the implementation plan.

4. Targets should be both achievable and ambitious enough to accomplish the necessary improvement in performance. This often means that physicians and staff will be asked to perform at levels they think are impossible.

5. Most people are uncomfortable with change and, therefore, often resist necessary changes. They also may become angry or confused as the process begins and expectations change.

6. Momentum and motivation must be maintained over the length of the implementation plan. Motivating staff and physicians in the beginning, when the biggest changes are required, can be especially difficult.

7. Physician and staff layoffs may be required, causing the remaining staff to feel insecure and anxious about their future. This anxiety can make it difficult to maintain motivation.

STRATEGIES FOR ACHIEVING SUCCESS

Although the challenges are numerous, the strategies available to minimize their impact are also numerous. The first task is to redefine the organization's culture. Because change is so stressful, it is important to set expectations for group behavior before the process begins. Also, the group often has to change its behavior constructively if the performance improvement is to succeed. The ground rules or code of conduct for physicians and staff going forward should be clearly stated. Key organizational principles should include the following:

1. *Teamwork and collaboration are valued.* Looking good at others' expense is not. Valuing the mistakes of others is inappropriate. Disruptive behavior is not tolerated.

2. *Data and facts are to be respected* and used to make decisions. Old information and anecdotes are rarely useful. Ideas are separate from judgment.

3. *Intellectual conflict is encouraged* but must be conducted with civility and respect for others. Issues will be fully aired. Then decisions will be made, and it is expected that the attitude will be, "I can live with the decision, even if I disagree."

4. *Risk taking is encouraged*, and mutual accountability is required.

Once the code of conduct has been established, it is important to ensure that the process is inclusive. Individuals are much more likely to support actions they understand and helped create. Therefore, group members and staff should be involved in all steps of the process, from data collection to plan implementation. This does not mean giving everyone veto power. It does mean providing the opportunity to be heard.

Regular feedback during the process is critical to keeping people motivated. This requires ongoing monitoring and measuring of progress. This also allows for celebrations. Celebration encourages success, so celebrate often and publicly. Celebrations reinforce the sense of achievement, and public recognition of success is a wonderful reward for hard work.

Changes in organizational structure and governance should be made quickly. Those who do not meet performance expectations should be dealt with in a timely manner, as poor performers can be disruptive to the improvement process and cannot be allowed to block progress. Appropriate action reinforces accountability and indirectly provides support for those who are working hard.

It is important to provide training and coaching so that people feel supported through the change process. It is unreasonable to expect that people will know how to make the necessary changes without guidance. At the same time, potential gainsharing opportunities through bonuses or other profit-sharing mechanisms can increase staff creativity and commitment to change.

Staff and physicians should be empowered to identify solutions. It is not necessary to dictate how the change should occur. It is important to set expectations or targets, but then give people the freedom to determine how to achieve them.

The effectiveness of the evaluation and planning stages will determine the success of the operations improvement plan. A thorough assessment identifies all the key variables affecting the group's performance. It creates an environment in which staff and physicians understand and accept the need for change and leads to adoption of an implementation plan that everyone can support and will be motivated to accomplish. In other words, it is the road map for improving performance. It is the task of group leaders, both lay and medical, to stay on course, focusing on the desired performance targets. Motivating and rewarding achievement will keep positive momentum. However, everyone in the organization must be accountable for his or her part in the group's success.

3

MEDICAL GROUP LEADERSHIP

Benjamin S. Snyder, MPA, FACMPE

Regardless of geographic location, every medical group practice is constantly challenged with maintaining physician income, managing expenses, and dealing with thin operating margins. Whether you call it improving practice performance or aggressively managing to a bottom-line result, the need for effective medical and administrative leadership is the same.

Group leaders are continually challenged to instill confidence in staff, articulate their vision and objectives, and effectively manage each detail associated with identified tasks and/or actions. Their ability to encourage innovation and internal support for change is also critically important. Given the turbulent nature of the medical landscape, successful governance and management are necessary requirements for improving medical practice performance.

This chapter describes the principles and approaches that are crucial in identifying and organizing medical group leadership.

THE NEED FOR EFFECTIVE LEADERSHIP

Leadership plays a key role in virtually every organization and business. The more people-oriented an organization is, the more critical leadership skills become for senior management and owners. For medical group practices, this reality is profound. On a national basis, medical group practices spend between 69 and 70 percent[1] of every net revenue dollar on physician, allied health, and support personnel. When coupled with the dynamics of a highly educated physician staff being supported by a majority of young, single employees who have only a high school education, the need for leadership and the ability to deal effectively with this workforce diversity becomes even more apparent.

Relative to their size, medical group practices are also "big" businesses. With gross revenue averaging a minimum of $200,000 to $300,000 per full-time equivalent physician, a busy three- to five-physician primary care practice will easily be a $1 million business. A 10- or 15-physician multi-specialty medical group more heavily weighted toward subspecialties rather than primary care could be a $25- to $50-million company. While most businesses of this size recruit nationally for their senior leadership, medical groups tend to select physician leaders from their own ranks, often without regard for actual qualifying experience. It is also not uncommon for a physician leader to be selected because no one else was interested. When this occurs, it is important to have an administrator or manager who complements the physician leader's knowledge and skills.

However, many smaller group practices select a manager or administrator through the same type of informal process. An employee who is viewed as loyal, dedicated, and hard-working may be placed in a management position without actual consideration of his or her skills and abilities in this area. When coupled with an inexperienced physician leader, the result can be devastating from both a financial and an operational basis.

---

[1] *MGMA Cost Survey: 1999 Report Based on 1998 Data.* Englewood, CO: Medical Group Management Association, 1999.

Balancing the roles of physician and administrative leadership has fostered the building of the "team approach" to management by the Medical Group Management Association (MGMA). While many think of this structure as merely having physician issues managed by physicians and non-physician issues addressed by lay administrators, it is actually a collaborative approach to management
that draws on the skills, knowledge, and abilities of
each individual.

ORGANIZATIONAL STRUCTURES

Depending on the size of the physician staff and the ownership model, a number of different approaches can be taken in organizing and managing a medical group practice. This chapter will discuss two specific organizational models. One relates to smaller medical group practices (fewer than 10 physicians), and the other applies to larger physician organizations (consisting of 30 or more physicians). Those practices in between are often a hybrid of the two structures.

Smaller Medical Groups

With a vast majority of medical group practices in the United States consisting of fewer than 10 physicians, this is clearly the area of practice management where the opportunity is the greatest to have a positive impact on organization, management, and operating results. At the same time, this size of organization is perhaps the most difficult to organize and operate because of ownership structure, leadership skill levels of physician and lay administration, and mix of support personnel.

Before even attempting to develop an organizational structure for this type of medical group practice, the physicians and owner physicians must reach agreement on how they view the medical practice and what they believe are the appropriate goals and objectives for the organization. If possible, the best starting point is the development of a mission, vision, and values statement that can be used to guide the organization in its decision-making process (see Chapter 1).

At the heart of the organizational design decision is the question of whether or not the physicians want to be managed. Depending on how this question is truthfully answered, the response will determine the direction that the development of the organizational structure should take. If the physicians are willing to relinquish individual control and allow themselves to be governed, then the group must determine and adopt an appropriate organizational structure, as well as identify the individuals who can potentially fill the senior physician and non-physician administrative positions. However, inherent in this decision is the understanding that both administrative and clinical issues will be subject to review, comment, and, most importantly, change.

Most physicians will support change that is based on data, particularly if operations or economics of the practice are not meeting the level of their expectations. The issue usually surfaces when changes begin to be implemented that affect a particular physician's practice area or the responsibilities of support personnel. It is not uncommon for a physician who fully participated in the discussion and agreement process to object to change when it will affect him or her personally. Minimizing this type of reaction and situation will be key in the process of discussing and approving an organizational structure.

The recommended organizational structure for small medical groups is diagrammed as Figure 3-1.

Figure 3-1. Organizational Chart
Small Medical Groups

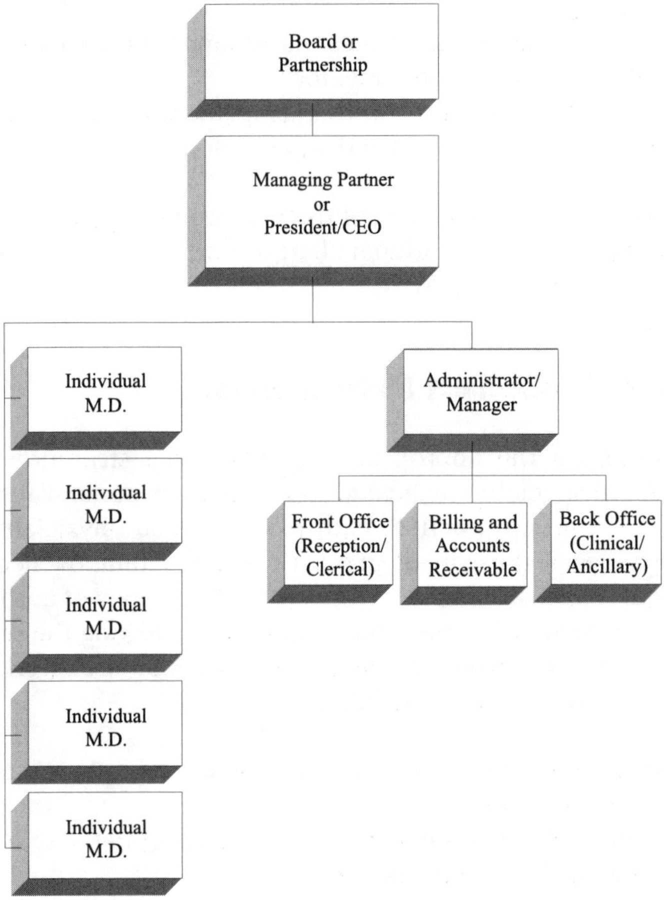

The management philosophy behind this organizational structure focuses on the team approach. The major factors that will contribute to making this an effective organization include:

- The physician appointed to the managing partner or president/CEO ("physician leader") position is sincerely interested in assuming the responsibilities of this position and has the most qualifications for assuming the position.
- The physician leader manages and oversees both the administrative and clinical components of the medical practice.
- The physician leader values the administrator/manager as a full management team member.
- A coordinated approach to management is portrayed consistently to physicians and support staff.

Job descriptions for each of the management positions detailed on the organizational chart are included in Exhibit 3-1 at the end of this chapter.

Large Multi-specialty Medical Groups

Developing the appropriate organizational structure for a large multi-specialty medical group is easier in some ways than for a small group practice. With more than 30 physicians and 120 employees, these medical practices understand the need for a formal organizational structure and defined lines of authority. However, certain key elements required for making the organization successful from an operations standpoint are often missing. These key elements include:

- Senior physician leadership who understand their role and responsibilities
- Senior administrative staff with demonstrated experience in medical group operations
- Senior physician and administrative leadership who are able to focus and manage the medical practice's core business without being diverted by external opportunities

- Operating committees that effectively address assigned responsibilities
- A board of directors that understands its governance role and fiduciary responsibility as differentiated from the role of management.

The organizational chart presented in Figure 3-2 details suggested reporting lines of responsibility and authority for a large medical group practice. The degree to which the president/CEO and medical director are full time in this capacity will depend on the size of the group. In most circumstances, physicians in leadership roles continue to practice medicine, until the responsibility becomes too great—in most cases in groups with more than 100 physicians.

Figure 3-2. Organizational Chart
Large Medical Groups

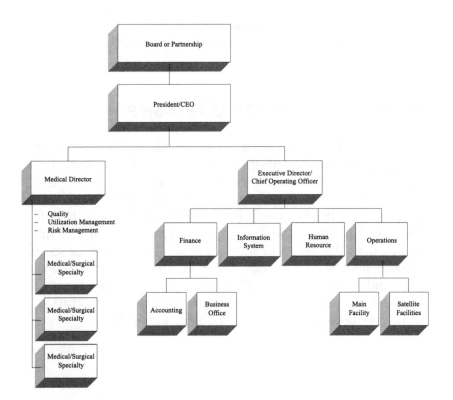

While the reporting relationships follow a more traditional approach, several issues will either help or hinder the organization in meeting its day-to-day functional needs.

The qualifications of each person who fills a senior-level position and how well each member of the senior management team works together toward agreed-upon goals are critically important. The wrong individuals holding a position in the most technically correct or appropriate organizational structure will not allow the organization to reach its maximum potential. If this wrong individual is the president, medical director, or chief operating officer, the organization will surely struggle to meet its operational and financial goals. A distracted or ineffective president/CEO could easily stymie the organization and negatively affect financial performance.

Job descriptions for each of these senior management positions are included in Exhibit 3-1 at the end of this chapter.

With this understanding of medical group organizational structure, what roles do physician and lay administrative leadership really play?

THE ROLE OF PHYSICIAN LEADERSHIP

Physician leadership plays a critical role in medical group management because physicians want to be led by physicians. Administrative personnel can be excellent at analyzing and organizing operations, including addressing some clinical—as opposed to medical—issues. However, success is usually only guaranteed in those functions where administration has full control over the entire change process. This change process includes analysis of the problem, development of recommendations, and implementation of actions. These identified areas of responsibility include accounting, purchasing, registration, medical records, patient business office, and facilities.

When processes start to affect physician office practices directly, an entirely different dynamic is at play. These processes could include changing a physician's clinical hours, introducing appointment schedule templates, beginning team nursing, or implementing a centralized scheduling function. These types of initiatives demand a higher degree of physician involvement to gain physician attention and effect necessary change.

When physician behavioral issues begin affecting patient care and the quality of service being provided, it is more appropriate for the physician head of that specialty or the medical director of the practice to become involved to manage the process effectively. In these types of circumstances, physicians will more likely respond positively to another physician, particularly if that physician is in a leadership role. Examples of physician issues that negatively affect patient care include:

- Consistently arriving late for scheduled patient appointments
- Canceling and rescheduling patients because of last-minute schedule conflicts (add-on surgical cases, on-call coverage, etc.)
- Canceling patient appointments because of last-minute plans to take time off.

Physician behavior issues such as these can best be resolved through strong medical leadership. The lay administrator would not be as likely to receive a positive response by managing this issue without the participation of the physician leader. Having effective medical leadership brings the physicians into the picture as partners with administration and helps facilitate a positive outcome.

To achieve performance improvement, every leader is being challenged to look at operations in a new way. Strong medical leadership encourages the practice to look critically at how care is being provided, review the quality of care, and experiment with new methods and processes to meet patient care needs and expectations more efficiently. The end result should be a higher quality of care arising from improved processes. Clinical outcomes should be better, and the care should become more cost-effective for patients.

Why do most medical groups find medical leadership a challenge? Historically, the entire training process for physicians has been focused solely on the clinical aspects of medicine. The development of leadership skills and business acumen has been left to physicians to develop on their own, post-residency training. Some have developed these skills without more formal training, and others have pursued postgraduate training in Masters of Business Administration (MBA) and Public Health (MPH) programs. The American College of Physician Executives (ACPE) also provides management education to physician leaders in all phases and sizes of group practice.

While larger medical groups have a higher probability of having several physicians with this advanced management training, smaller medical groups tend to depend on their colleagues learning these skills on the job. Unfortunately, not all physicians have the interest or desire to become effective medical leaders, even though they serve in that senior leadership role. At some point these physicians will understand that they are in the business of medical group practice and need to use essential business skills to manage effectively.

THE ROLE OF LAY ADMINISTRATION

Lay administration has the responsibility to oversee and manage the quality of the non-clinical activities of the medical group. It is their responsibility to manage effectively the assigned business processes of the medical practice and achieve the stated financial performance for the organization. In large medical groups, the expectation and understanding are that senior management has these skill levels.

However, in small medical groups, there is a higher likelihood of having a void in formal business management training and the development of leadership skills. Most medical group managers with these smaller medical groups have primarily on-the-job training, and their skill levels vary greatly. Part of this skill variance is a direct correlation to the compensation level the medical practice is willing to pay for administrative talent.

Regardless of the size of the medical group and the skill levels of the individuals in senior management positions, the basic job of managing must be performed. Using the suggested organizational structures and making every reasonable effort to select the most qualified people will make all the difference.

As part of the process to identify the right individuals for a given management position, Figure 3-3 delineates the roles of medical and administrative leadership, noting the areas where they overlap.

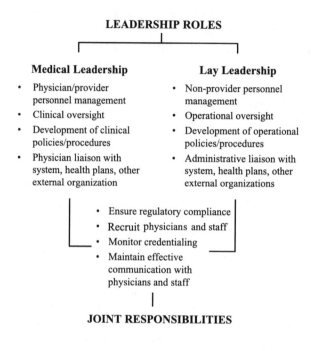

Figure 3-3
Roles of Medical and Administrative Leadership

REQUIRED LEADERSHIP COMPETENCIES

Required leadership competencies include those developed by ACMPE as well as other abilities.

ACMPE Body of Knowledge for Medical Practice Management

The American College of Medical Practice Executives (ACMPE), the professional development and credentialing affiliate of MGMA, has also recognized the need for individuals in medical group management to have specific demonstrated skills, knowledge, and abilities. As a result of a long-term research endeavor, ACMPE has identified and categorized the professional knowledge requirements of a successful medical practice executive.

The outcome of this ACMPE study has been the identification of eight professional domains critical to the successful medical practice executive's body of knowledge. These domains include:

- Financial management
- Human resources management
- Planning and marketing
- Information management
- Risk management
- Governance and organizational dynamics
- Business and clinical operations
- Professional responsibility.

These eight domains essentially define what physicians and lay administrative leaders need to know and do as part of their executive management responsibilities. Specific competency tasks have been identified for each identified domain. These competency tasks are included in ACMPE's Body of Knowledge for Medical Practice Management, included as Exhibit 3-2 at the end of this chapter.

Other Key Requirements

In trying to match qualified individuals to a senior management position within a medical group, several other basic requirements need to be addressed.

Clear Organizational Vision
For an organization to achieve its stated goals and objectives, it is important that leadership be clear about its mission and strategic vision. In today's environment, it is difficult if not impossible to reach the desired end point if there are constant questions of "why are we doing this?" Having a clearly stated mission and strategic vision will answer this question.

Degree of Participation

Leaders also must be able to determine when it is appropriate to encourage participation in decision making and when they need to make the decision on their own. As a general rule, effective leaders need to encourage participation and feedback from staff. It is important to seek input, particularly when making major decisions. However, it should also be understood that under certain circumstances, some decisions may be made without input or participation.

Leadership Talent

Senior management needs to serve as a cheerleader and coach of the team. It is important to understand this role and to mentor staff. The development of leadership skills and abilities of middle management staff will only strengthen and enhance management's overall capabilities. With this depth of management staff, senior leaders should have more time to focus on strategic issues rather than on day-to-day operational issues. Reliance on middle management becomes crucial when trying to improve operations or financial performance. Depending on timeframes and urgency for improvement, "all hands on deck" may be required.

Necessary Risk-taking

Don't be afraid to make mistakes! A sign of an effective leader is to make overall sound decisions. There is nothing wrong with a bad decision as long there are enough good decisions to offset it. The success of the organization needs to be viewed from a long-term perspective. And the sign of a strong leader is the ability to admit when he or she has made a mistake. This illustrates to the organization that it's okay to reach and take a reasonable risk. It also illustrates the importance of being accountable for one's own actions. If it turns out to be the wrong decision, it is important to highlight the lessons that were learned to prevent a similar error in the future.

In addition, being able to keep a sense of humor through dramatically changing times should not be minimized. With the seriousness and high degree of difficulty in making many of the decisions required, showing a lighter side at opportune times can often keep motivation alive.

AVOIDING THE TRAPS DURING AN OPERATIONAL IMPROVEMENT EFFORT

Leading a medical group during times of financial crisis is perhaps the greatest challenge for medical and lay management. Often the difficult decisions required during this period, including changing physician compensation, laying off providers and support staff, and setting higher performance requirements, can be "career-limiting" decisions of medical group executives. Table 3-1 identifies the typical leadership "traps" that need to be avoided during a period of focused operational or financial improvement.

Physician leaders can be particularly susceptible to these traps:

- *Relying on anecdotes*—Physician leaders can be reactive. This can be an asset during a turnaround, when immediate action is required. However, it can also obscure the organization's focus if actions are taken in response to anecdotal stories or "the squeaky wheel." Validate facts through analysis or additional discussions before taking action, particularly regarding significant decisions.
- *Shouldering the burden alone*—Physicians are accustomed to making independent decisions in their clinical practices and are often reluctant to delegate authority. Remember that there is a difference between delegating authority and responsibility. Leaders retain ultimate responsibility regardless of the authority delegated. But a successful operational improvement plan requires that managers (including other physician leaders) be held

Table 3-1. Avoiding The Traps

The Trap	How to Avoid It
• Relying on anecdotes/responding to the squeaky wheel	• Use data where appropriate; interview others; market research
• Shouldering the burden alone	• Lead through others
• Impatience	• Pick some low fruit while reaching for the high ones
• Analysis paralysis	• Use what you can and move on; use common sense
• Blame it on the structure	• Even entrenched systems can change -- don't accept old rules
• Dwelling on what you can't change	• Allow a little "steam blowing"; but then refocus on the action required
• Assuming the right team is in place	• Make personnel changes swiftly if necessary
• Ruling vs. leading	• Be the coach and the player, but know when to take the lead
• Governance vs. management	• Empower management

Source: The Camden Group

accountable as well as be given the authority for making the necessary changes.

- *Impatience*—Physicians become extremely inpatient with the process that is often required to facilitate change. Physician leaders must balance the need for immediate action during a performance improvement with the need for long-term improvement. Often this can be accomplished by pursuing short- and long-term objectives simultaneously. In other words, pick the "low-hanging fruit" and claim the victory, but don't forget to keep reaching for the fruit at the top.

- *Analysis paralysis*—On the other hand, some executives are stymied by decision-making processes and use "lack of data" as a reason to delay. Recognize that decisions must be as informed as possible, but it is the job of leadership to apply judgment and simple common sense when necessary. After all, not all data can be organized into useful information.

- *Blaming it on the structure*—This often occurs in hospital-based groups. The reason for poor performance is blamed on "hospital" decision making. In more established groups, leaders often get trapped in entrenched systems and policies that prevent change. That is, "we've always done it that way," or worse, "we tried that five years ago, and it didn't work then." It is the leader's responsibility to identify those issues—both structural and procedural—that must change to effect the vision and goals of the organization. Sometimes this involves changing the operating culture of the group—perhaps the most difficult challenge of all.

- *Dwelling on what you can't change*—This is the reverse of the previous point. Sometimes leaders get caught in the trap of focusing energy on endless discussions of historical decisions or environmental factors that are out of their control. A leader must recognize when to allow others to "vent" about their frustrations with the medical practice and when to focus on what action can be taken.

- *Assuming the right team is in place*—As noted, matching capabilities with organizational needs is critical to successful management. During a period of focused operational improvement, it is vital that these capabilities be analyzed critically. Sometimes it is necessary to introduce a different management style to effect a improvement. This can be accomplished by bringing in interim or temporary assistance to facilitate the change or, if necessary, by replacing management. Unfortunately, there is no time to waste in making these crucial decisions if the organization is facing a financial or operational crisis.

- *Ruling versus leading*—Knowing the difference between ruling and leading is the mark of an effective leader. During a period of focused operational improvement the difference may be difficult to distinguish, given the importance of decisiveness and the magnitude of some of the decisions required. However, the leader who can live through and survive change must be both the coach and a player, encouraging participation when appropriate and taking action when required.The development of strong "lieutenants" will facilitate effective leadership for the long haul.

When there is a need for immediate improvement, this is not the time to lead through consensus. While the organization must understand the rationale behind management decisions, many decisions required during this period are not appropriate for "putting it to a vote" of a committee or the physicians at large.

- *Governance versus management*—Medical groups often suffer from a lack of ability among their leaders in distinguishing between governance and management. While the governing body has the ultimate fiduciary responsibility for the medical group, it must empower management to make operating decisions. During periods of focused operational and financial improvement, this can become particularly important. When decisions must be made quickly and cannot always be brought before a governing body for discussion, the board needs to support management. If the board sets clearly articulated goals and objectives, and roles and responsibilities are clear, physician and lay management will be more effective in leading the organization and effecting the changes that are required.

Leadership is truly an art. There is no time that this is more apparent than during a financial crisis or when there is a need for major operational improvement. However, it is also crucial that leaders balance the need for knowledge and facts with the need for action and change.

Organizations that survive major change are those that seize the opportunity to create new leaders at all levels of the organization to build strength for the long term. At the same time, there must be followers. The greatest challenge to leaders of medical organizations during a crisis is to create a platform for change without destroying the positive culture and the "glue" of the group that has held it together in the past. Finding this balance is the key to both short- and long-term success.

Exhibit 3-1
SAMPLE JOB DESCRIPTIONS

Position: President/CEO   **Reports To:** Board of Directors

Position Summary

The President/CEO provides the senior leadership for both the medical and administrative management for the medical practice. This physician has the responsibility for all aspects of the operation: practice management, finance, and business development, as well as quality management and improvement.

Job Responsibilities

- Provides administrative leadership and direction to management staff and practices.
- Works in conjunction with the board to establish and implement goals, objectives, and the short- and long-term business plans.
- Maintains effective communication with employee and physician staff.
- Directs the organization's strategic planning process.
- Pursues opportunities to create physician links and develops new business opportunities.
- Continually monitors financial performance and takes appropriate actions when needed to correct budget variances.
- Keeps current with trends in medical management, regulations, and administration. Keeps the administrative staff, physicians and board members apprised of issues that may affect the medical group.
- Maintains a safe and healthy working environment that meets all federal and state regulatory requirements.
- Performs other specific duties as assigned.

Qualifications

Education and Experience
At least five years of increasingly responsible management positions in health care organizations; demonstrated leadership and medical group management experience required; enthusiasm and high energy. Medical degree and current license to practice medicine in the state of [name of state] and master's degree in business administration or public health preferred.

Knowledge
Strong medical management skills; strong interpersonal skills; strong written, financial, and analytical skills.

Abilities
Ability to communicate effectively; proven ability to work successfully with physicians and non-physicians; demonstrated skills in building new business; ability to set priorities and manage multiple tasks to achieve stated objectives; broad understanding of the health care industry.

Note: This description indicates in general terms the type and level of work performed and responsibilities held by the employees. Duties described are not to be interpreted as being all-inclusive.

I acknowledge receipt of this job and can fulfill all the requirements of this position.

Signature: _____ Date: _____

Job Description/Summary

The Executive Director/CEO provides the leadership and direction needed to achieve business objectives. This individual manages all aspects of operations: site management, finance, business development, practice marketing, human resources, and quality improvement.

Performance Standards[1]	Performance Tracking[2]
• Meet or exceed budgeted performance	• Actual vs. budget reports
• Employee turnover less than 5%	• Terminations and voluntary resignations
• [1-20%][3] growth in revenue	• Financial statements
• 90% overall patient satisfaction	• Patient survey
• 90% employee satisfaction	• Employee satisfaction surveys
• 100% compliance to state, federal, and health plan audits	• Internal and external audits

Definitions

[1] Performance standards: expected measures of individual performance.

[2] Performance tracking: process activities to track achievement of performance standards.

[3] Based on your group's strategic or budget assumptions.

Position: Executive Director/COO   **Reports To:** Board of Directors

Position Summary

The Executive Director/COO provides the leadership and direction needed to achieve business objectives. This individual manages all aspects of operations: practice management, finance, business development, practice marketing, human resources, and quality improvement.

Job Responsibilities

- Provides administrative leadership and direction to management staff and practices.
- Works in conjunction with the board, management, physicians, and staff to establish and implement goals, objectives, and the short- and long-term business plans.
- Maintains effective communication with physician staff.
- Directs the organization's strategic planning process.
- Pursues opportunities to create physician links and develop new business opportunities.
- Continually monitors performance compared to budget and takes appropriate action when needed to correct budget variances.
- Keeps current with market, regulations, and legal trends and activities that may affect clinic site activities. Keeps physicians and board members apprised of issues that may affect the medical group.
- Maintains a safe and healthy working environment that meets all federal and state regulatory requirements.
- Performs other specific duties as assigned.

Qualifications

Education and Experience
At least five years of increasingly responsible management positions in health care organizations; strong medical group management experience required; track record of exhibiting ini-

tiative and leadership with a minimum of supervision; enthusiastic and high energy; bachelor's degree required, master's degree preferred.

Knowledge
Strong interpersonal skills; strong written, financial, and analytical skills.

Abilities
Ability to communicate effectively; proven ability to work successfully with physicians; demonstrated skills in building new business; ability to set priorities and manage multiple tasks; broad understanding of the health care industry.

Note: This description indicates in general terms the type and level of work performed and responsibilities held by the employees. Duties described are not to be interpreted as being all-inclusive.

I acknowledge receipt of this job and can fulfill all the requirements of this position.

Signature: _____ Date: _____

Job Description/Summary
The Executive Director/COO provides the leadership and direction needed to achieve business objectives. This individual manages all aspects of operations: site management, finance, business development, practice marketing, human resources, and quality improvement.

Performance Standards[1]	Performance Tracking[2]
• Meets or exceeds budgeted performance	• Actual vs. budget reports
• Employee turnover less than 5%	• Terminations and voluntary resignations
• [1-20%][3] growth in revenue	• Financial statements
• 90% overall patient satisfaction	• Patient survey
• 90% employee satisfaction	• Employee satisfaction surveys
• 100% compliance with state, federal, and health plan audits	• Internal and external audits

Definitions

[1] Performance standards: expected measures of individual performance.

[2] Performance tracking: process activities to track achievement of performance standards.

[3] Based on group's strategic or budget assumptions.

Position: Practice Manager   **Reports To:** Medical Group President
                                                  or Board of Directors

Position Summary

The Practice Manager manages specific administrative functions related to the operations of the clinic site as assigned.

Job Responsibilities

- Establishes and maintains an operating environment that ensures effective, efficient, and safe operation of the office practice that responds to patient, physician, and staff needs.
- Establishes and implements policies, procedures, and systems for the assigned administrative areas.
- Participates in the development and implementation of long-range plans and budgets for the medical practice.
- Selects, trains, and ensures development of component personnel. Apprises employees of the policies and procedures stipulated in the employee handbook and adheres to them. Schedules staff to meet the needs of the practice. Reviews and approves employee time sheets or payroll cards. Generates and completes employee performance reviews in conjunction with the physicians.
- Schedules and performs OSHA training. Ensures compliance of exposure control program and establishes and maintains employee medical records in compliance with OSHA regulations.
- Ensures a positive working relationship with physicians.
- Coordinates the purchase of medical and office supplies and equipment. Establishes and maintains an inventory system to ensure adequate levels of office supplies.
- Monitors and controls clinic expenditures within budget.
- Establishes and maintains an evaluation program to ensure timely repairs and proper functioning of office and medical equipment.
- Monitors and analyzes patient schedules and practice operations to determine opportunity for improvement in patient services.

- Ensures the submission of timely, accurate, and complete information for billing and insurance claims processing
- Ensures that patient accounts receivable are worked in a timely and efficient manner.
- Reviews each physician's accounts receivable at month-end to track collection percentages and aging of account balances.
- Reviews and approves all invoices for payment.
- Reviews practice expenses compared to budget and implements action when appropriate.
- Implements reporting system as requested by physicians.
- Assists with the expansion of the office practice, as necessary.
- Works with the board of directors, the president, the medical director, and practice physicians to ensure that quality patient care and services are provided.
- Participates in professional development activities to keep current with health care trends and practices.
- Maintains strictest confidentiality regarding medical group information, including patient information.
- Maintains appropriate inventory control and approves all purchase orders made by clinic staff.
- Performs other duties as requested.
- Ensures that OSHA, federal, and state regulatory guidelines are met.

Qualifications

Experience and Education
Bachelor's degree or an equivalent of five years of management experience preferred, including three years managing a clinic; certificate/license not required.

Knowledge

Knowledge of organization policies and systems; knowledge of health care administration practices; knowledge of computer systems and applications; knowledge of government and reimbursement regulations and requirements.

Abilities

Ability to take initiative, exercise independent judgment, and solve problems; ability to work effectively with staff, patients, public, and external agencies; skill in planning, organizing, delegating, and supervising; skill in gathering and interpreting data; skill in verbal and written communication; skill in researching, preparing, and presenting comprehensive reports.

Note: This description indicates in general terms the type and level of work performed and responsibilities held by the employees. Duties described are not to be interpreted as being all-inclusive.

I acknowledge receipt of this job and can fulfill all the requirements of this position.

Signature: _____ Date: _____

Job Description/Summary

The Practice Manager manages specific administrative functions related to the operations of the clinic site as assigned.

Performance Standards[1]	Performance Tracking[2]
• 90% or greater overall patient satisfaction	• Patient surveys
• 100% physician satisfaction	• Physician feedback
• Meet or achieve positive variance of medical practice budget	• Actual vs. budget variance report
• Meet budget guidelines	• Budget
• Maintain appropriate inventory of supplies	• Perform inventory audits
• Attend two seminars for professional development	• Attend meetings, seminars, and conferences
• Less than 5% staff turnover rate	• Track staffing patterns
• 100% accuracy of demographic information	• Number of accounts missing data for billing and insurance claim processing
• Less than 70 days of revenue in accounts receivable	• Accounts receivable aging

Definitions

[1] Performance standards: expected measures of individual performance.

[2] Performance tracking: process activities to track achievement of performance standards.

Position: Medical Director   **Reports To**: Board of Directors

Position Summary

The Medical Director interfaces with administration, providing physician input on development and implementation of all policies and procedures. He or she has overall responsibility for guiding the enhancement of the clinical functioning of the clinic sites.

Job Responsibilities

- Acts as the physician liaison between the clinic sites and the health plans. Assists administration with outside regulatory and accrediting agencies.
- Participates in establishing performance guidelines for physicians; ensures that all physician performance is measured against these guidelines and advises on disciplinary action when necessary.
- Assists administration with the implementation of policies and procedures relating to clinical practice.
- Assists administration in physician recruitment decisions.
- Assists administration in orienting the new physicians and in establishing procedures to monitor performance of all new physicians.
- Develops work procedures to expedite and improve the level of medical care to all patients.
- Provides leadership as a member of the utilization review and peer review committees.
- Is available to consult with other providers for consultation related to health care delivery.
- Participates as the lead physician in all quality assurance programs to ensure documentation of clinical procedures and maintenance of up-to-date protocols and medical care standards.
- Assists administration in ensuring compliance with medical group bylaws and required policies from regulatory and accrediting agencies.

- Monitors all medical staff activities and periodically reports the findings to the medical group's governing board and administration.
- Assists administration in establishing and maintaining review, analysis, and evaluation of medical staff performance in all department and services.
- Establishes and maintains effective channels of communication among physicians and between physicians and administration.
- Assists administration in monitoring the credentialing of clinical staff.
- Performs other duties as assigned.

Qualifications

Experience and Education

Valid license in [insert state(s)], with no pending or previous disciplinary action from any state licensing entity; board-certified in specialty.

Knowledge

Working knowledge of administrative practices, procedures, polices, and standards as they relate to medical services; awareness of all health care financing and payer trends; knowledge of applicable federal and state requirements for quality assurance, credentialing, and coding guidelines for billing.

Abilities

Ability to communicate effectively; demonstrated leadership abilities applicable.

Note: This description indicates in general terms the type and level of work performed and responsibilities held by the employees. Duties described are not to be interpreted as being all-inclusive.

I acknowledge receipt of this job and can fulfill all the requirements of this position.

Signature: _____ Date: _____

Job Description/Summary

The Medical Director interfaces with administration, providing physician input on development and implementation of all policies and procedures. He or she has overall responsibility for guiding the enhancement of the clinical activities.

Performance Standards[1]	Performance Tracking[2]
• 95% compliance health plan audits	• Internal assessment of health plan audit results
• Less than 5% disenrollment rate	• Eligibility reports
• 100% credentialing compliance	• Credentialing reports
• 95% overall physician satisfaction	• Physician satisfaction survey
• 90% physician adherence to clinical protocols	• Chart audits
• 100% annual completion of physician evaluation	• Number of physician evaluations completed
• 95% compliance with coding guidelines for billing	• Chart audits

Definitions

[1] Performance standards: expected measures of individual performance.

[2] Performance tracking: process activities to track achievement of performance standards.

Exhibit 3-2

The Body of Knowledge for Medical Practice Management
American College of Medical Practice Executives

I. Financial Management

- Prepare and manage budgets
- Develop accounting and financial control systems
- Prepare financial statements and conduct financial analysis
- Develop and manage material procurement and payment systems
- Develop coding and reimbursement policies and procedures
- Facilitate investment planning, management, and compliance
- Establish business relationships with financial advisors
- Establish fee schedules
- Negotiate third-party contracts
- Develop reconciliation systems for third-party payer reimbursement
- Facilitate retirement planning, management, and compliance
- Maintain compliance with tax laws and filing procedures

II. Human Resources Management

- Develop compensation and benefits programs
- Establish job classification systems
- Develop employee placement programs and facilitate workforce planning

- Establish employee appraisal and evaluation systems
- Develop and implement employee training programs
- Establish employee relations and conflict resolution programs
- Maintain compliance with employment laws

III.   Planning and Marketing

- Create marketing plans
- Pursue and establish partnerships and strategic alliances
- Develop and evaluate strategic plans
- Develop and implement community outreach, public relations, and customer relations program

IV.   Information Management

- Conduct information system needs analysis
- Facilitate information system procurement and installation
- Develop and implement information system training and support programs
- Oversee database management and maintenance
- Develop information network security systems
- Provide electronic education resources and systems

V. Risk Management

- Maintain legal compliance with corporate structure
- Maintain corporate history and develop record-keeping procedures
- Develop conflict resolution and grievance procedures
- Develop systems of managing at-risk health care delivery under capitation
- Assess and procure liability insurance
- Establish personnel and property security plans and policies

- Develop and implement quality assurance and patient satisfaction programs
- Establish patient, staff, and organizational confidentiality policies
- Conduct audits of at-risk financial activities
- Develop professional resource networks for risk-related activities
- Negotiate and comply with contractual arrangements
- Maintain compliance with government contractual mandates

VI. Governance and Organizational Dynamics

- Develop leadership and change agent skills
- Construct and maintain governance systems
- Evaluate and improve governing bylaws, policies, and processes
- Conduct stakeholder needs assessments and facilitate relationship development
- Facilitate staff development and teaming
- Facilitate physician understanding and acceptance of good business management
- Develop and implement quality assurance programs
- Provide mechanisms for administrative and clinical input and collaboration

VII. Business and Clinical Operations

- Facilitate business operations planning
- Conduct staffing analysis and scheduling
- Develop ancillary clinical support services
- Establish purchasing procurement and inventory control systems
- Develop and implement facilities planning and maintenance programs
- Establish patient flow processes
- Develop and implement patient communication systems

- Develop clinical pathway structure and function
- Create monitoring systems for licensure, credentialing, and recertification
- Develop and implement process improvement programs for clinic operations

VIII. Professional Responsibility

- Advance professional knowledge and leadership skills
- Balance professional and personal pursuits
- Promote ethical standards for individual and organizational behavior and decision making
- Conduct self-assessments
- Engage in professional networking
- Advance the profession by contributing to the body of knowledge
- Develop effective interpersonal skills

American College of Medical Practice Executives, 104 Inverness Terrace East, Englewood, CO 80112-5306
Toll-free (888) 608-5601 ext. 869; Fax: (303) 643-4427; email acmpe@mgma.com.

4

PERFORMANCE, BENCHMARKING, AND REPORTING TOOLS

Mary J. Witt, MSW

With declining reimbursement and increasing costs, medical groups can no longer take a lackadaisical approach to performance. Instead, they need to challenge themselves constantly to operate at optimal levels. This becomes even more critical when problems exist. Practices must continually measure key practice indicators, compare them against industry standards, and use them to strengthen performance. While most groups, even those in trouble, often report the existence of performance measures, these measures are rarely used consistently. More importantly, they are rarely integrated into the daily operations of the practice, used to create accountability, or effective in driving performance improvement. It is critical that groups not only benchmark their performance, but that these benchmarks facilitate the reengineering process required for performance to improve.

This chapter explores processes for establishing performance standards, using benchmarks to reengineer processes, and creating management tools to monitor performance on an ongoing basis. It identifies key practice indicators and discusses how to apply these to process and performance improvement. It also includes sample "dashboard" report formats that medical groups can use to monitor ongoing performance.

BENCHMARKING OVERVIEW

Benchmarking provides a continuous process of measuring productivity, costs, and quality using standard measures.[1] The process directs problem identification by providing a framework in which to critically analyze the drivers contributing to medical group success.

Benchmarking is helpful in a improving performance for a number of reasons. It can:

- Identify strengths and weaknesses
- Provide objective, measurable support for desired change
- Promote the development of realistic performance targets
- Help differentiate operational losses from strategic imperatives
- Assist in the allocation of resources
- Shorten the process improvement timeline.

The four types of benchmarking are delineated in Table 4-1, noting their advantages and disadvantages.[2]

Internal benchmarking is generally the easiest type to implement. However, it is probably not the most appropriate type to use when pursuing performance improvement because it is unlikely that internal data can provide the clues needed for this task. A more appropriate starting point would be to use industry or competitor data.

[1] Dobosenski, Thomas and Brad Vaudrey. Cost per Relative Value Unit—A Benchmark Tool for the Future. *Group Practice Journal* 46(6):21, 1997.
[2] Cleverly, William D., PhD., CPA. *Balanced Scorecards for Medical Groups.* 1998. Speech delivered at the Medical Group Management Association 72nd Annual Conference.

Table 4-1. Types of Benchmarking

TYPE	DEFINITION	EXAMPLES	ADVANTAGES	DISADVANTAGES
Internal	Similar activities in different parts of the organization or over time	• Check-in at various sites • Expenses for this year compared to same time period last year	• Data often easy to collect • Similarity/consistency in environment	• Narrow focus • Internal bias
Industry	Organizations in same business but not competing for same customers	• Geographically dispersed medical practices	• Similar issues/ practices • Willingness to share data • Can lead to best performance targets	• May be unknown difference in organizations
Competitors	Competitors for the same patient base	• Practices in the same town • Other local providers on HMO provider list	• Comparable environment • Measures against local threats	• Difficulty collecting data • Ethical issues • Antagonisms
Functional	Compares similar functions across industry lines	• Registration process of hotels • Call centers for airline registration	• Increases likelihood of discovering innovation • Creates new alliances/ networking	• Difficulty translating to different industry • Some information not transferable

The goal of benchmarking to improve performance is to identify optimal performance based on the industry and competitors. While its focus is not on cutting costs, cost reductions may result as problems are identified and resolved. Nor is the use of performance targets and benchmarking a quick fix or short-term solution. Rather, it is an ongoing, disciplined methodology that creates accountability and provides a structured approach to problem solving. As Steven Shortell states, benchmarking should "add value, not merely limit the use of resources and/or cut costs. Value is the combination of attributes desired by purchasers and other stakeholders."[3]

BENCHMARKING PROCESS

The benchmarking process has two distinct phases. Phase 1 focuses on identifying problems and establishing practice-specific performance targets. Phase 2 involves developing and implementing an action plan to achieve the targets established in Phase 1. Figure 4-1 details the steps involved in the performance improvement process.

Figure 4-1. Performance Improvement Process

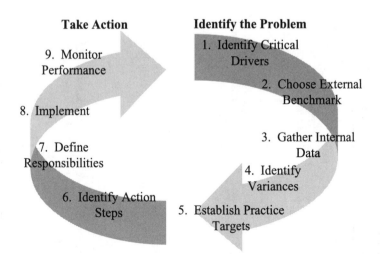

Take Action

9. Monitor Performance

8. Implement

7. Define Responsibilities

6. Identify Action Steps

Identify the Problem

1. Identify Critical Drivers

2. Choose External Benchmark

3. Gather Internal Data

4. Identify Variances

5. Establish Practice Targets

[3] Benchmarking Must Add Value to Communities, Patients. *Medical Group Management Update* 31(15):1,1997, p. 8A.

Step 1: Identify Critical Drivers

The identification of critical drivers for the practice is intrinsic to the successful use of benchmarks in a reengineering or performance improvement process. Unless everyone is clear on the critical factors that lead to improved performance, it will be difficult to gain the support and cooperation required to move forward. Thus, it is necessary to identify the key players who need to be involved in this first step before the process begins and to ensure that findings throughout the process are communicated throughout the organization.

Step 2: Gather Internal Data

The use of a simple decision tree can start the identification process. For example, assuming that the medical group is experiencing financial losses, using the decision tree in Figure 4-2 can narrow the search for the critical factors causing the group to lose money.

Figure 4-2
Decision Tree for Identifying Critical Factors

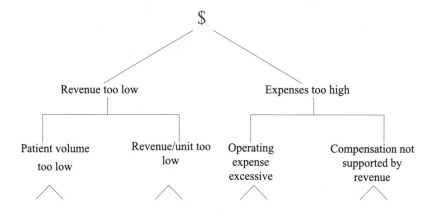

Steps 3 and 4: Select External Benchmarks/Identify Variances

As a starting point, one critical revenue driver and one expense variable could be compared to selected external benchmarks. Since visits per physician FTE drive revenue for most specialties, and quickly identify expense issues and operating expense as a percentage of net revenue expenses, they provide a good starting point for benchmarking. Sources for external benchmarks include:

- American Medical Group Association
- American Medical Association
- The Camden Group
- Center for Heathcare Industry Performance Studies
- McGladrey & Pullen, LLP
- Medical Economics
- Medical Group Management Association
- Merritt Hawkins
- Weatherby Associates
- Other consulting firms.

By comparing internal measures to external benchmarks and identifying significant negative variances, it quickly becomes clear what the critical drivers will be in improving performance. It also allows managers to recognize where success has been achieved—where actual performance compares favorably to the benchmarks. Alternatively, it could indicate a lack of research devoted to a particular function, which could just as easily lead to missed performance opportunities.

However, because of the interdependence of most variables within the practice, it is important that the initial variables identified not be analyzed in isolation or only at the macro level. For instance, while number of visits often drives revenue, many factors impact the number of visits. Thus, looking at visit volume can identify problems, but it does not necessarily clarify either the cause or the solution. That requires analysis at a more detailed level. The variance analysis should also include identification of any unique characteristics of the practice that could affect its ability to achieve the benchmark.

Step 5: Establish Practice Targets

Once these drivers are known and cause and effect determined, it is time to create practice-specific performance targets based on internal history and external benchmarks. The targets should be designed to minimize the variance between your group's performance and the external benchmark, thereby maximizing performance. It should be emphasized here that reaching benchmark performance immediately may not be feasible, particularly in a troubled group. Therefore, the group's targets must reflect realistic, near-term expected performance, with the "benchmark" being perhaps a longer-term goal.

Practice history is important in determining reasonable time frames in which to achieve the new targets, but it should not be the only factor. Others include cash available for the improvement process, complexity of process reengineering, and retraining requirements for providers and staff. The targets need to be aggressive enough to move the organization forward in a timely manner while providing opportunities for quick success to build physician and staff confidence that the targets are achievable.

Physicians and staff need to be involved during this step, just as they were in the identification of critical drivers and as they will be in the development of action plans. This does not necessarily mean they have veto power over potential changes or targets. Rather, they need to be involved in identifying the reasons for the problems so that they have a context for understanding and accepting the new standards. At the same time, because they will be required to make changes to achieve the new targets, it is critical that they provide input on the action plan. Their input will help ensure that the action plan is realistic and that they have buy-in to its success.

Steps 6-9: Develop and Implement Action Plan

The identification of practice-specific targets and implementation of an action plan to achieve them is where the process breaks down for many groups. While targets may be identified and even communicated to staff and physicians, it is often assumed that specifying the target will automatically lead to its being met. Generally, the target has not been met in the past because of system and knowledge barriers. Therefore, it is not sufficient to identify targets without creating an action plan to achieve them. At the same time, another common problem is that the standards are not consistently measured, nor feedback provided. The silence, of course, implies that the performance measures are not important and can be ignored.

The action plan often is more complex than initially anticipated because of the interdependency of critical variables related to the target. To accomplish a single target often requires reworking multiple processes, as well as re-training. For instance, to increase provider productivity, changing the schedule, staffing, and work flow processes may be necessary. Therefore, the action plan should list all the processes and system changes required, as well as any necessary training. Time frames and individuals responsible for implementation of each step of the action plan should be included. It is then critical to monitor implementation carefully so that any issues can be quickly resolved, time frames met, and goals achieved. The information gained from this process can then be fed into the next round of problem solving and the setting of new performance targets.

LIMITATIONS TO BENCHMARKING

While the use of benchmarking can lead to improved performance, it is important to understand the limitations of benchmarking, as well as the requirements to make the process successful:

- Benchmarking does not end with identification of the benchmark or data collection. To gain maximum benefit, it should be used not only to identify areas for improvement and establish performance measures, but also to drive the development of action plans that will actually improve performance.

- Because this is a change process, it is critical to make an objective assessment of the organizational culture, staff, and management to identify any potential barriers to the performance improvement process, as well as to determine the organization's capability to create and manage change internally. Leading a change process requires a different skill set than day-to-day management. Therefore, outside resources may be necessary to assist in the implementation of the benchmarking process. If painful decisions are required, it may be more successful to have someone from the outside lead the process so that the long-term effectiveness of the management team is not impaired. Also, an outside perspective may be helpful in overcoming resistance to the need for change.

- One benchmark may not tell the whole picture. There are multiple indicators of a successful practice. In addition, these factors are interdependent and cannot be used in isolation. For example, staffing may look appropriate when using FTEs per provider ratios. However, using salaries or benefits as a percent of net revenue may yield a very different conclusion.

• Benchmarks are not absolute. Instead, they serve as road maps that point to potential problem areas. Unique practice characteristics, such as geography, age of practice and patients, service mix, and practice style, can have an impact on the validity of national benchmarks for a particular practice. Therefore, it is important that national benchmarks be modified to reflect any differences. At the same time, however, differences should not be used to rationalize variances inappropriately. Also, practices may want to look outside health care to benchmark functions that are performed in other industries. For example, the hotel industry can provide benchmarks for registration, and many service businesses have phone standards that may be applicable.

POTENTIAL REVENUE INDICATORS

Potential revenue indicators include productivity, scheduling, revenue per unit of service, and the accounts receivable process.

Productivity

As the decision tree in Figure 4-2 indicates, revenue problems are due to either low volume or low revenue per unit of service. Obviously, provider productivity is the critical driver for revenue because revenue is generated only through the provision of services (except in capitated environments, when volume is measured by enrollment). The indicators listed in Table 4-2 are the most common measures of productivity. While all are effective measures, each has its limitations.

Table 4-2. Productivity Indicators

INDICATOR	DEFINITION	ADVANTAGES	DISADVANTAGES
Visits	E & M encounters	• Easy for providers and staff to understand • Industry standards are easily available	• May encourage unnecessary visits • Do not reflect all work performed
RVUs	Relative value units as defined by the Medicare RBRVS system; include work units only	• Measure all work activity • Allow for comparison among specialties • Provide measurement for patient acuity	• May encourage up-coding to increase RVUs • Difficult for physicians and staff to equate to actual work produced
Hours worked/patient care sessions	Number of scheduled patient care hours/sessions	• Easy to document	• Do not measure work units
Enrollment	Patients assigned to provider; typically applies to capitated payers	• Measures total practice "size" • Can be adjusted to reflect age/sex mix	• May not measure actual workload in groups where physicians share patients • Difficult to measure for non-capitated patients

Because number of visits is a measure easily understood by both physicians and staff, we generally recommend its use as a baseline measure of practice productivity. Visits, whether in the office or hospital, drive the performance of other professional and ancillary services. Therefore, visit minimums or targets should be established for all providers.

Performance against targets should be monitored monthly, and the data should be shared with providers and staff. Any negative variance should be immediately addressed and an action plan developed to meet targets, if appropriate. Ignoring negative variances reinforces negative behavior and undercuts the potential to improve performance.

RVUs are most useful in measuring work productivity. They provide a mechanism to compare work across specialty lines and can be helpful in addressing the common complaint, "my patients are sicker than yours" because sicker patients require more work effort, thereby resulting in higher RVUs. It also provides a useful basis for compensation, which is addressed in more detail in Chapter 5.

Hours worked or patient care sessions are a starting point for defining expectations for provider office hours and accessibility. It is crucial to clarify this standard for all specialties. In today's economic climate, it is often necessary to increase expectations for physician office hours and accessibility to accommodate required increases in patient volume.

Scheduling

One cannot evaluate productivity without examining scheduling templates and processes. For example, the number of appointment slots affects patient access, as well as patient revenue. Scheduling will be discussed in detail in Chapter 6.

Revenue per Unit of Service

A number of indicators help evaluate revenue per unit of service. The first step is to review the practice fee schedule to ascertain if the fee schedule appropriately captures all revenue. Charges for the most common CPT codes should reflect the costs incurred in providing the service and should be high enough to receive the full payment provided by the practice's major payers. Generally, this means that charges are generally 10 percent higher than your highest preferred provider fee schedule.

The next step is to examine the charge per visit. The coding patterns that drive the charges must be analyzed. Frequently, if a provider has a lower charge per visit, it is because most visits are coded at a 99212 level. While this may be appropriate for simple, acute visits with younger patients, it is often not appropriate for visits with older patients with multiple system problems and many medications. Figure 4-3 not only shows the distribution of evaluation and management codes by a specific provider, but it also compares the distribution to Medicare averages for the specialty and can serve to identify potential compliance issues.

Figure 4-3. Type of Visit

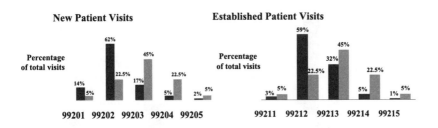

Source: www.hcfa.gov/stats/resource.htm

In this example, the physician uses a preponderance of low codes compared to others in his specialty, suggesting that the physician might be undercoding his visits. This hypothesis can be validated by reviewing both the patient demographics of the physician's panel as well as his documentation. Because of compliance fears, it is not unusual to find physicians coding at a lower visit level than the documentation actually supports. Generally, it is useful to perform this analysis on a quarterly or biannual basis. During periods when coding and compliance training are occurring, it is useful to monitor coding on a monthly basis along with a review of samples of the documentation of the visits to assess the impact of the training.

The service mix of the provider also influences revenue. Physicians performing more procedures or seeing more hospital patients have higher revenue per unit of service. A more complex service mix obviously also generates higher RVUs. A baseline analysis of service mix (shown in Figure 4-4) with periodic (semiannual) reviews thereafter can be useful in evaluating the strengths and weaknesses of the service mix, as well as any significant trends.

Figure 4-4. Service Analysis—1999/2000 Charges Comparison

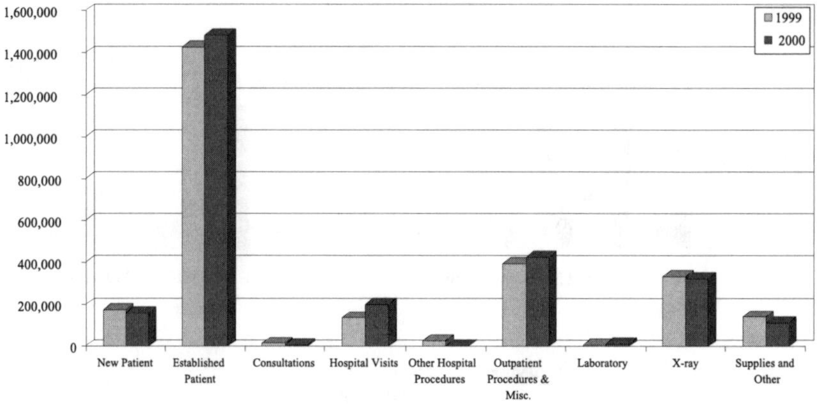

Source: The Camden Group

Accounts Receivable (A/R) Process

Another critical practice driver is the quality of the accounts receivable process. Because this is discussed in depth in Chapter 10, the discussion here will focus on those indicators that senior management should monitor on a consistent basis. The monthly practice report is not complete if it does not include an overall review of accounts receivable, as shown in the sample dashboard report in Exhibit 4-1 (at the end of this chapter): collection percentage, days in A/R, and percent of A/R over 90 days old. Definitions of these indicators are included in Chapter 10.

Many practices use a single indicator, days in A/R, to measure the effectiveness of their A/R process. However, that provides only part of the picture because days in A/R can be affected by the practice's write-off policy. Without also looking at bad debt and the net or adjusted collection percentage, you cannot assess whether staff is being too aggressive with their write-offs. If we do not look at percentage of A/R over 90 days, we cannot be sure that staff is performing the follow-up necessary to maximize collections.

When trying to improve performance, there is one other revenue indicator that needs to be monitored on a daily, weekly, and monthly basis: cash flow. By monitoring cash flow, smooth cash management can be ensured, progress toward the objectives quickly identified, and the performance of the collections process monitored. Table 4-3 is a sample spreadsheet that can be used to project expected collections based on charges from the previous months and budgeted charges for the current months. It requires that the gross collection percentage be calculated and that the timing of payments be estimated, i.e., the percentage of each month's charges that are collected over subsequent months until all the charges are collected. In the example, 15 percent of the current month's charges are collected in the current month. Most (30 percent each) are collected two and three months later.

Table 4-3
Sample Spreadsheet for Projecting Collections

Month	Charges	Total Expected Collections (61%)	Jan-99	Feb-99	Mar-99	Apr-99	May-99	Jun-99	Jul-99	Aug-99	Sep-99	Oct-99	Nov-99	Dec-99	Jan-00	Feb-00	Mar-00	Apr-00	May-00	Jun-00	Jul-00	Aug-00	Sep-00	Oct-00	Nov-00	Dec-00	Total
Dec-98	2,715,489	1,629,293	488,788	488,788	244,394	81,465	81,465																				
Jan-99	2,621,788	1,573,073	235,961	471,922	471,922	235,961	78,654	78,654																			
Feb-99	2,547,503	1,528,502		229,275	458,551	458,551	229,275	76,425	76,425																		
Mar-99	2,853,131	1,711,879			256,782	513,564	513,564	256,782	85,594	85,594																	
Apr-99	2,570,203	1,542,122				231,318	462,637	462,637	231,318	77,106	77,106																
May-99	2,455,523	1,473,314					220,997	441,994	441,994	220,997	73,666	73,666															
Jun-99	3,193,242	1,915,945						287,392	574,784	574,784	287,392	95,797	95,797														1,915,945
Jul-99	2,637,113	1,582,268							237,340	474,680	474,680	237,340	79,113	79,113													1,582,268
Aug-99	2,923,992	1,754,395								263,159	526,319	526,319	263,159	87,720	87,720												1,754,395
Sep-99	2,675,963	1,605,578									240,837	481,673	481,673	240,837	80,279	80,279											1,605,578
Oct-99	2,829,740	1,726,141										258,921	517,842	517,842	258,921	86,307	86,307										1,726,141
Nov-99	2,723,375	1,661,259											249,189	498,378	498,378	249,189	83,063	83,063									1,578,196
Dec-99	2,769,902	1,689,640												253,446	506,892	506,892	253,446	84,482	84,482								1,520,676
Jan-00	2,664,908	1,625,594													243,839	487,678	487,678	243,839	81,280	81,280							1,219,195
Feb-00	2,618,056	1,597,014														239,552	479,104	479,104	239,552	79,851	79,851						718,656
Mar-00	2,952,269	1,800,884															270,133	540,265	540,265	270,133	90,044	90,044					270,133
Apr-00	2,468,368	1,505,704																225,856	451,711	451,711	225,856	75,285	75,285				0
May-00	3,146,852	1,919,580																	287,937	575,874	575,874	287,937	95,979	95,979			0
Proj 6/1/2000	3,334,098	2,033,800																		305,070	610,140	610,140	305,070	101,690	101,690		0
Total	36,937,877	22,417,802						1,603,883	812,124	1,312,623	1,529,227	1,600,051	1,686,775	1,677,336	1,676,029	1,649,897	1,659,731	1,656,609	1,685,227	1,763,918	1,581,764	1,063,406	476,334	197,669	101,690	0	13,891,184
Actual								1,447,006	1,705,647	1,866,174	1,464,839	1,683,342	1,835,315	1,656,427	1,808,639	1,579,438	1,718,483	1,707,831	1,839,309								1,762,938
Variance								(156,877)	893,523	553,551	(64,388)	83,291	148,540	(20,909)	132,611	(70,459)	58,752	51,221	154,082								

Source: The Camden Group

POTENTIAL EXPENSE INDICATORS

If productivity and revenue per unit of service indicators are at benchmarks, then it is necessary to assess the expense structure of the organization. Negative variances in expenses are related to either operating expenses or physician compensation (Figure 4-2). As we discuss in Chapter 7, an income and expense statement that common-sizes expenses as a percentage of net revenue provides a good starting point to assess practice operating expenses because national benchmarks are available for the most common expense categories for comparison to your practice. The first item to compare to benchmark is total operating expenses. Benchmarking standards based on MGMA's surveys as well as those used by The Camden Group are included in Exhibit 4-2 (at the end of this chapter). A negative variance leads to an examination of expenses by category to identify major negative outliers. Exhibit 4-3 at the end of this chapter provides examples of key expense categories and sample benchmarks. Chapter 7 includes a detailed discussion of cost management strategies for operating expenses.

Non-provider Staffing Expenses

As we look at operating expenses, the largest variance often occurs in non-provider staffing. Because it is the largest operating expense of the practice, decreasing this expense can have a significant impact on overall costs. Three measures related to staffing can quickly identify whether non-provider staffing expenses are a problem:

- Staff salaries and benefits as a percentage of net revenue
- Number of non-provider staff per provider FTE
- Non-provider staff hours per visit.

As with other practice indicators, however, none of these measures should be examined in isolation. Negative variances in the salary and benefit percentage may be a function of revenue (volume), rather than excessive staffing. Non-provider staffing per provider may be higher than expected, but if those staff members also generate a higher-than-expected revenue, the higher staffing is probably appropriate.

Other Operating Expenses

Other major expense categories that may require scrutiny include medical supplies, ancillary expenses (laboratory and radiology), and facility expenses. Ancillary expenses should be carefully reviewed on a regular basis because the rapidly changing reimbursement in these areas now often makes these services a cost center rather than a profit center. Also, it is important to consider the hidden costs when evaluating the profit margin in ancillary services. Extra staffing may be required in other areas, such as check-in/check-out and billing to provide these services, yet those costs are frequently not included in an analysis. Additional space is required as well, and is not always included when looking at costs.

Physician Compensation

The starting benchmark to consider when looking at physician compensation is compensation as a percentage of net revenue. For most specialties, compensation, including all benefits, will be no greater than 50 percent of net income. Surgical and hospital-based specialties are the exceptions, where physician compensation may be 60 percent of net revenue. In a performance improvement situation, there often is a significant negative variance in this percentage. This generally occurs either because (1) the compensation formula does not include a strong productivity incentive, or (2) there are too many physicians for patient demand. Solving the first problem requires redesign of the compensation plan, which is discussed in more detail in Chapter 5. Resolution of the second problem requires a realistic look at the patient demographics of the service area to determine the required number of physicians. Often performance improvement can be accomplished only by downsizing physician staff.

ONGOING MONITORING

Benchmarking or measuring against targets cannot cease with an initial improvement in performance. Numerous indicators should be monitored on an ongoing basis by selected individuals within the organization to ensure that the success is not temporary. Table 4-4 lists key indicators to measure and identify who within the organization should review and monitor their performance.

Table 4-4
Key Measures for Ongoing Monitoring

| | Distribution | | | |
Performance Measure	SENIOR MANAGEMENT	PROVIDERS	CLINIC MANAGEMENT	BUSINESS OFFICE
Productivity				
Visits by provider by site	X	X	X	X
RVUs by provider by site	X	X	X	X
Net revenue per visit by provider by site	X	X	X	
Financial				
Income/expense statement to budget & previous year by site & roll-up	X	X	X	X
Staff FTEs/provider	X	X	X	
Overhead as percentage of net revenue by site	X	X	X	
Collection percentage	X	X	X	X
Days in A/R	X	X	X	X
A/R percentage by aging category	X	X	X	X
Credit balance report	X		X	X
Operations				
Access wait times	X	X	X	
Telephone abandonment rate			X	X
Wait time/visit		X	X	
Wait time for return call		X	X	X
Accounts worked/biller				X
TOS collections by site			X	X
Missing ticket report			X	X
Denial & edit reports			X	X

Source: The Camden Group

As indicated, responsibility for monitoring and reviewing are spread throughout many levels of the organization. It is important that those who have an impact on the achievement of targets know and understand the practice's performance on those key indicators. Some information may be distributed to heighten awareness, whereas some may be reviewed to cause action. For example, it is the business office manager's responsibility to ensure that appropriate action is taken with respect to the credit balance report. On the other hand, senior management and clinic managers should be aware of its implications.

Benchmarking is a valuable tool in assisting practices in improving their performance and achieving at the optimumlevel. It creates the context in which to identify issues, set targets, and take action to improve performance. To be successful in the long term, however, the use of benchmarks must be an ongoing five-step process: identifying problems, setting benchmarks, taking action, continually monitoring, and reassessing. As Todd Lambertus has said: "Benchmarking is the practice of being humble enough to admit that someone else is better at something and wise enough to try to learn how to match and even surpass them at it on a continuous basis."[4]

[4]Lambertus, Todd. Understanding Benchmarking. *Journal of Healthcare Resource Management* 11(9):36, 1993.

Exhibit 4-1
Executive Summary Monthly Dashboard Report
FY 2000 Income/Expenses Statement

Expense	July Actual $	July Actual % Net Revenue	YTD Actual [1] $	YTD Actual [1] %	YTD Budget $	YTD Budget % Net Rev	YTD Variance [2] $	YTD Variance [2] %
Charges	2,534,285		30,411,418		$31,360,000		(948,582)	-3.0%
Contractual Allowances	962,165		11,545,974		9,408,000		2,137,974	22.7%
Net Revenue	1,572,120		18,865,444		21,952,000		(3,086,556)	-14.1%
OPERATING EXPENSES								
Staff Salaries/Benefits	547,375	34.8%	6,225,596	33.0%	7,018,054	32.0%	(792,458)	-11.3%
Medical Supplies	82,106	5.2%	943,272	5.0%	878,080	4.0%	65,192	7.4%
Lab/Radiology	62,885	4.0%	754,618	4.0%	939,546	4.3%	(184,928)	-19.7%
Facility	102,110	6.5%	1,225,321	6.5%	1,578,349	7.2%	(353,028)	-22.4%
Malpractice	31,442	2.0%	377,309	2.0%	335,866	1.5%	41,443	12.3%
Professional Services	15,721	1.0%	188,654	1.0%	166,835	0.8%	21,819	13.1%
Marketing	10,520	0.7%	126,235	0.7%	90,003	0.4%	36,232	40.3%
General & Administrative	135,217	8.6%	1,885,632	10.0%	1,751,770	8.0%	133,862	7.6%
Total Operating Expenses	987,376	62.8%	11,726,638	62.2%	12,758,502	58.1%	(1,031,865)	-8.1%
PROVIDER EXPENSES								
Mid-level Salaries/Benefits	31,625	2.0%	365,038	1.9%	425,655	1.9%	(60,617)	-14.2%
Physician Salaries/Benefits	693,782	44.1%	8,325,388	44.1%	8,724,635	39.7%	(399,247)	-4.6%
CME	7,947	0.5%	95,367	0.5%	112,325	0.5%	(16,958)	-15.1%
Total Provider Expenses	732,149	46.6%	8,785,793	46.6%	9,262,615	42.2%	(476,822)	-5.1%
NET INCOME(LOSS)	(147,405)	-9.4%	(1,646,987)	-9%	(69,117)	0%	(1,577,870)	2282.9%

(1) YTD 2000 includes 11 months
(2) Comparisons should also be done for monthly performance. We have not included them here, given space constraints.

Source: The Camden Group

Exhibit 4-1a
Executive Summary Monthly Dashboard Report (cont'd)

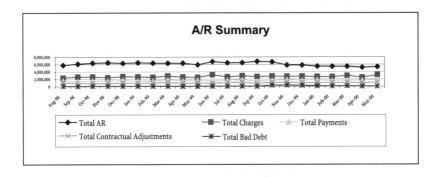

A/R Summary

Exhibit 4-1a (cont'd)
Executive Summary Monthly Dashboard Report (cont'd)

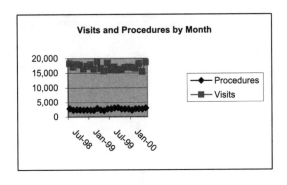

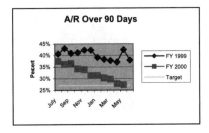

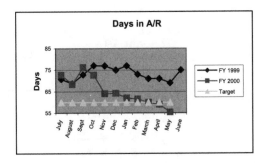

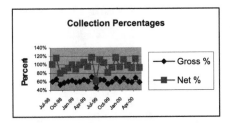

Source: The Camden Group

Exhibit 4-2
Practice Performance Indicators

Indicator [1,2]	Family Practice		Internal Medicine		OB/GYN		Pediatrics		MGMA Best Practice [5]	
	MGMA	Camden	MGMA	Camden	MGMA	Camden	MGMA	Camden	Medicine	Surgery
Production [9]										
Total Annual Office Visits (Table 37)	4,382	6,210	2,998	4,554	3,201	3,381	5,067	6,210	n/a	n/a
New Patient %	n/a	10-20%	n/a	10-20%	n/a	10-20%	n/a	10-20%	n/a	n/a
Total Work RVUs (Table 49)	3,786	5,900	3,350	5,465	9,135	9,636	4,386	5,900	n/a	n/a
Average RVU/Visit	0.86	0.95	1.12	1.20	2.85	2.85	0.87	0.95	n/a	n/a
Total Annual Deliveries	n/a	n/a	n/a	n/a	n/a	180	n/a	n/a	n/a	n/a
C-Section %	n/a	n/a	n/a	n/a	n/a	20%	n/a	n/a	n/a	n/a
Revenue [9]										
Annual Charges (Table 18)	$338,554	$484,380	$296,718	$478,170	$746,510	$760,725	$401,209	$465,750	n/a	n/a
Average FFS Charge/Visit	$77	$78	$99	$105	$233	$225	$79	$75	n/a	n/a
% Ancillary	n/a	5-10%	n/a	5-10%	n/a	5-10%	n/a	5-10%	n/a	n/a
Operating Expenses [10]										
Staff Salary + Benefit Expense [3]	31.9%	33.0%	28.7%	33.0%	25.2%	30.0%	30.1%	34.0%	n/a	n/a
FTEs per Provider	3.92	4.20	3.62	4.20	3.38	3.65	3.44	4.20	n/a	1.78
Productive employee hours/visit [4]	n/a	2.0-3.0	n/a	1.9 - 3.2	n/a	1.9 - 3.2	n/a	1.9 - 3.2	n/a	n/a
Operating Overhead % [3]	57.7%	55.0%	57.4%	55.0%	50.7%	50.0%	54.9%	55.0%	35.6%	37.3%
Accounts Receivable [6,10]										
Gross FFS Collection % [9]	75%	TBD	70%	TBD	68%	TBD	81%	TBD	n/a	58%
Net FFS Collection %	98%	TBD	97%	TBD	97%	TBD	98%	TBD	n/a	99%
Discount % [8]	25%	TBD	30%	TBD	32%	TBD	19%	TBD	n/a	42%
Days in A/R	53.1	50.0	57.0	50.0	59.7	60.0	57.0	50.0	n/a	45.9
% A/R Over 90 Days	25%	25%	25%	25%	24%	25%	22%	25%	n/a	15%

Notes:

1   All indicators are shown on a per provider FTE basis unless otherwise noted

2   MGMA data is based on single specialty practices

3   Expressed as a percentage of net revenue (collections)

4   Includes all employees (including MSO); the smaller the group, the higher the # of productive hours per visit

5   Based on MGMA report of *Performance and Practices for Successful Medical Groups; 1999 Report Based on 1998 Data* Information for "better performers" was utilized.
    Detail for all specialties not available.

6   MGMA A/R data found in Tables 10.2, 11.2, 12.2, 13.2, 14.2 of the Cost Survey

7   Collections as a percent of total charges

8   Adjustments as a percentage of payments ÷ adjustments

9   *MGMA Physician Compensation and Production Survey, 1999 Report Based on 1998 Data,* Tables 18, 37 and 49

10 *MGMA Cost Survey, 1999 Report Based on 1998 Data*

n/a   Data not available/not applicable

TBD   The Camden Group collection benchmarks are determined by the practices' actual payer mix

Data used with permission from the Medical Group Management Association, 104 Inverness Terrace East, Englewood, Colorado 80112-5306; 303-799-1111
www.mgma.com. Copyright 1999.

Exhibit 4-3
Expense Benchmarks

	FP - Not Hsp Owned		FP-Hsp Owned		Internal Medicine		OB/GYN	
	MGMA	Camden	MGMA	Camden	MGMA	Camden	MGMA	Camden
Gross Charges/FTE (Table 18)	$338,554	$484,380	n/a	$465,750	$296,718	$478,170	$746,510	$760,725
Collection Percentage	75%	TBD	73%	TBD	70%	TBD	68%	TBD
Net Revenue								
OPERATING EXPENSES [1]								
Staff Salaries/Benefits	31.8%	33.0%	31.1%	33.0%	28.7%	33.0%	25.2%	30.0%
Medical Supplies	4.0%	4.0%	3.5%	3.5%	2.3%	2.8%	3.0%	3.0%
Lab/Radiology	3.3%	3.0%	3.9%	3.0%	4.5%	3.5%	2.5%	3.0%
Facility	6.7%	6.5%	8.6%	6.5%	6.1%	6.5%	5.7%	5.7%
Malpractice	1.5%	1.5%	1.1%	1.5%	1.4%	1.0%	3.7%	3.5%
Professional Services	0.7%	1.0%	0.4%	0.2%	0.6%	1.0%	1.0%	0.6%
Marketing	0.4%	0.4%	0.3%	0.4%	0.3%	0.5%	0.5%	1.0%
General & Administrative	2.8%	5.6%	9.2%	9.9%	8.5%	6.7%	3.6%	3.2%
Total Operating Expenses	57.7%	55.0%	62.9%	58.0%	57.4%	55.0%	50.7%	50.0%
Total Operating Expenses for Better Performing Groups	0.0%	n/a	57.4%	n/a	n/a	n/a	n/a	n/a
PROFESSIONAL EXPENSES								
Provider Salaries/Benefits 2,3	138,277	163,086	n/a	n/a	140,951	149,698	216,307	259,559
CME/Licenses								
Other								
Total Professional Expenses	42.3%	45.0%	37.1%	42.0%	42.6%	45.0%	49.3%	50.0%
Other Income								
NET PHYSICIAN INCOME								

Notes:

[1] All MGMA specialty information is from Tables 10.5b, 11.5b, 12.5b, 13.5b and 14.5b with the exception of the multispecialty data from Table 1.5b (median); and Tables 56-76A.

[2] Camden based on: (charges)x(MGMA collection percentage)x(total professional expense percentage)

[3] Salaries are defined as the following:
MGMA: (Salary)+ (bonuses)+(incentive payments)+(research stipends)
Camden:(Base Salaries)+(Benefits)

Sources: *MGMA 1999 Cost Survey, 1999 Report Based on 1998 Data* and the *Physician Compensation and Production Survey, Report Based on 1998 Data* and The Camden Group proprietary database

Data used with permission from the Medical Group Management Association, 104 Inverness Terrace East, Englewood, Colorado 80112-5306; 303-799-1111. www.mgma.com. Copyright 1999.

5

DESIGNING AN EFFECTIVE COMPENSATION PLAN

Laura P. Jacobs, MPH

As part of a performance improvement process, virtually nothing is more crucial nor more controversial than provider compensation. Representing the single largest expense item for medical groups, physician compensation must be an important consideration as part of improving financial performance. In addition to its pure economic impact, the effect that the incentive structure has on physician behavior, including productivity and attention to group goals, will touch virtually every aspect of an effort to enhance performance. This will include the group's ability to increase revenue through volume, accurate coding, willingness to cooperate with expense reduction efforts, attention to patient service, and many other factors.

While the importance of reviewing the compensation structure is paramount, it also touches one of the most sensitive spots in the group: the physician's wallet. This will heighten physician anxiety throughout the assessment process, until decisions are made and communicated regarding any changes in the methodology for determining physician compensation.

Therefore, it is critical that any changes in physician compensation be made early in the improvement process. This will not only ensure that physicians are engaged in the overall effort, but it also will maximize and expedite the positive economic impact on the medical group.

COMPENSATION TRENDS

The Medical Group Management Association (MGMA) conducts annual surveys of physician compensation and productivity, as does the American Medical Group Association (AMGA) and other firms. MGMA's survey is often used as a benchmark of compensation trends because it represents a wide spectrum of medical groups, from small (three physicians) to very large, multi-specialty groups across the country. Tables 5-1 and 5-2 depict the compensation and productivity trends from 1994 through 1998, based on MGMA surveys.[1] What is clear from these figures is that while compensation has increased during this time frame, it has grown through higher levels of productivity.

For example, primary care compensation experienced lower increases through 1996 and 1997, with increases of 1.42 and 0.42 percent. In 1998, however, this trend was reversed, with a 2.54 percent increase in median compensation between 1997 and 1998. The increase in productivity was also at its highest level during this period, with a 4.67 percent increase in median charges between 1997 and 1998. Even with the imperfections of charges as a measure of productivity, it is clear that the way for most groups to achieve higher levels of compensation is through increases in productivity.

[1]Medical Group Management Association. *Physician Compensation and Production Survey: 1999 Report Based on 1998 Data.* Englewood, CO, 1999, pp. 14-15.

Table 5-1. Change in Physician Compensation*
1994-1998

	94-95 Change	95-96 Change	96-97 Change	97-98 Change	94-98 Change
Family Practice	5.86%	2.54%	2.69%	1.67%	13.34%
Internal Medicine	4.30%	0.49%	-0.09%	0.91%	5.66%
Pediatric Medicine	2.12%	2.29%	-0.18%	2.43%	6.80%
All Primary Care	4.46%	1.42%	0.42%	2.54%	9.10%
All Specialties	1.79%	2.58%	-0.48%	5.22%	9.34%
All Mid-level Providers	1.39%	0.53%	4.41%	4.93%	11.68%

*Represents median compensation for specialties listed
Source: MGMA, *Physician Compensation and Production Survey: 1999 Report Based on 1998 Data*, Table A, p.14.

Data used with permission from the Medical Group Management Association, 104 Inverness Terrace East, Englewood, Colorado 80112-5306; 303-799-1111. www.mgma.com. Copyright 1999.

Table 5-2. Change in Physician Productivity (Charges)*
1994-1998

	94-95 Change	95-96 Change	96-97 Change	97-98 Change	94-98 Change
Family Practice	1.12%	2.62%	2.44%	1.97%	8.40%
Internal Medicine	-1.93%	3.74%	5.90%	-0.52%	7.18%
Pediatric Medicine	0.03%	9.39%	-0.12%	3.59%	13.21%
All Primary Care	0.57%	3.36%	2.56%	4.67%	11.59%
All Specialties	5.59%	10.61%	3.97%	6.51%	29.33%
All Mid-level Providers	14.57%	-5.52%	8.26%	15.77%	35.67%

*Represents median gross charges for specialties listed
Source: MGMA, *Physician Compensation and Production Survey: 1999 Report Based on 1998 Data*, Table B, p.15.

Data used with permission from the Medical Group Management Association, 104 Inverness Terrace East, Englewood, Colorado 80112-5306; 303-799-1111. www.mgma.com. Copyright 1999.

During the 1990s, many integrated delivery systems were formed and, as part of the process of acquiring practices, established guaranteed salaries for the physicians. This single factor has been attributed to the sizable losses experienced by many hospital-owned groups. With no incentive to maintain or increase patient volume and with compensation fixed, it is no wonder the result was a deterioration in the practice financial condition, not to mention physician motivation. Many PPMs experienced this same "financial meltdown" as a result of poorly designed compensation formulas.

For these reasons, many compensation models today are refocusing on production as a primary basis for paying providers. The 1999 MGMA survey indicates that 53 percent of established primary care physicians' compensation is based on productivity. For specialists the figure is virtually the same (51 percent).[2]

WHEN IS IT TIME TO CHANGE THE COMPENSATION PLAN?

It is a truism in health care that there are three types of physician compensation plans: last year's, this year's, and next year's. Changes in reimbursement, medical group composition, economic realities, ownership structure, and many other factors will have an impact on the effectiveness of the compensation methodology. If the medical group is in financial trouble, it is a virtual certainty that the compensation plan will be reviewed. The following statements are other warning signs that the compensation plan is a problem:

- What plan? Our physicians are on income guarantees.

- Everyone hates it...the other guy is making too much money, and I'm not making enough.

- It's a plan that has been in place for the last 5 years; it was so painful to create that we're afraid to change it.

[2] Medical Group Management Association. *Physician Compensation and Production Survey: 1999 Report Based on 1998 Data*. Englewood, CO, 1999. pp. 14-15.

- It takes 30 days and 3 computers to calculate bonuses and 365 days to explain them.

- If our administrator/medical director were ever to leave, we'd never be able to explain our compensation plan.

- It seems to provide incentives for all the wrong behavior.

- The group is in financial trouble, yet physicians are making greater than market incomes.

- There's no sense of commitment to the group's performance; everyone's out for his/her own good.

Compensation plans should be evaluated annually for many reasons. Comparing compensation internally will identify any unintended differences in compensation among physicians in the group. Changes in strategy or payer mix may require adjustments in incentives. Comparisons to external benchmarks will illustrate variations as compared to market rates. Various sources for external comparisons are available, as noted, including MGMA, AMGA, AMA, as well as publications such as *Medical Economics*. These resources can be extremely valuable, but the following issues should be considered when using any external physician compensation resource:

- How large is the sample from which the data were gathered? Obviously, smaller sample sizes may be less reliable as a comparison.

- Are comparable productivity data available from the same survey? Any compensation comparisons should include measures of productivity as well. This could be charges, net revenue, visits, or relative value units (RVUs). Higher or lower compensation could be explained by higher or lower levels of productivity. Therefore, compensation figures alone can be misleading unless accompanied by productivity indicators.

- Are data available for your region? Physician compensation varies by region, depending on managed care penetration, physician supply, and other environmental factors. Be careful, however, in defining the region too narrowly, as competition for physicians often extends across a multi-state region.

- How are the survey data compiled? In general, large national surveys such as MGMA and AMGA use standardized survey instruments and are conducted by independent organizations. Surveys compiled by publications might be less reliable because they rely on the participation of subscribers. Given the complexity of defining terms and the difficulty of ensuring that data are submitted in a consistent manner, no survey will be perfect.

FACTORS INFLUENCING COMPENSATION PLAN DESIGN

Numerous factors influence compensation plan design (see Figure 5-1). The complexity of physician compensation is compounded by the fact that physicians are not only employees, but typically are also owners of the medical group.

Figure 5-1. Factors Influencing Compensation Plan Design

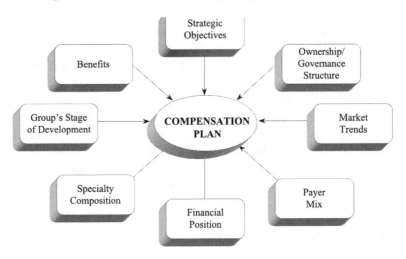

Strategic Objectives

Is the group poised to expand into new geographic regions? As a result of expansion, will it need to place physicians in sites with a different payer mix or opportunity for growth? Are there other strategic goals that could affect revenue, individual physician performance, or financial results?

What are the group's primary values? Is it focused on building stronger group culture, or does it value individualism? How important to the group's success is improving patient service or access? The answers to these and other significant questions will affect the design of the compensation plan. For this reason, it will be crucial for the strategic objectives of the group to be clear before beginning the review of the plan.

Ownership/Governance Structure

Shareholders or partners in the group will have a different compensation structure than physicians who have recently joined the medical group. By definition, the compensation of owners of the medical group will be affected by its profitability. Employed physicians will have less of their compensation at risk, but they may also have a lower potential maximum compensation level. The degree to which the group has empowered the governing body and group leadership with the ability to review physician performance will affect the degree to which "subjective" measures are used in the compensation formula.

Market Trends

The strategic objectives of the group should be based on the trends in the local marketplace. Changes in managed care penetration and the reimbursement strategies of local payers could influence the structure of the compensation plan. For example, many groups have created a compensation methodology assuming high levels of capitated revenue. When capitation fails to materialize or is eliminated as a payment mechanism by payers, it may require a revamping of the compensation formula.

Payer Mix

As noted, payer mix must be considered, particularly in designing productivity incentives. If emphasized without regard to sources of revenue, productivity can create disastrous financial results in a fully capitated environment. On the other hand, in a fee-for-service marketplace, straight salaries will also lead to less-than-desirable performance.

Financial Position

Comprising the single largest expense item in a medical group, physician compensation will always be affected by the medical group's financial resources. In addition, physician behavior has significant impact on both revenue and the operating expenses of the practice. Depending on the priorities of a financial improvement plan, the compensation structure may need to emphasize physician participation in operating expense reduction and revenue or volume enhancement in various degrees.

Specialty Composition

Whether the group is single- or multi-specialty will affect the complexity and flexibility required in the compensation formula. Single-specialty groups can use fairly straightforward formulas, in some cases simply splitting group profitability equally among all members. In multi-specialty groups, the differences in compensation levels and revenue/expense structures of the various specialties create the need to consider multiple factors in designing the group's compensation plan. For example, in multi-specialty groups, using RVU-based productivity formulas will require multiple conversion factors to convert RVUs to income appropriate to the specialty.

Group's Stage of Development

While not often discussed, the medical group's longevity and stage of development can have a major impact on the most suitable type of compensation formula. Well-established groups often have an ingrained culture that dictates the type of compensation formula. They may also have leadership in place that allows more complex methods of evaluating physician performance. Newer groups usually rely on pure quantitative measures to drive individual physician compensation. They are more likely to use a methodology driven solely by individual production.

Benefits

Benefits are often not factored in adequately when compensation plans are evaluated. This is a mistake, if only because of the economic impact that benefits have. Groups can offer a wide range of benefits, including the following:

- Vacation, sick, holiday (paid time off) allowance
- Allowance for CME, including time off and expenses allowed
- Health, life, and disability insurance
- Sabbatical (paid or unpaid)
- Pension/deferred compensation.

The direct cost of these benefits, as well as the indirect cost (e.g., time off), must be taken into consideration when determining the cash compensation targets for the physicians in the group.

KEYS TO DESIGNING A SUCCESSFUL PLAN

Taking into consideration these factors, an effective compensation plan will include the following elements:[3]

- The plan is responsive to the vision and strategic objectives of the group.
- Compensation is reviewed annually to reflect external and internal conditions.
- Clear expectations of physician performance are established prospectively.

[3] Jacobs, Laura P. The Compensation-Governance Connection. *Group Practice Journal,* Volume 47, No. 7, July/August, 1998, p.18.

- A system is established and consistently executed to review and communicate individual physician performance.
- Measures and incentives for "team" (site, "pod," or group) performance are included.
- Performance targets are achievable and take into consideration external and internal benchmarks.
- Cash compensation is coordinated with benefit plan design and the group's ownership structure.
- KISS: keep it simple and easy to communicate and administer.

COMPENSATION STRUCTURES

There are about as many types of compensation formulas as there are medical groups. Based on the factors discussed, each group will develop a plan unique to its set of circumstances. Table 5-3 illustrates the basic formats for compensation plan design and the ability of the plan to engender certain behaviors.

Salary

Many large groups and some hospital-based groups use a salary structure as the basis for physician compensation. Straight guarantees are to be avoided at all costs, as compensation bears no relationship to behavior or performance. More sophisticated groups will use the salary structure but will vary individual physician salary based on performance reviews conducted annually. This can be used successfully to affect physician behavior, but it has two important drawbacks: lack of frequency in rewarding positive behavior and limited incentives for productivity.

Table 5-3. Individual Physician Compensation Methods

Compensation Method	PERFORMANCE GOALS						
	Physician Productivity	Revenue Enhancement	Expense Reduction	Approp. Utilization	Quality Care/ Outcome	Patient Service	Citizenship
Salary	—	—	—	•	•	•	•
Salary + Productivity Bonus	+	+	•	—	•	•	•
Salary + PerformanceBonus (multi-measures)	+	+	+	+	+	+	+
% Individual Net Revenue*	+	+	•	+	•	•	•
Equal Split of Group Income	•	•	•	•	•	•	+
% Equal split of Group Income and % Individual Net Revenue	+	+	•	+	•	•	+

* Assumes net revenue includes capitated payment for assigned enrollees and share of risk pool distribution.

Legend:	
+	Incentive to achieve goal
•	Neutral
—	Negative incentives; work against goal

Salary + Bonus

The salary and bonus structure is becoming the most common methodology for many medium-to-large groups because it provides a baseline income for physicians while allowing for flexibility in designing incentives to influence performance. The biggest debate in using this structure is the level of salary to be provided. The rule of thumb is that the base salary should be no greater than 80 percent of targeted compensation, allowing at least 20 percent of compensation to be at risk. This provides enough incentive to influence behavior, while leaving a reasonable floor to provide a predictable income to the physician. The success of this design will depend on the measures used and the frequency with which incentives are paid. It is suggested that incentive pay be awarded at least three to four times per year to ensure that regular feedback is being provided.

Percentage of Net Revenue

This pure economic model is appropriate for groups where there is generally similar payer mix among the physicians in the group. Many smaller groups use this model effectively. It provides an emphasis on individual performance, and it is for this reason that many groups prefer it. It can lead to excessive competition among members of the group, so the potential for this dynamic within each group must be determined. The percentage of net revenue assigned to individual physicians can be determined based on total group operating expenses, or it can be based on the site's operating expenses. Some groups prefer to allocate expenses to individual physicians, but this can become extremely difficult to administer as groups get larger in size. One of the case studies described in this chapter uses this model.

Equal Split of Group Income

This model is most often used in single-specialty groups of less than eight or ten physicians. It encourages internal referrals within the group and is often used in such specialties as cardiology or orthopedics, where there are sub-specialties but where the group values the contribution of each member equally. It is also used in groups where some members have teaching responsibilities that cannot be measured with productivity indicators. This can work as long as each member has roughly the same work ethic and devotion to producing for the group. More common in groups that have been together for a long time, this method tends to break down as some members wish to slow down or as new members join. It can be used in combination with other compensation structures, including the percentage of net revenue and salary/bonus formulas.

Incentive Structures

The most complex aspect of physician compensation plan development is determining the incentive structure. Of course, the simplest compensation plans are either those that are straight salary or are an equal split of practice income. The instances that these methodologies work effectively are few and are usually limited to small, tightly knit groups. Even groups with compensation that is fixed annually typically use some performance measures to determine annual salary to ensure that compensation can effectively drive preferred behavior. And of course, the effect of salary guarantees has already been discussed as a major contributor to failed or failing medical groups.

Therefore, the challenge to medical group leadership is the determination of how and to what degree various incentives should be used in the compensation formula. Figure 5-2 illustrates the variety of measures that can be used to evaluate and pay physicians.

Figure 5-2. Performance Measures

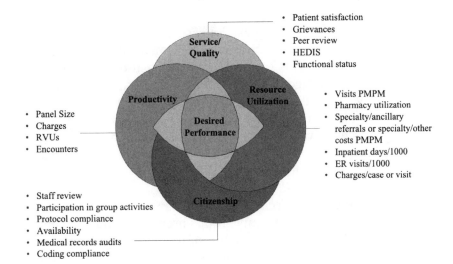

- Patient satisfaction
- Grievances
- Peer review
- HEDIS
- Functional status

- Visits PMPM
- Pharmacy utilization
- Specialty/ancillary referrals or specialty/other costs PMPM
- Inpatient days/1000
- ER visits/1000
- Charges/case or visit

- Panel Size
- Charges
- RVUs
- Encounters

- Staff review
- Participation in group activities
- Protocol compliance
- Availability
- Medical records audits
- Coding compliance

Productivity

Productivity incentives are often emphasized today, typically because it is necessary to increase revenue, hence patient volume, to facilitate performance improvement. Also, many troubled groups are emerging from situations with a lack of productivity incentives (e.g., guaranteed salaries) or have lapsed into a culture that fosters low productivity.

The measure of productivity utilized will vary depending on the group's ability to track it. For this reason, many groups use *charges* as a surrogate for productivity. The weakness of this measure is that it often has no relationship to either what will be collected or the physicians' work effort. The exception is if the fee schedule is built as a function of the RVUs designated for each CPT code, such as that used in the Medicare RBRVS schedule. However, another weakness with using charges is the difficulty in using it to compare productivity to external surveys. Because fee schedules vary between practices and across the country, it is not a uniform measure of work effort.

Visits are a commonly used measure of production, particularly in primary care practices or other medical specialties that are office based. This can be a useful measure, but definitions of a "visit" are varied: e.g., are procedures or nursing visits treated as a "visit," and are hospital, home, or skilled nursing facility visits counted? If the definition is at least standardized within the group, however, this can be a simple and appropriate measure of production. Its weakness lies in the inability to distinguish between acuity and length of visit.

Net revenue or *collections* by physician is an appropriate productivity measure, and many groups prefer it because it bears a direct relationship to the amount of money available to spend. Its use forces physicians to understand the impact their coding and documentation have on the ability to collect from payers. The weakness is that it can create inequities within the group if some physicians practice at sites with a greater proportion of Medicaid or other sources of payment with lower reimbursement rates.

Relative value units, or RVUs, have increased in popularity in recent years with the widespread use of Medicare's RBRVS fee schedule. RVUs probably provide the most accurate measure of physician work effort and can reflect a "sicker" or older patient population. The complexity of RVUs comes with the creation of a conversion factor to determine how much an RVU is worth when it comes to physician compensation. For this reason, RVUs are often linked with individual or specialty net revenue or group net income to ensure that a linkage with the financial resources is available.

In capitated groups, *panel size* can be used as a measure of the total patient population managed by the physician. The weakness with this measure is that there are often patients seen by multiple physicians within the group, thus requiring various "credits" or other measures of actual work performed by each physician.

Service/Quality

With the current focus on the need to ensure appropriate levels of patient service and quality outcomes, many groups have responded by placing more emphasis on service and quality measures in the compensation formula. The difficulty this presents for many groups is that they often lack adequate means of measuring these indicators.

Patient satisfaction is the measure most commonly used, but physicians often criticize it for not being gathered in a statistically meaningful way. Chapter 8, which offers some insight into patient satisfaction survey instruments, can provide a reference for determining a reasonable means of capturing this kind of data. In this age of consumer empowerment, physicians must be aware of how they are perceived by the most important customer, their patients. And the degree to which they pay attention to the results may depend on the dollars that are at stake through the compensation formula. Other measures of service include patient complaints or grievances and average wait times in the office.

Quality measures are even more controversial because most groups do not have effective means of collecting clinical data. The simplest means of monitoring quality is through medical record audits and a traditional peer review process. HMOs commonly require HEDIS (Health Plan Employer Data Information Set) measures and will include providers' compliance with standards for preventive care (Pap smears, mammography, blood pressure screening, etc.). Many providers, however, do not believe that they are an accurate indicator of quality of care. The most sophisticated groups are beginning to use functional status surveys (e.g., SF-36 forms) to measure improvement in patients' health status over a period of time.

The degree to which quality and service, as well as "citizenship," are emphasized in a group's compensation structure will depend largely on its physician leadership structure. If there is no organized mechanism within the physician leadership structure for reviewing physician performance, the relevance of these evaluations will be reduced. Most physicians will have difficulty accepting a lay administrator's evaluation of their performance. In these situations, limiting the dollar impact that these types of incentives have on physician compensation must be considered.

Citizenship

This category of performance measures refers to the wide array of activities that may indicate that the physician is a "good citizen of the group." From willingness to adhere to established policies and procedures, ability to get along with peers and support staff, attendance and participation in group meetings and community activities (marketing), there are many indicators that can be used. Some groups use internal staff surveys to obtain feedback from support staff and peers regarding performance. This information is submitted to a department head or medical director for review and to be factored into the performance review.

The difficulty with this range of measures is the pettiness that can result once it is identified as a factor in determining compensation. Which community events get counted (e.g., coaching soccer or teaching Sunday school versus attending health fairs and delivering lectures), and which meetings get the most credit will have to be specified. Remember, the most important axiom in designing the compensation formula: Keep it simple!

Medical groups must establish clear policies regarding how income from outside positions (e.g., hospital medical directorships) will be taken into account. Will it flow directly to the physician, or will it be considered "group revenue," with a portion allocated to the group?

Resource Utilization

These measures are typically factors in groups that receive reimbursement from HMOs in the form of capitation or are otherwise at risk for utilization management. They might include outside referrals, emergency room visits, hospital utilization, adherence to drug formularies, as well as others identified on Table 5-4. Given the controversy over the potential for limiting patient care, many groups use these measures as indicators of individual physician performance with caution, often in conjunction with the quality measures described earlier.

Table 5-4 summarizes these measures and their impact on performance goals. As illustrated, many of these measures have conflicting impacts on each other, which may be beneficial by providing some "checks and balances" in the formula. For example, measuring both RVUs and utilization measures may be necessary in capitated groups. Likewise, net revenue and RVUs may be used as productivity measures to ensure fair measure of work effort as well as adherence to appropriate coding and business office policies.

Table 5-4. Assessment of Performance Measures

Compensation Method	PERFORMANCE GOALS						
	Physician Productivity	Revenue Enhancement	Expense Reduction	Approp. Utilization	Quality Care/ Outcome	Patient Service	Citizenship
Encounters	+	—	•	—	•	+	•
RVUs	+	+	•	—	•	+	•
Charges	+	•	•	—	•	+	•
Net revenue	+	+	•	+	•	•	•
Visits/member* ER utilization Out-of-network	•	•	+	+	—	•	•
Specialty referrals*	•	+	+	+	—	•	•
Availability	+	+	•	•	•	+	+
Patient waiting time	+	•	•	•	•	+	+
Patient satisfaction surveys	•	•	•	•	•	+	+
Medical record review	•	•	•	•	+		+
HEDIS results	•	•	•	•	+	+	+
Meeting participation	—	•	•	•	•	•	+
External marketing activities	—		•	•	•	•	+

* Used in capitated models

Legend:
+   Incentive to achieve goal
•   Neutral
—   Negative incentives; work against goal

Don't Forget the KISS Rule

With the plethora of measures available and the tendency to want to ensure that physicians won't "game" the system, there invariably develops an "incentive creep" in the design of the compensation plan. As a result, so many measures are used and included in the incentive plan that no one measure has much impact. The plan becomes so cumbersome to manage and measure that no one understands it anymore. For this reason it is suggested that no more than five indicators be used in the compensation model, and preferably fewer. This doesn't mean that a wider variety of factors can't be used to measure physician performance. On the contrary, it can be very beneficial to keep physicians apprised of their performance on a number of levels. Every factor need not carry with it an economic impact, however. It is well known that physicians are motivated by data, often competitive, and are driven to perfection. Therefore, the sheer presence of comparative data may have the desired impact on physician behavior without trying to quantify the dollar impact.

REDESIGNING THE PLAN

The importance of leadership has been stressed throughout this book. Nowhere is leadership more important than during the process of redesigning the compensation plan. This is not an instance where there should be widespread participation in the decision. In smaller groups, of course, there should be unanimous consent to the plan. In larger groups, however, decisions about how compensation will be determined must be made by the governing body. Figure 5-3 illustrates the role of management and governance with regard to compensation plan design and management.

Figure 5-3. The Compensation-Governance Connection

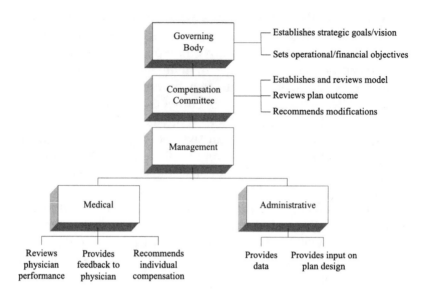

In most groups it will be necessary to form a compensation committee to discuss and review the various options and impact on the group. However, the governing body must give this committee direction regarding organizational and financial goals. From these, the compensation committee can articulate the goals specific to the compensation plan. Once these are established, the compensation committee can produce recommendations regarding the methodology and expected outcome of the model. The committee should be fairly representative of various specialties within the group, but most important, it should be composed of the individuals with experience in group leadership. It is a recipe for disaster if the compensation committee is perceived (or is) self-serving because its members are looking out for their own welfare instead of the group's.

INTRODUCING A NEW PLAN

Putting a new compensation plan up for a vote by the members is not recommended, except in smaller groups. In these situations, members will vote based on the expected impact of the new formula on themselves individually, rather than on the effect on the group overall. The governing body, therefore, must approve the plan and introduce it to the group through clear communication channels, explaining the rationale behind its make-up and the need to focus on the group's goals. Department chairs or other leadership representatives should be responsible for communicating and discussing the plan's impact on individual compensation with each physician.

Depending on how different the proposed plan is from the previous one, some groups prefer to run a "shadow" plan for three to six months prior to the real introduction of the plan. This can be helpful, particularly where new measures of productivity, such as RVUs, are being used for the first time. In crisis situations, however, there may not be time for such transitions. This, again, will be the decision of the governing body.

CASE STUDY 1: USING RVUs

This 20+-member family practice group had been using a compensation formula with a high base salary, with additional incentives driven by charges. The physicians were distributed in five different locations, some of which were in remote, rural areas. The group wished to move to an RVU-based system, with a greater proportion of compensation at risk. In addition, they wished to begin to use other non-productivity measures, such as patient satisfaction and medical record completion, in the incentive structure. There was also a need to clarify the minimum expectations of full-time physicians regarding scheduled office hours and meeting attendance. The biggest weakness in the previous compensation structure was a wide range of productivity among individual physicians in the group, without corresponding differences in compensation levels.

Established Goals

The clinic directors of each site comprised the governing body and compensation committee. The group's medical director chaired the committee. The following goals for the compensation plan were identified during an initial planning session:

- The plan must be fair and utilize achievable standards in establishing the incentive structure.
- The plan must be market-driven with respect to the compensation provided as well as the work effort expected.
- The plan must take into consideration differences in practice style: hospital coverage, emergency coverage, obstetrics, and the market dynamics of the rural locations.
- Incentives should be largely focused on productivity, with some consideration for service and group "citizenship."

Plan Structure

Figure 5-4 illustrates the basic model developed by the committee.

Figure 5-4. Plan Design

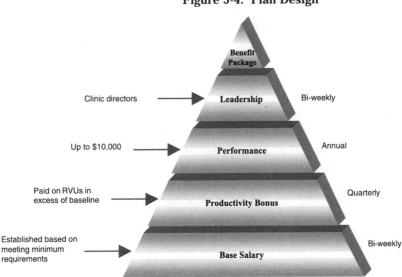

To initiate the process, the governing body established a target compensation rate based on external survey data and internal historical results. For the proposed year, this target was set at $140,000, excluding benefits. Base salary was established at approximately 60 percent of this base ($85,000), leaving the remainder at risk. However, the physicians' ability to earn the base salary was dependent on their adherence to the requirements of a full-time physician. This included a standard for days worked per year, hours of scheduled patient contact hours, participation in call coverage, and participation in group committees. In future years, physicians' base pay could be adjusted based on their fulfillment of these requirements.

The productivity incentive was driven by RVUs. Table 5-5 summarizes the rationale behind the methodology selected.

Table 5-5. Productivity Incentive Rationale

Component	Objective/Rationale
Productivity incentive is RVU (as defined by RBRVS) based (work unit only).	• Accounts for hospital and emergency activity as well as type of patient (older/more complex problems, OB, etc.). • Eliminates the problem of physicians who see patients assigned to other physicians not getting appropriate "credit" for the productivity.
Capitated dollars and fee-for-service revenue will be taken into account in calculating $/RVU to be paid for RVUs in excess of the baseline.	• Takes into account the primary care utilization management of capitated patients. That is, with the capitated payment fixed, as the number of RVUs increases, the revenue per RVU decreases. This places the incentive on increasing enrollment, and not "churning" existing patients. • Maintains consistency with reimbursement "reality" for managed care.
The baseline productivity will be established assuming 40 percent of net revenue required for physician compensation.	• Incentives will not be paid until this modified breakeven on base salary has been reached. • Minimizes the financial exposure to the group.
Net revenue per RVU is calculated using total group revenue versus site or physician specific data.	• Encourages intra-division referrals. • Minimizes impact of different payer mix based on location.
The percent of dollar/RVU paid will increase at high levels of productivity.	• Recognizes the value of incremental volume.
Incentives in addition to productivity have been included.	• Adds incentive for maintaining high levels of patient satisfaction and quality of care. • Recognizes contributions to the group due to administrative or leadership positions.

The model was based on the belief that physicians would receive incentive pay as soon as a calculated "break-even" was reached in the number of RVUs produced. The value of each RVU was based on the net revenue and RVUs generated by the group. There was also an interest within the group in rewarding physicians at higher productivity levels. For this reason, physicians received higher compensation/RVU for those RVUs greater than 150 percent of the baseline. In this case, "breakeven RVUs" were calculated assuming that physicians would receive 40 percent of net revenue as compensation, but incentive compensation paid 45 percent of net revenue for productivity up to 150 percent of baseline RVUs and 50 percent of net revenue for RVUs greater than 150 percent. Table 5-6 provides an example.

This plan was modeled using historical data to illustrate the impact on each individual physician to ensure that the group met the financial objectives. It also was used to communicate to physicians the incremental productivity required to achieve their desired level of compensation.

Table 5-6. Sample Productivity Calculation

Indicator	Assumption	Explanation
Step 1: Establish Baseline RVUs		
A Base salary	$85,000	Approximately 60% of target compensation ($140,000)
B Net division revenue	$6,000,000	1999 Net Group Revenue
C Total division RVUs	80,000	1999 Total Group RVUs (includes all providers)
D Revenue per RVU	$75.00	B/C
E % Physician compensaton	40%	Percent allocated for physician compensation
F Baseline comp per RVU	$30.00	D*E
G Baseline RVUs	2,833	A/F
Step 2: Calculate Individual Physician Productivity Incentive		
H RVUs	4,300	Physician's RVUs for the period
I RVUs over baseline	1,467	H-G
J % RVUs over baseline	52%	I/G; Determines % to apply
K RVUs at 0 - 50% greater than baseline	1,417	.50*G
L % Applied to RVU 0-50%	45%	Based on productivity grid
M Comp/RVU paid for 0 - 50%	$33.75	D*L
N RVUs paid at second increment	50	I-K
O % applied to RVUs 50%+	50%	Based on productivity grid
P Comp/RVU paid for RVUs 50%+	$37.50	D*N
Q Productivity bonus	$49,688	(M*K) + (P*N)

Source: The Camden Group

In addition to productivity, the group set aside up to $10,000 per physician for performance-related objectives. These objectives would be established annually and could be focused on quality, service, or other priorities. Because the group was only in the process of establishing patient survey tools, they decided to focus the first year's efforts on medical records and adherence to documentation requirements. The process for performance review is illustrated in Figure 5-5.

Figure 5-5. Performance Review Process

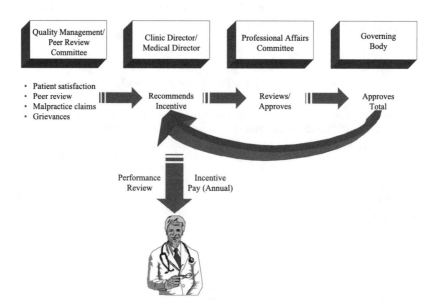

To reward clinic directors for their administrative responsibilities, they also established a stipend of $2,000 per year per provider supervised. No other board or committee positions would receive stipends because the group felt that it was everyone's responsibility to participate in these activities. Table 5-7 summarizes the compensation for a sample, relatively high-performing physician.

Because some physicians were going to be negatively affected by greater emphasis on productivity, the group was given a 90-day transition period, during which their productivity would be monitored but no change in compensation would be made.

Table 5-7. Total Sample Compensation

Base Salary	$ 85,000
Productivity	49,688
Performance	7,500
Leadership	<u>8,000</u>
Total Cash Compensation	$ 150,188

CASE STUDY 2: PERCENTAGE OF NET REVENUE

This group was composed of approximately 70 providers, representing all primary care specialties (internal medicine, pediatrics, and family practice). It had been developed through the acquisition and expansion of local primary care providers as part of the development of an integrated delivery system. While the compensation plan had been productivity-driven (charge-based), the system's goal was to create a formula that more closely resembled a private practice model, thereby making the physicians more sensitive to the net revenue and expenses of their locations.

Plan Design

Figure 5-6 illustrates the core elements of the compensation plan.

Figure 5-6. Core Elements of Compensation Plan

* Excludes Stark II Designated Health Services

The productivity incentive was site-driven with respect to the determination of the percentage of net revenue the physician would receive. That is, all physicians in the same office location received the same percentage of net revenue. This was designed to give the physicians incentive to work together more closely in each location to manage expenses and overall site performance. Each site's percentage would be established according to the targeted performance of the site. Table 5-8 illustrates a sample calculation for a particular site

In this example, each of the physicians in this location would

Table 5-8. Sample Productivity Calculation

		$	% of Net Revenue
A	Net Revenue – Dr. A	350,000	
B	Net Revenue – Dr. B	275,000	
C	Net Revenue – Dr. C	400,000	
D	Subtotal – Eligible Physicians	1,025,000	
E	Net Revenue – Dr. New	150,000	
F	Net Revenue–Mid-level	125,000	
G	**Net Revenue – Site***	1,300,000	
H	**Operating Expenses***	700,000	54%
I	Benefit Costs	75,000	6%
J	Other Incentives	60,000	5%
K	New Physicians	100,000	8%
L	Mid-level Providers	65,000	5%
M	**Subtotal–Other Provider Expenses**	300,000	23%
N	**Budget Target**	(120,000)	-9%
O	**Available for Productivity Incentive**	420,000	32%
P	**As Percentage of Eligible Physician Net Revenue**	41%	

*Excludes Stark II Designated Health Services

Source: The Camden Group

receive 41 percent of his or her net revenue, based on the budgeted loss of $120,000 for the site, or referencing Table 5-7, Site Net Revenue (A) minus Operating Expenses (H) minus Other Provider Expenses (M) minus the Budget Target (N). This produces (O), the dollars available for the productivity incentive ($420,000), which, as a percentage of their Net Revenue (D), is 41 percent. Therefore, Dr. A would receive 41 percent of $350,000, or $143,500, as productivity-based compensation.

The percentage is determined semi-annually for the following period to ensure that physicians feel the impact of changes (positive or negative) in the financial performance of the site. At the same time, the impact of seasonal changes in revenue needed to be minimized. While the calculation appears complex, the physicians focus on the percentage and can easily calculate what their compensation potential will be for the upcoming period.

It is important to note that net revenue is defined as capitated payments as well as fee-for-service net revenue, excluding any revenue from Stark II-designated services (radiology, lab, physical therapy, etc.). Also relevant is the fact that the eligible physicians will feel the impact of the profitability (or the lack thereof) of mid-level providers. Therefore, the determination of how and whether or not to utilize these providers should be a site decision.

The peer review committee determines the *individual performance* incentive using a set of criteria established prospectively each year. Patient satisfaction and peer review of designated cases, as well as assessment of peer interaction, are part of this review. Up to $20,000 per physician may be awarded for this aspect of performance. In the future, managed care utilization factors (such as ER admits and outside referrals) could also be used to measure performance in this category.

Team performance is awarded to the group as a whole, based on the group's achievement of goals established by the system at the beginning of the year. These goals could include such factors as group-wide patient access, development and implementation of designated group policies and procedures, performance to group budget, group-wide patient satisfaction, and utilization targets. The system determines this incentive award annually.

Leadership stipends were provided to individual physicians based on committee chairs, selected committee attendance, and supervision of mid-level providers.

A discussion of compensation is a critical aspect of a performance improvement effort. The degree to which physicians will be held accountable for the financial results will depend largely on group ownership structure. However, many integrated delivery systems are seeking ways to provide physicians with both revenue and expense incentives, thereby increasing accountability for the overall financial performance of the practice. While compensation plans can be extraordinarily powerful in facilitating the desired performance, a word of caution must be stated: Groups should be careful about trying to attach too many indices to physician compensation. While more attention must be placed on both qualitative and quantitative performance measures, select those that have the potential for having the broadest impact rather than on several specific ones.

Concern is invariably expressed about the potential for physicians to "game" whatever compensation system is created. Undoubtedly, some will. But groups must distinguish between those actions that require leadership intervention and those that will be driven out by a "pure" compensation formula. No one compensation plan will solve the problems encountered in managing physicians in a group structure. A well-designed compensation plan can encourage the performance essential to group success, but it has its limitations. It cannot eliminate inappropriate behavior or make inefficient physicians suddenly efficient. Strong leadership intervention will be required in any group, whether to coach non-performers or recognize high achievers, to maximize the overall success of the medical group.

6

IMPROVING PROVIDER PRODUCTIVITY

Mary J. Witt, MSW

With decreasing reimbursement and increasing costs, it is critical that medical groups maximize their profit margin on the services provided. Approximately 75 percent of total expenses are fixed (staffing, facility, malpractice, professional services, marketing, and some general and administrative expenses).[1] It is clear that a practice's volume has the biggest impact on both its cost and revenue per unit of service. However, it is rare to find a medical group that is not struggling with the issues of provider productivity and how to increase volume. Consequently, the first priority of most performance improvement plans is to increase the volume of services provided or the number of patients served. This chapter focuses on practical techniques to increase provider productivity without sacrificing quality.

[1] Medical Group Management Association. *Cost Report: 1999 Report Survey on 1998 Data.* Englewood, CO, 1999, p. 12.

DEFINING PRODUCTIVITY

Traditionally, productivity in a medical group has been measured by numbers of visits or services rendered by the provider. For many providers, however, this definition engenders more anger than motivation because in their minds, it means working harder, faster, and longer with no reward. At the same time, in this era of managed care, physician organizations must be sure that the services provided are an appropriate use of resources. Thus, practices pursue ways to improve productivity. Numbers (visit/service) cannot be the sole focus—the appropriateness and the input required to get there must also be considered. Marshall Zaslove, M.D., in his book T*he Successful Physician*, describes the following productivity equation:[2]

Productivity = (Appropriate outcomes) - (Inappropriate Outcomes) / (Effective Inputs) + (Ineffective Inputs)

In this definition, input reflects the efficiency with which the outcome is achieved. Consequently, as we look at strategies for improving productivity, we will examine approaches that improve both volume and efficiency. In many cases, providers should not be working harder. Rather, they should be striving to eliminate those ineffective inputs that accomplish nothing but wasted time and effort.

Physicians have three tools with which to improve productivity: time, knowledge and skills, and relationships,[3] as shown in Figure 6-1. Each of these has numerous work habits associated with it that can strengthen its effectiveness.

[2] Zaslove, Marshall O., M.D. *The Successful Physician: A Productivity Handbook for Practitioners*. Gaithersburg, MD: Aspen Publishers, 1998, p. 22.
[3] Ibid., p. 29.

Figure 6-1. Physician Productivity Tools

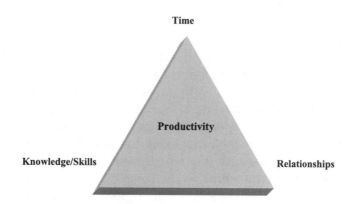

The following elements affect productivity:

- *Time* is required to produce, and without it production is zero.
- The application of *knowledge and skills* facilitates or produces the outcome.
- *Relationships* help produce or accomplish outcomes because physicians work for, with, and through people.

For production strategies to be meaningful, therefore, they must address the efficient use of time. They also must provide easy access to information and knowledge so that they can be readily applied. Last, they must facilitate the development of helpful relationships that affect productivity.

ACCESSIBILITY AND SCHEDULES

It is impossible for productivity to improve if providers are not accessible. Therefore, providers must have an adequate number of patient care hours. One of the reasons that hospital-owned practices have struggled is that their physicians spend 10 percent less time seeing patients.[4] Family practitioners have discovered that they need to be in the office to generate revenue, and they now spend 37 hours weekly in the office in direct patient care,[5] no longer performing many out-of-office surgeries or assists. Often, they look for others to take care of their hospitalized patients because it is not efficient for them to see one or two hospitalized patients a day. Today's primary care physicians should see patients a minimum of four and one-half days per week, with at least seven hours of scheduled patients per day. However, it is not unusual to see eight hours of scheduled patients in better-performing practices. In addition, practices often add supplemental evening hours to maximize patient access.

Physician Schedules

It is common to find schedules that are unfriendly to both patient and staff in poorly performing practices. Patient-unfriendly schedules result in long patient waits and offer little access, even when patients are sick. Staff-unfriendly schedules are complex to administer and provide little opportunity for staff to meet patient needs. In these situations, staff also have little latitude in scheduling and constantly need to consult the physician before scheduling patients.

To maximize scheduling efficiency, schedules must be simple to understand and administer. At the same time, they must have enough slots to accommodate patients in a timely manner. In the past it was not uncommon to find physicians scheduling on

---

[4] Kikano, G. et al. Physician Employment Status and Practice Patterns. *Journal of Family Practice* 46:6, 1998.
[5] Borglum, Keith. Practical Tips to Boost Your Efficiency and Cut Practice Costs. *Family Practice Management,* October 1997.

a fixed-wave schedule, an approach that scheduled four patients at the top of the hour who would be seen during that hour on a first-come, first-served basis. Unfortunately, patients were often unhappy with this approach because it seemed to show little respect for their time. The advantage of the schedule for the physician was that no one wasted time waiting for patients to arrive.

Today, a modified wave schedule is often used. Long and short appointments are interspersed throughout the day, and patient times are staggered based on when it is expected they will be seen. This approach can reduce waiting times, assuming that the patient has properly explained the problem and that no delays occur during the visit. However, it can become complex to administer if too many categories of patient appointments are created, and it can limit the ability to accommodate patients who need to be seen the same day.

Recently, many practices have begun moving toward an open-access model, in which anywhere from 40 to 60 percent of the appointment slots are allocated for same-day or follow-up appointments. Experience shows that about 0.8 percent of the average patient panel will visit on any given day under this scenario. This generally translates into about 18 to 27 patients per day.[6] Both staff and physicians find it easier to deal with a patient on the day he or she calls than with a patient who has been put off. Not only is the patient more satisfied, but the practice has saved multiple phone calls, which lead to additional work for the staff. In moving toward open-access scheduling, it is first necessary to eliminate any backlog demand for appointments. This generally requires that extra sessions be added for the short-term until the demand is satisfied.

[6] Grandinelli, Deborah A. You Mean I Can See the Doctor Today? *Medical Economics* March 20, 2000, p.6.

Another scheduling approach that is gaining acceptance is the use of "drop-in group medical appointments," or DIGMAs, which can improve care, enhance the physician-patient relationship, cut waiting lists, reduce phone calls, and enable physicians to manage resources better.[7] During these 90-minute group visits, the physicians do much of what they would routinely do on a visit: refill or change prescriptions, order tests and discuss results, answer medical questions, and, if appropriate, conduct a brief private medical exam in an adjacent room. At the same time, patients can gain support from other participants and learn that others are facing similar problems.

Regardless of the scheduling system, some common sense rules can make any scheduling system more efficient and lead to increased productivity:

- **Start on time**. Maintaining productivity levels is impossible if the physician and staff are always behind schedule. While all patients may eventually be seen, starting late creates stress for patients, staff, and the physician. Besides, in today's busy world, patients have little tolerance for tardy physicians who abuse their time.
- **Give the staff and physician an incentive to stay on time.** Perhaps they should face monetary or other penalties for tardiness. In some instances patients are not required to pay for their appointment or are provided other "consolation prizes" for waits. Of course, payer and other reimbursement regulations must be considered.
- **Keep the schedule simple.** Minimize the number of appointment types by categorizing appointments according to length of time they require or how quickly they are scheduled, and keep the categories to a minimum. For example, categories could include: same day, recheck (scheduled out no more than two weeks), and prescheduled appointments (annual exams and routine checkups for chronic disease patients). Even if open access does not seem appropriate for your practice, be sure that a number of same-day slots are available for those patients who need

[7] Noffsinger, Edward B., Ph.D. Increasing Quality of Care and Access While Reducing Costs through Drop-in Group Medical Appointments. *Group Practice Journal.* Vol. 48, No. 2, February 1999.

to be seen immediately, and scatter these appointments throughout the day. This will accommodate patient need and minimize the impact on the schedule if the slots go unfilled.

- **Schedule a brief (five-minute) meeting between physician and medical assistant at the beginning of each day** to review the schedule, identify potential problem areas, and identify spaces for add-on patients.

- **Create a visit map and monitor it on an ongoing basis.** This road map details what happens to the patient during the visit and the time it takes to complete each step. Quickly resolving roadblocks that derail patient progress ensures that systems remain sensitive to the smooth progression of the patient through the visit.

- **For more efficient use of staff and resources, bundle similar short visits in blocks of time.** At the same time, it also makes sense to schedule a short visit at the beginning of a longer one. This allows the physician to remain productive while the nurse and the patient are preparing for the physician. Certainly any long appointment (longer than 15 minutes) should be confirmed the day before to minimize no-shows.

- **Develop protocols for common problems, diseases, and patient types** to ensure consistency in treatment and to provide documentation of the visit process so that physicians and staff can be prepared. Protocols ensure that the right thing is done at the right time in the right way for the right cost.

- **Avoid interruptions to the day's work flow.** Pulling a physician out of an exam room to address another issue is generally much more disruptive than trying to wait for an appropriate break. Research indicates that it takes four minutes to recover from an interruption. Since studies show that workers in an average office are interrupted every six minutes,[8] eight interruptions can lead to 20 hours per week of low productivity. While avoiding interruptions, minimize breaks in the schedule as well so that momentum is maintained throughout the day.

- **Focus, focus, focus.** More work can be done in a given period, with better quality, when workers are focused—clearer directions will be given, and people respond more carefully to those requests.
- **Develop a schedule that maximizes the physician's natural rhythm.** If the physician is a night person, which make an 8:00 a.m. appointment difficult to be on time for, start later in the day and run longer. Perhaps a noon to 7:00 p.m. schedule would work better. This also would accommodate those patients who work during the day.
- **Be sure that the space is adequate to the volume demands.** It is highly unlikely that a family practitioner can routinely see 30 patients a day if he has only two examination rooms in which to work. Primary care physicians generally require at least three exam rooms to see efficiently the 25-30 patients needed to support the normal group practice. Having three exam rooms provides for patients who need extra time while, at the same time, a nurse performs a procedure or teaches another patient in a second, and the physician sees a patient in a third. Creating a seamless flow with minimum interruption and maximizing the physicians' time is also easier.
- **Set up examination rooms to support the physician's efficiency.** These should be completely stocked at all times so that the physician does not need to leave the exam room searching for supplies. They also should include pertinent, routinely used information. For example, it can be helpful to have available in each room a matrix that lists common procedures requiring authorization by plan so that the physician does not spend time trying to get that information. Another helpful matrix is a listing of network labs and radiology providers, as well as specialists frequently used for referrals.
- **Invest in good front office staff who understand the practice's schedule and can use it well.** This investment should include both time spent training and salaries that recognize the value of this skill to the practice.

[8] Zaslove, Marshall O., M.D. *The Successful Physician: A Productivity Handbook for Practitioners*. Gaithersburg, MD: Aspen Publishers, 1998, p. 70.

The following also suggest clearly defining the key roles and responsibilites related to scheduling and patient flow:

- **Check-in and patient greeter:** acts as receptionist and validates that demographic information is accurate; monitors patient waiting times and informs appropriate clinical personnel; collects co-pays.
- **Scheduling/patient triage:** responsible for telephone interaction with patients and scheduling appointments; should not be located at the front desk if possible.
- **Check-out:** collects encounter forms and payment at time of service; makes follow-up appointments when appropriate.

Data and Time Management

Without the effective use of time, it is difficult to see the number of patients that are required in today's environment. The first step to improving use of time is to identify major time wasters and then develop strategies to minimize their impact. Major items on the time-waster list include:[9]

- Interruptions
- Down time
- Paperwork
- Rework
- Unnecessary work
- Insufficient knowledge or skills
- Clinical errors
- Missing or misplaced patient information
- Phone calls
- Administrative duties better done by others
- Useless meetings
- Friction and misunderstandings with others on your team.

[9] Zaslove, Marshall O., M.D. *The Successful Physician: A Productivity Handbook for Practitioners.* Gaithersburg, MD: Aspen Publishers, 1998, p. 61.

Everyone in health care complains about the paperwork volume, and many feel helpless to change it. The most important paperwork that practices deal with is that related to patient care. Our clients have identified numerous strategies to manage paper flow:

- **Use comprehensive forms whenever possible** to document the care provided during a visit and to minimize the handwriting or dictation required. This saves both time and money.
- **Complete the information while with the patient or immediately thereafter**, while it is still fresh in your memory. Often you can give patients copies of these forms to reinforce the information you gave during the visit. Not only does using forms save time, but it also makes the documentation more legible for others.
- **If you prefer to dictate, dictate while in the room with the patient.** Patients like this because they get to hear what you are putting in their chart, which can strengthen what they were told during the visit.
- **Use templates for dictation when possible.** This not only saves the physician's time but also reduces the cost of transcription.
- **Review standard correspondence requirements** to determine if another document can suffice. For instance, if making a referral, can the chart note suffice? If a specialist, can the hospital discharge summary provide the primary care physician with the necessary patient information?
- **Pull only those charts that are needed.** It is possible that many requests and calls could be handled without the chart. This not only eliminates the need for the physician to handle more paper but also frees staff to focus on other priorities such as keeping filing up to date so that results and reports are easily found.
- **Create a tracking system to ensure that ordered results are received.** This will minimize missing information, the need for rework, or clinical error. Moreover, by

identifying ordered results proactively, they can be secured before the patient visit or call so that time is not wasted. It also limits potential liability that could result from lack of follow-up on a positive test result.
- **Triage as much as possible of the paper that crosses the desk.** Determine if someone else can handle it, and provide the appropriate instructions. Create a separate process for urgent items or those that need only a moment or two to resolve. Those can be clipped to the examination room chart holder or on a "do now" clipboard and addressed as the physician moves to the next patient. Try to standardize responses whenever possible, thus enabling the use of standard letters. Aggressively eliminate anything that is not relevant to current needs, including journals. Keep a list of educational needs and let those determine your review of journal items.

Phone Calls

Unnecessary phone calls can add several hours to the workday of both physician and staff. Some phone tips are:

- **Schedule return phone calls** so staff can inform patients when to expect the physician's call. This will cut down on multiple phone calls and messages.
- **Bundle phone calls** to minimize disruptions and to answer them more efficiently.
- **Convey a positive attitude.** Calls seeking reassurance require few details. Rather, they require your confidence, so being positive and energetic can save time on the phone and give better results.[10]
- **Establish a protocol for telephone calls with patients.** The average phone call lasts six minutes.[11] A protocol will ensure that time is not spent on the phone with a patient who should be seen.
- **If leaving a message, be as complete as possible** (being sensitive to confidentiality issues with patients) to eliminate the need for a return phone call.

- **Use handouts, videotapes, e-mail, and the Internet** aggressively to help educate patients about their health. Not only does this help them care for themselves, but it also can limit the number of calls made by patients because they cannot remember what they were told or have more questions about their disease.

Relationship Management

As physicians face increasing pressure to see more patients, creating a positive physician-patient relationship becomes harder. With the average office visit now at 15 minutes,[12] it is critical that physicians know how to make a short visit seem longer. Patient anger at what seems like a short visit has less to do with the actual time spent and more to do with inadequate communication skills of the provider. It can be helpful to regard a patient visit as an interview. The success of the interview is based more on communication and less on actual diagnosis and treatment. As you meet with the patient, remember the steps in an interview:

- Gather background information; identify problem/feelings
- Understand how they have handled the problem thus far
- Attempt to inform, educate, and enlist the patient in his or her care
- Show empathy.

Effective communication requires the following:

- **Know what your goal is before you enter the examination room** so you can use the time to best advantage. Organize your interview. Ask questions that can accomplish multiple purposes, even in informal conversation. For example, asking about the children also provides an oppor-

[10] Zaslove, Marshall O., M.D. *The Successful Physician: A Productivity Handbook for Practitioners.* Gaithersburg, MD: Aspen Publishers, 1998, p. 61. p. 88.
[11] Wheeler, S.Q. and B. Siebelt. How to Perform Telephone Triage. *Nursing.* July 1997.
[12] Belzer, Ellen J., MPA. Improving Patient Communication In No Time. *Family Practice Management.* Vol. 6, No 5, May 1999.

tunity to ask about their health and immunizations.

- **Build rapport by greeting the patient and exchanging pleasantries.** Have your staff note personal items about the patient on the progress note along with the presenting problem. Make a note of any special personal characteristics in the chart so you can refer to them in a future visit.
- **Focus on the patient and do not appear rushed.** Establish eye contact from the moment you enter the room. Be direct but do not stare. Do not refer to your watch, keep your hand on the door, or remain near the door. Sit down so that the patient feels like he or she has your undivided attention. Allow an unstructured moment during the visit so that the patient can guide the discussion.
- **Allow interruptions only in the case of emergencies.** Also, be aware that for some, interruptions may be no more than turning your back to write something in the chart.
- **Listen without interrupting.** Let the patient talk for three to four minutes. However, gently keep the patient on track if he strays too far from the purpose of the visit.
- **Sit close to the patient and do not be afraid to touch.** It can comfort and reassure the patient of your concern.
- **Be sure to say something positive to the patien**t.
- While conducting the examination or performing a procedure, **keep the patient informed** about what is happening

REWARDS FOR IMPROVED PRODUCTIVITY

It is important that both physicians and staff understand the relationship between profitability and volume. The assessment process (see Chapter 2) provides the perfect opportunity to create the link between volume, cost, and revenue so that all understand the need for productivity. However, it is not enough to achieve this understanding. The reward structure of the organization also needs to provide incentives for volume. While there has been considerable discussion in the literature about the need for appropriate physician incentives for productivity, little discussion has occurred relating to staff.

Staff, however, play a significant role in the group's ability to see more patients. Thus, it is important that organizations develop appropriate incentives to encourage improved productivity on the part of staff as well as providers. Certainly, profit-sharing formulas or bonuses based on profitability can encourage productivity. There are other, less costly approaches that also foster a commitment to increased productivity. Celebrations, such as pizza lunch parties or quarterly dinners, when targets are met consistently for a period of time, can be effective incentives. Other rewards can include free movie tickets or fast food coupons when visits for the week exceed the target by a percentage.

For many physicians and staff, the need to increase volume can be overwhelming. Many strategies, however, can be pursued to help them see more patients with little extra effort. The keys to improving volume are:

- Establishing clear goals, monitoring progress, and celebrating successes.
- Focusing on the goal. Minimize interruptions and distractions. It is much easier to achieve the goal when devoting all energies to its achievement.
- Improving physician time management skills. Improving volume does not necessarily require adding hours to the work day. Often managing time and processes can lead to improved productivity.
- Making each contact memorable to the patient. Look patients in the eye and give them your full attention. Refine physician interpersonal skills.
- Developing and supporting a strong team to help providers manage their work load. Ensure that providers are performing work that requires their skills and knowledge. Delegate work that does not.

7

MANAGING COSTS IN TODAY'S ENVIRONMENT

Mary J. Witt, MSW

A cornerstone of any operational improvement process and plan is the focus on expenses. As indicated by the gross collection percentages in Figure 7-1, medical groups have seen larger and larger discounts applied to their fees. According to MGMA's 2000 Cost Survey,[1] the median gross collections for all groups surveyed indicate a collection rate of only 68 cents of every dollar charged.

At the same time, MGMA reports that median practice operating expenses now consume 58 percent of net revenue.[2] Consequently, fewer dollars are available to pay expenses and maintain physician income.

This chapter focuses on the problems that lead to runaway expenses and explores various strategies to control costs overall. Although these strategies are applicable to most practices, hospital-owned medical groups face particular challenges in managing costs, and those are discussed in a special section at the end of this chapter.

[1] Medical Group Management Association. *Cost Report: 1999 Report Survey on 1998 Data.* Englewood,CO, 1999, p. 12.
[2] Ibid., p. 17.

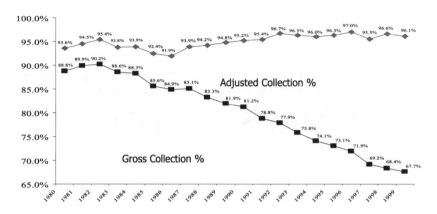

Figure 7-1
**Mean Gross and Adjusted Fee-for-Service Collection Percentages
1980-1998**

Source: *MGMA Cost Survey: 1999 Report Based on 1998 Data*

Data used with permission from the Medical Group Management Association, 104 Inverness Terrace East, Englewood, Colorado 80112-5306; 303-799-1111. www.mgma.com. Copyright 1999.

THE BUDGET PROCESS

The first step in the improvement process in controlling operational expenses is to develop and manage from a budget or financial plan. The budget provides a road map and guides management in evaluating financial trends, setting goals, establishing financial targets, and determining priorities. Yet many practices either do not have a formal budgeting process, or they ignore the budget once it is developed. Through the budgeting process, consensus can be reached regarding priorities and, perhaps more importantly, expense parameters and expectations can be established. Participation in this process creates buy-in by all of the key constituencies and can minimize battles about how money is spent during the year.

It is not enough to have a budget, however. The budget must be grounded in reality to have any credibility with physicians or staff. Thus, it must be based on previous history and compared to industry norms or standards. By using practice history as a base, it considers the practice's current spending habits. Comparing to industry benchmarks provides a reality check for practice behavior and will help to establish operating objectives. Also, comparing expenses over time provides additional insight. Analyzing horizontal trends by raw dollars, percentage of total expense or revenue, and per unit (visit or enrollee) is helpful.

Understanding the relationship of expense to volume is important in creating an accurate budget. Expenses can be:

- **Fixed:** expenses that remain stable, regardless of volume
- **Variable:** expenses that vary with volume
- **Semi-variable:** expenses that have both a fixed and a variable component
- **Step variable:** expenses that remain stable for a range of volume.

Table 7-1 lists common expenses and their relationship to volume.

Strategies to affect fixed costs focus on increasing volume to reduce the per-unit expenses. Variable expense strategies are more likely to focus on tactics to lower specific costs.

Managing to budget needs to be integrated into both individual job expectations and practice goals as a whole. Everyone in a position to influence expenditures should be aware of what is in the budget and receive regular monthly updates as to performance against budget. It should be a key component in the evaluation of management performance (both physician and lay leadership), as well as any staff with responsibilities affecting expenses (e.g., an employee responsible for ordering supplies).

Table 7-1. Expense Classifications

Expense	Fixed	Variable	Semi-Variable	Step Variable
Staff salaries/benefits				X
Rent				X
Utilities/building maintenance			X	
Office supplies		X		
Medical supplies		X		
Laboratory/radiology expenses			X	
Professional expenses			X	
Information services			X	
Marketing	X			
Mid-level provider salaries/benefits				X
Physician salaries/ benefits				X

During a performance improvement process, this culture is particularly important. The budget may be superseded by a short-term, specific financial plan. This plan, and management's ability to meet the specified expense targets, will be a cornerstone of the performance improvement effort itself.

Financial Reporting

Expense management is only as good as the financial data available to management. Expense items must be tracked, methodologies for analysis agreed upon, and their relationship to volume clarified. A report detailing expenses is only data until it is put in a context that measures and analyzes the information.

Variance Analysis

The use of variance analysis to create financial reports provides a context in which to understand the financial performance of the medical practice. While variance analysis can take a variety of forms, it always involves a comparison to another factor. Table 7-2 identifies common tools for variance analysis and lists some sample questions to ask when variances are noted.

Table 7-2. Tools for Variance Analysis

Tool	Measurement	Sample Questions
Budget	Comparison to target	Has the environment changed from that on which assumptions were made? How? Why? Is the change permanent or temporary? What action can be taken in the short-term and long-term?
Prior period	Comparison to history	What is different this year from prior years? Volume? Staffing? Reimbursement? Supply costs? Permanent or temporary?
Benchmark	Comparison to a standard	What is different about our practice from a benchmark practice? Different staffing ratio? Difference in service mix, patient type, utilization patterns?
Per unit	Per visit, percent of total revenue/expense or per member per month	What have the trends been? And why? Has this been caused by enrollment, revenue, visits, etc.?

It is frequently beneficial to consolidate a number of variance tools into one report to review multiple factors at one time, as illustrated in Table 7-3.

Table 7-3. Multi-specialty Group Annual Income/Expense Statement

	Current Year		Budget			MGMA		
Expense	$	Pct. Net Revenue	$	Pct. Net Revenue	Variance Budget to Actual	$	Pct. Net Revenue	Variance MGMA to Actual
Charges	5,463,768		6,233,000		769,232	$8,037,972		($2,574,204)
Contractual Allowances	1,420,580		1,558,250		137,670	1,848,734		(428,154)
Net Revenue	4,043,188		4,674,750		631,562	6,189,238		(2,146,050)
OPERATING EXPENSES								
Staff Salaries/Benefits	1,462,017	36%	1,449,173	31%	(12,844)	1,836,966	30%	-6%
Medical Supplies	198,116	5%	186,990	4%	(11,126)	250,045	4%	-1%
Lab/Radiology	94,611	2%	186,990	4%	92,379	222,813	4%	1%
Facility	331,946	8%	331,946	7%	0	371,354	6%	-2%
Malpractice	46,497	1%	46,550	1%	53	94,076	2%	0%
Professional Services	36,793	1%	41,500	1%	4,707	46,419	1%	-1%
Marketing	22,238	1%	46,748	1%	24,510	25,376	0%	0%
General & Administrative	570,090	14%	748,158	16%	178,068	1,109,112	18%	4%
Total Operating Expenses	2,762,306	59%	3,038,054	57%	275,747	3,956,161	57%	-2%
PRACTICE GROSS INCOME	1,280,882	32%	1,636,697	35%		2,233,077	43%	11%
PROVIDER EXPENSES								
Mid-level Salaries/Benefits	0		0		0	0		
Physician Salaries/Benefits	1,800,000		1,620,500		(179,500)	2,215,077		
CME	18,000		16,000		(2,000)	18,000		
Total Provider Expenses	1,818,000		1,636,500		(181,500)	2,233,077		
NET INCOME (LOSS) BEFORE COPORATE ALLOCATIONS								
	(537,118)		197			0		

Source: The Camden Group and *MGMA Cost Survey: 1999 Report Based on 1998 Data*

Data used with permission from the Medical Group Management Association, 104 Inverness Terrace East, Englewood, Colorado 80112-5306; 303-799-1111. www.mgma.com. Copyright 1999.

In this variance report, expenses have been common-sized as a percentage of net revenue. At the same time, current expenses have been compared to benchmarks (MGMA median percentages as a percentage of net revenue based on MGMA's 1999 Cost Report[3]). This format also clearly separates direct operating expenses from provider salaries, making it easier to analyze actual operating expenses and identify areas for improvement. It also allows for more accurate comparison to other medical groups, as can be seen from the use of MGMA benchmarks.

Financial performance should be reported and reviewed on a monthly basis. The monthly financial report should include:

[3] Medical Group Management Association. *Cost Report: 1999 Report Survey on 1998 Data.* Englewood, CO, 1999, p. 24.

- Statement of income and expenses for the month and year to date
- Provider productivity (visits, RVUs)
- Accounts receivable measures (days in A/R, A/R over 90 days old, collection percentages as compared to expected)
- Staffing measures (as a percentage of the total net revenue, non-provider FTE/provider, staff hours/patient visit)
- Major successes and negative variances
- Conclusions and revised forecast
- Action plan to address issues and variances.

When focusing on performance improvement, some expenses should be monitored more frequently, e.g., by daily review of overtime, staffing hours compared to patient volume, and daily cash management reports, if necessary.

Frequently, physicians are reluctant to share budget and financial information with anyone other than the partners of the practice. Unfortunately, this approach allows everyone else in the practice to disengage from any responsibility for financial performance. The message becomes, "Since they don't know want me to know anything about it, I don't have to worry about it." Therefore, it is critical that enough financial data be shared with both employed physicians and staff to ensure their understanding and buy-in to the financial goals of the practice. In a performance improvement environment, expense management has to be everyone's business to ensure the success of the effort.

IDENTIFYING AREAS FOR IMPROVEMENT

Obviously, if a practice is losing money, the expense structure is too high for the revenue being generated. To sort out the issues, it can be useful to apply a simple decision tree to identify the problems (see Figure 7-2). Applying the decision tree to ask key questions, and using historical data and industry benchmarks as comparisons, will enable the practice to spot problems quickly and identify solutions.

Figure 7-2. Using a Decision Tree to Identify Problems

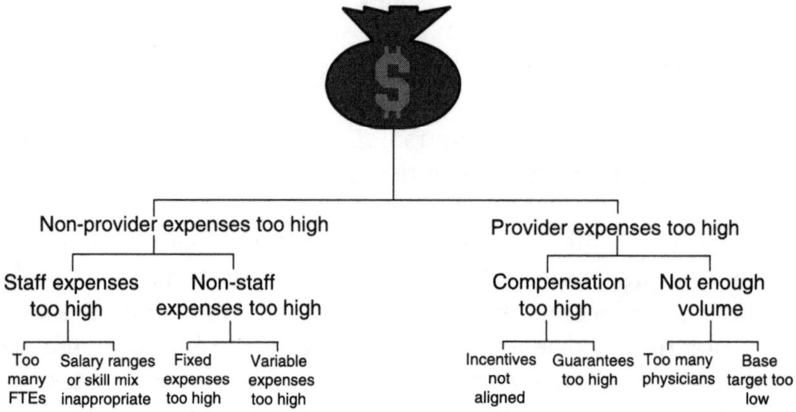

For example, in the financial summary in Table 7-3, non-provider staffing, facility, and medical supply costs exceed industry standards and budget. Thus, it is appropriate to focus on these three areas initially to develop expense management strategies. Other areas also present opportunities for managing expenses.

Non-provider Staffing

Given the dollars involved, changes in non-provider staffing can have the most significant impact on operating expenses. However, in resolving high staffing costs, one cannot look at non-provider staffing in isolation. Numerous other factors, as discussed below, require consideration and suggest potential solutions. Additional suggestions are discussed in Chapter 9.

Volume, along with the number of providers and hours spent seeing patients, must be used to set staffing ratios. Using only the number of providers, especially in startup or low-volume practices, can lead to excessive staffing. For example, while it is important to have at least one staff member present during office hours to answer phones, it may not be necessary to have clinical personnel available if patients are not being seen because there may be little for them to do.

At the same time, if the practice is seeing a high number of patients or offering special services, staffing may need to be higher. However, it is critical to complete a cost-benefit analysis on a regular basis for those special services to ensure that they are profitable. For example, many practices have had in-house laboratories that often require additional staffing. In today's environment, however, providing lab services could easily cost money rather than make it.

Staff skill mix should be carefully assessed and the appropriate skill level used. For example, many outpatient nursing functions can be performed by a medical assistant rather than a registered nurse. In a heavily captitated environment, where appropriate triaging of patients is critical, the use of a registered nurse in a triage position is more appropriate and cost-effective.

The hiring process should minimize the number of inappropriate hires. Clearly define job descriptions and performance expectations before beginning the hiring process. Communicate those expectations during the interview process. Doing so assists not only the interviewer, but also the interviewee, to assess fitness for the position. Employees should be held accountable for performance from the first day on the job. This allows for any mistakes to be identified quickly so they can be resolved and also provides for early resolution if a hiring mistake has been made. Unhappy, unproductive staff serve neither themselves nor the practice and become a disruptive influence.

Create an environment that recognizes and reinforces solid performance, thus minimizing turnover. This includes:

- Clearly defining performance expectations
- Rewarding good performance
- Developing, documenting, communicating, and enforcing personnel policies to ensure consistency in treatment of employees
- Establishing realistic salary ranges based on market conditions
- Rewarding performance, rather than longevity. At the same time, if you expect staff to be peak performers, you must be prepared to provide salaries near the top of the range, not at the bottom.
- Providing training when new skills are required.

Several key staffing indicators should be monitored on a regular basis, especially when focusing on performance improvement (see Table 7-4).

Table 7-4. Key Staffing Indicators

Indicator	Frequency
• Staff overtime	• Daily
• Staff hours/visit	• Payroll period or monthly
• Staff FTE/provider	• Monthly
• Staff salaries and benefits as percent of net revenue (be sure to include temporary staff)	• Monthly
• Use of temporary staff	• Daily/weekly

Staff overtime and using temporary staff often become easy solutions when there is increased pressure to see more volume. It is often simpler to increase staff hours than to reconfigure processes and work flow, even if it is reconfiguration that is required. Continuous monitoring of these variables helps both staff and providers understand the need to reengineer the way they do things, rather than to add costs by increasing staff hours.

Work Flow Processes

The way work is performed affects efficiency, effectiveness, and cost. Often, work processes take on a life of their own and continue to be performed long after their usefulness has expired. Thus, work flow processes must be continually re-evaluated to ensure their validity in the current environment. A review of patient flow, for example, often identifies unnecessary tasks or duplicate steps. Also, it is important to use processes that minimize, not maximize, exceptions. The use of work flow diagrams like that in Figure 7-3 makes it easier to analyze processes and identify extraneous steps and inefficiencies. This process is discussed in more detail in Chapter 2.

Facility Expenses

Short-term budget implications are not necessarily considered as space is chosen and designed. Financial pro formas are often too optimistic in their revenue projections to support the space identified. Space plans are often created without adequate input from the staff and providers using the space. In addition, tenant improvements and equipment purchases are often excessive for the basic needs of a medical practice. While the resulting facility may be beautiful, the cost structure is higher than the medical practice can support.

Figure 7-3. Patient Check-Out

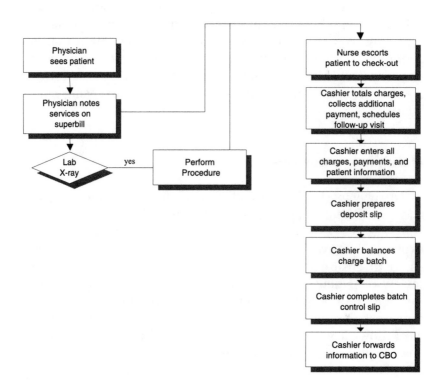

To estimate correctly the size of facilities needed, practices must incorporate the following into their facility planning:

- Analysis of market demand to project realistic volume and provider FTE needs and space requirements
- Creation of financial pro formas to ensure that the practice can support the facility
- Use of space planners who understand medical practice workflow so that space is efficiently designed (including staff and providers in review of the design)
- Conservative selection of interior decor and equipment.

Other strategies to manage facility costs include:

- Consider expanding office hours or adding providers to maximize the use of the space. Use flexible scheduling so that the space can be used throughout the day, including during lunch hours.
- Monitor utility and common space costs. Identify those factors that are under your control and those that are not. Negotiate expense caps or exclusions of those that you cannot control. Consider the use of timers on lights, heat, and air conditioning. Use your local utility as a resource to identify potential cost savings. Monitor telephone usage regularly, especially long distance.

Supply Costs

Supply costs can easily get out of hand in a practice, particularly when there are multiple parties involved in the purchasing process. Establishing better inventory control, as well as instituting an approval process for supply purchasing, are often the first steps in gaining better control of these expenses. Specific actions may include the following:

- Formalize the purchasing process to ensure competitive pricing through the use of requests for proposal. Use sole-source purchasing when appropriate to take advantage of volume discounts.
- Centralize control. Limit who can purchase items for the practice. Create inventory control policies and records to avoid duplicate and unnecessary purchases.
- Check all orders on arrival to ensure that the orders are accurate and match the packing slip and the invoice. Institute a purchase order system to provide an orderly process for allowing departments to request purchases and approvals to be centralized. This will require determining levels of authority for both dollar amounts and types of purchases. For example, a clinical supervisor may be

authorized to order certain vaccines or other medical supplies, but use of temporary staffing or other purchased
services would require a manager's approval.
- Explore the use of purchasing cooperatives through local
medical societies, MGMA, or other sources to achieve
greater volume discounts.
- Investigate Internet-based supply purchasing (e.g.,
Neoforma, MediBuy) to reduce per-unit costs. Continually
test these prices against other services.
- Monitor supply costs regularly as a cost per visit and as a
percentage of revenue. Use MGMA and other specialty
practice guidelines as a benchmark.

Equipment Costs

While largely fixed, there may be opportunities to reduce the
costs of existing equipment the practice uses. Any new expenditures must receive particular scrutiny. Some questions you
might ask include:

- Is existing equipment, particularly ancillary equipment,
being utilized effectively? For example, if a dexascan for
performing bone density screenings was purchased or
leased, how much is it currently being used? Do all
providers know that it exists?
- Are all providers educated about appropriate referrals?
- If volume can't be increased, can the equipment be sold?
Although the capital expenditure may already have been
made, underutilized equipment takes space that could be
used for other revenue-generating functions. It also could
be increasing staffing expenses unnecessarily and limiting
the use of an examination room for other providers.

Always perform a cost-benefit analysis when considering capital purchases or the addition of new services. Include costs such as new employees or supplies, as well as sunken costs (i.e., costs already incurred or committed). Also, include the opportunity costs or the costs of the alternative uses of the money. Be sure to evaluate the economic impact on the whole organization. Often new equipment and services affect other aspects of the operation. This same analysis may need to be performed on existing equipment as part of the effort to improve performance.

Although information systems (IS) are discussed in detail in Chapter 13, it is important to consider their impact on the expense structure of the practice. Given the availability of application service providers (ASPs) via the Internet and other options for working with IS vendors, practices should explore all options for accessing needed IS software and hardware. At the same time, it is important that practices maximize use of software to simplify work processes and capture the data required to monitor practice performance.

Other Operating Costs

Two other costs require review: professional services and transcription. Professional services expenses are those costs associated with practice advisors, such as accountants and attorneys. Practices should clearly define their needs for assistance in both areas so that realistic agreements about potential costs can be reached before the service is delivered. With the availability of easy-to-use financial software, the accounts payable function and preparation of monthly income and expense statements can easily be handled internally. The accountant can then focus on preparing quarterly financial statements and paying taxes. The use of an outside payroll service can simplify management of employee payroll, making it less time-consuming and generally ensuring that legal requirements are met.

Transcription costs have increased significantly in many practices as physicians become more concerned about adequate documentation and compliance. Therefore, outsourcing versus employing transcriptionists should be carefully evaluated. Generally, transcription costs are between $0.10 and $0.13 per line. In addition, the use of standardized dictation formats can both ensure adequate documentation and maximize the efficiency of the transcriptionists. As voice-activated software improves, test this capability to reduce the practice's reliance on transcriptionists.

Physician Compensation and Right Number of Providers

While physician compensation is discussed in detail in Chapter 5, any review of practice expenses must consider physician compensation. The importance of physician behavior on practice profitability has been proven by the impact of physician income guarantees. Without incentives tied to performance, achieving optimal performance is difficult. Because major practice expenses, such as facilities and staff, are largely fixed, there are limited options in cutting expenses to compensate for inadequate volume. Without aligning incentives and linking compensation to performance, it will be difficult, if not impossible, to improve practice profitability.

Total physician compensation is also a function of the number of physicians receiving compensation. In some practices, physicians have been added for strategic reasons. Unfortunately, the financial and market realities have not always supported these strategic initiatives. Thus, practices have been supporting physicians who cannot generate the revenue required to support the expenses of the practice because the patients are simply not there.

HOSPITAL-OWNED PRACTICES OR INTEGRATED DELIVERY SYSTEMS

For many integrated delivery systems (IDSs), the seeds for significant losses were planted during their initial development process. Acquiring medical practices was often a defensive response to competition. Also, it was frequently assumed that any problems identified during due diligence were the result of the physician's lack of "business sense" or sophistication. The corollary was then that the hospital, with its sophisticated systems and expertise, would have no trouble making the practice financially sound and could help achieve economies of scale, thereby reducing practice expenses.

Unfortunately, many hospitals underestimated the significant differences between running a hospital and running a medical practice. It was a matter of putting people in charge who manage dollars to now manage nickels—they couldn't do it. As Table 7-5 illustrates, those differences clearly suggest that a hospital approach to practice management is likely to fail given the contrasting organizational characteristics and needs.

Not only have many IDSs lacked appreciation for the differences between medical groups and hospitals, but they have also failed to focus on the critical drivers for either costs or revenue. At the same time, IDSs frequently have not hired management with medical practice experience, thereby compounding the knowledge gap.

Based on our experience and substantiated by MGMA cost data, hospital-owned medical groups traditionally have had higher costs as a percentage of net revenue in three critical areas: physician compensation, non-provider staffing, and facilities. Since these also happen to be the largest expense items in any practice, the impact of these variances takes on added significance.

Table 7-5
Hospital vs. Physician Approaches to Management

	Hospital	Physician
Orientation	Big Business	Small Business
Revenue/Unit	Gross revenue/adjusted discharge $11,967	Gross revenue/patient visit $55-$120 per visit
Financial Reporting	Accrual accounting	Cash accounting
Expense Management	Multiple number of cost centers Average cost by department	Limited number of cost centers Cost by site and across specialties
Decision Making	Hierarchical	Benevolent dictator or consensus
Speed of Decision-Making	Months	Days
Management Structure	Complex, multiple levels	Flat with 1 to 2 levels

Because hospital-owned practices have lower gross revenue ($455,314 per FTE physician) compared to non-hospital owned practices ($699,831 per FTE physician[4]), they also have less revenue to cover practice expenses. This is another reason why expenses as a percentage of patient revenue are higher for hospital-owned practices. Thus, cost management becomes even more critical.

If hospitals are going to achieve long-term success with their medical groups, they not only have to understand the cost structure of a successful medical group, but they also need to operate under that cost structure. These medical practices must be operated more like independent medical groups. The issues and strategies discussed in this chapter are as applicable to IDS practices as they are to free-standing medical groups. In fact, they take on added significance given the lower gross revenue per physician FTE. Perhaps the biggest challenge faced by these groups is the need to balance the desire for "systemness" with the need to recognize the added costs this can create for a medical group.

[4] Medical Group Management Association. *Cost Report: 1999 Report Survey on 1998 Data.* Englewood,CO, 1999, p. 27.

Expense management does affect financial and operational performance. By addressing each of the critical components of a viable cost structure, as identified in Figure 7-4, medical groups can control expenses and improve performance.

However, expense management is not a one-time task. To be successful, it must become an ongoing process that requires constant data collection, analysis, and feedback. At the same time, while we have identified numerous strategies for controlling cost, they will not, on their own, ensure financial success. Revenue generation is still a critical component of long-term success. Because many practice expenses are fixed or have a large fixed component, volume remains an important factor in driving per-unit costs. Thus, strategies to enhance revenue per visit or service must also be implemented, and volume must be increased or maintained.

Figure 7-4
Components of a Viable Cost Structure

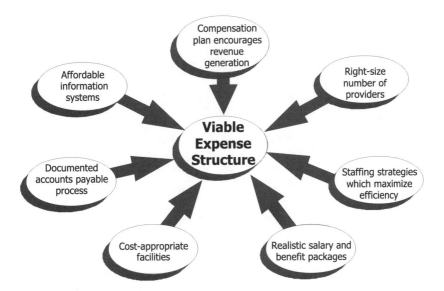

8

KEEPING A FOCUS ON QUALITY AND SERVICE

Karen E. Dunbar, MBA, MHS
Benjamin S. Snyder, MPA, FACMPE

Patients are the reason a medical practice exists. Recognizing the need to grow and expand, many medical groups spend tremendous time and effort on improving name recognition to attract new patients. A major initiative to improve financial performance should also include plans to increase patient volume. Depending on size, medical groups can spend from thousands to hundreds of thousands of dollars per year on this quest. However, if a medical group is unable to satisfy these new patients, or, for that matter, existing patients, all this effort and expenditure may be for naught.

Numerous research studies on patient satisfaction have all reached similar findings and conclusions. Even in those medical groups that receive over 90 percent responses to the question of whether the patient would return to the physician seen, often only 70 to 80 percent of patients would recommend their provider to family or friends. This difference in positive response indicates just how difficult it is to satisfy patients to the extent necessary to have them become active referral sources for the medical practice. This is particularly true for family practice and general internal medicine as opposed to specialty care physicians.

It also has been consistently shown that dissatisfied customers will tell on average 10 to 20 others about their negative experience. Only 20 percent of dissatisfied customers will give businesses an opportunity to correct a problem.[1] And because this percentage may be even higher in the health care industry, it must be managed by any medical group that hopes to grow and expand its patient base.

Industry research has demonstrated that it is five to seven times more expensive to attract a new patient to a medical practice than it is to keep an existing patient. Based on these consistent findings and conclusions, it is critical for medical groups to do all that is reasonably necessary to satisfy patients. Even in difficult financial times for medical groups, it is important to satisfy existing clients.

Patient satisfaction benchmarks (see Table 8-1) can help guide medical groups in establishing standards.

Table 8-1. Patient Satisfaction Benchmarks

Performance Indicator	Industry Benchmark
Overall satisfaction	At least 90%
% of patients who recommend your medical practice to others	85 to 90%
Managed care disenrollment rate	Less than 5%

[1] Brown, Stephen, Ph.D. *Customer Based Management Strategies*. Third National Forum, Phoenix, AZ, date unknown.

When Jan Carlzon assumed the position of Chief Executive Officer at Scandinavian Airlines System (SAS) in the early 1980s, he found this state-run airline to be a lackluster performer with high dissatisfaction ratings by customers. In a few short years, he turned the airline into a profitable business that consistently won passenger preference surveys. The central element to this turnaround was Carlzon's adoption of the concept of the "moment of truth" first described by Richard Normann in 1984.[2] This concept puts forth the notion that a service organization's overall performance is the sum of countless interactions between customers and employees. These so-called moments of truth will either help to retain a customer or send one to a competitor.

Larger medical group practices experience eight to ten moments of truth related to each and every scheduled office visit. Given this volume of interfaces, successful medical organizations need to be flat in structure, make sure everyone understands the vision of the company, and empower front-line employees. This approach and commitment need to be an absolute starting point to improve satisfaction. Without this occurring, organizations will have a difficult time making sure that each moment of truth is a positive experience.

As medical groups focus on improving patient satisfaction, they should not lose sight of the fact that some dissatisfied patients may actually have a valid quality-of-care issue. These medical issues need to be addressed effectively by the medical leadership as well. However, it is critical that quality be viewed from the physician's perspective as well as the patient's perspective.

As medical groups struggle with having enough overhead dollars available to accomplish all they want to do, they can follow a number of basic strategies and actions at minimal cost. The balance of this chapter will focus on these strategies and actions that will make a positive impact on quality and service.

[2] Carlzon, Jan and Tom Peters. *Moments of Truth*. New York: Harper Collins, 1989.

PREPARING FOR A QUALITY INITIATIVE

Before embarking on a major initiative focusing on quality and service, the organization must make sure that there is agreement to support such an ongoing project actively. If the organization does not have a formally approved mission, vision, and values statement, this would be an excellent time to develop one (see Chapter 1).

If the organization does have such a statement, make sure it clearly supports moving the organization in this new direction. If the answer is no or if it is unclear, then these statements need to be revisited and modified. It would not be in the interest of the organization to begin a major, ongoing quality and service initiative without having physician and senior management support.

If a mission, vision, and values statement is either developed or changed, the statement needs to be effectively communicated to all physicians and employees. Once this task is completed, no one should have to ask the question, "Why are we giving this quality improvement program or activity such priority?"

View the Quality of Service from the Patient's Perspective

Quite often, organizations become so involved with process they lose sight of trying to reach their goal through simpler means and methods. Improving the quality of patient service levels can be one of those areas caught up in elaborate review and survey processes. Not that some of these processes do not make the most sense to pursue—the problem is that easier and more direct methods may be just as effective for less cost and shorter process time.

Improving patient satisfaction may mean simply looking at activities and functions from a patient's perspective. Step back and take a hard look at how your practice runs from the patient's point of view. Have one or two people new with the organization participate as patients. Have them try calling the medical practice. How long does it take for staff to answer the phone? Was the person courteous and helpful? Was he or she knowledgeable in the subject matter relating to the question? Was the question posed satisfactorily answered?

Try scheduling an appointment. Were you placed on hold for an excessive amount of time? Were you able to get an appointment within a time frame that met your expectations? Were an adequate number of options offered?

Assuming you arrived on time for your appointment, how long did you have to wait before the physician began the physical examination? Did the physician appear rushed or disinterested? Did the physician understand your medical needs and meet your expectations for diagnosis and treatment? Were all of your questions answered?

Did you receive laboratory and x-ray services? Were the employees who performed these services courteous and professional? Did the physician or a member of the staff provide you with your laboratory results? Were these results timely and understandable?

With answers to these basic questions, you can begin to understand how patients would view the service level of your organization. After you have validated and analyzed these responses either by doctor, area, or specialty, you will have gathered valuable information to raise awareness about your practice's level of service.

Another method is to conduct patient focus groups. Again, these can be conducted internally as long as the facilitator can be objective and non-defensive during the discussion. A focus group should consist of no more than 10 patients, who can be grouped according to age, location, and services received. It is generally not a good idea to have the physician conduct the session because it may limit patients' willingness to speak. Participation can be encouraged by giving out gift certificates or other low-cost giveaways to those who take part. Keep discussion questions brief, and allow everyone to express opinions. If possible, pose questions that will help prioritize those problems (or solutions) that are most important to patients.

A "mystery shopper" or focus group will give you a feel for the kinds of things patients use to evaluate your medical practice. While physicians and administrators may view these issues as determining a level of service, many patients actually interpret the activities as the quality of care. If that is the patient's perception of quality, then the organization needs to deal with these issues on that basis. Perceptions need to be dealt with as if they are reality.

The diagram in Figure 8-1 was developed by Stephen Brown, Ph.D., and Andrew P. Morley, Jr., M.D., as part of a recent study on marketing strategies for physicians.[3] Most patients who leave a practice to receive their care elsewhere do so because of staff discourtesy or product (care or health insurance) dissatisfaction. Whether the issues are real or only perceived, the end result is the same: the patient leaves the medical practice.

---

[3] Brown, Stephen Ph.D., and Andrew P. Morley, Jr., M.D. *Marketing Strategies for Physicians.* Medec Books, 1986.

Figure 8-1
Why Patients Leave a Practice

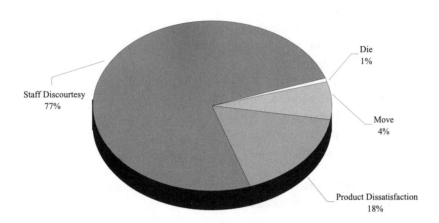

Source: Brown, Stephen Ph.D. and Andrew P. Morley, Jr., MD. *Marketing Strategies for Physicians*, Medec Books, 1986.

Listen to Patients

Nine times out of ten, people will tell you what they are looking for. All you have to do is be willing to hear it. Often, we do not hear people because we are too busy anticipating what they will say next. We think we already know what they are about to say and miss what they do say. Our emotions and thought processes can make us deaf to what people are really telling us.

To make employees and physicians better listeners, teach them to concentrate. Focus on the person, what he is saying, and how he is saying it. Body language can speak louder than words. When medical organizations have employees serving as both receptionists and schedulers, they are violating this basic service tenet—listening uninterrupted to the customer. The following table lists examples of things you can do to make you and members of your organization better listeners:

- Limit your own talking
- Concentrate on what people are saying
- Think like the customer
- Take notes
- Ask questions—at the end
- Listen for ideas—not just words
- Do not interrupt
- Don't interject your own thoughts or feelings
- React to the ideas, not the person
- Turn off your own words
- Do not jump to conclusions
- Listen for overtones.

Behaviors that are considered to be patient-friendly physician characteristics include:

- Communicative
- Caring
- Takes time
- Competent
- Listens
- Friendly
- Thorough
- Interested
- Sincere
- Prompt.

Negative characteristics include:

- Hurried
- Doesn't care
- Arrogant
- Inattentive
- Keeps me waiting
- Doesn't explain
- Careless with prescriptions
- Ineffective treatment
- Uninterested
- Reluctant to refer or consult.

Conduct a Formal Patient Satisfaction Survey

As discussed, medical practices can conduct an informal review of operating performance through personal observations or a more formal "mystery shopper" program. However, if an organization has more than 20 providers in several locations, it may be more cost-effective to have the same type of questions posed to a statistically valid random sampling of patients through a formal survey instrument. These surveys would be tabulated with results reported to physicians and employees. Estimating a 30 to 40 percent survey return rate, a minimum of 50 patients per physician would need to be mailed surveys for completion to have a statistically valid sample size.

There may be several advantages to using a formal survey process, particularly if it is conducted by a third party. For one, the results would appear to be more independent. As such, the medical practice could share them with payers to differentiate themselves from the competition. They could also be shared with patients to serve as a baseline to show improvement. Consumers are beginning to demand data from health care providers, and this may be a valid way of providing that data.

A good starting place for developing a written patient satisfaction survey instrument is to review the one developed by the Group Health Association of America (GHAA). A copy of GHAA's basic suggested patient satisfaction survey is presented in Table 8-2.

Table 8-2

GHAA Patient Satisfaction Survey

In terms of satisfaction, how would you rate each of the following:
(On a scale of 1 to 5. 1=Excellent, 2=Very Good, 3=Good, 4=Fair, 5=Poor)

	<Excellent to Poor>				
	1	2	3	4	5
Getting through to the office by phone?					
How long you waited to get an appointment?					
Convenience of the office location?					
Length of time spent waiting at the office?					
Time spent with physician?					
Explanation of the problem/what was done for you?					
The technical skills (thoroughness, carefulness, competence) of the physician?					
The personal manner (courtesy, respect, sensitivity, friendliness) of the physician?					
The visit overall?					

Source: Prometrics website: www.prometrics.com/ghaa.htm

This instrument could easily be modified to incorporate areas about which you are concerned. However, it is recommended that you ask the same set of questions over a period time so that you can evaluate improvement. Also, the grading scale should be consistent (i.e., poor to excellent, 1 to 5, etc.).

Some medical practices have used this instrument with a fixed number of questions that remain the same for every patient, and three or four questions added for a specific medical specialty or facility. By taking that approach, you can have questions across the organization as well as those that are specific to a medical specialty. In either case, you should validate the questions for clarity prior to putting the survey instrument to use.

Included in Table 8-3 are sample questions included in the patient satisfaction survey utilized by HealthCare Partners, a large successful 300-physician multi-specialty medical group located in Southern California. This survey is sent to randomly selected patients every month. At least 50 patients per physician are surveyed every 12 months.

Table 8-3
Sample Questions for Patient Satisfaction Survey

	Poor	Fair	Good	Very Good	Excellent
Access to a specialist, if needed	☐	☐	☐	☐	☐
Access to medical care after hours	☐	☐	☐	☐	☐
Ease of making appointments for medical care by phone	☐	☐	☐	☐	☐
The forms you must fill out (their number, ease of complexity)	☐	☐	☐	☐	☐
The ease of finding a parking space	☐	☐	☐	☐	☐
The office wait time to see the **DOCTOR/PROVIDER**	☐	☐	☐	☐	☐
The courtesy and support shown to you by the staff	☐	☐	☐	☐	☐
Thoroughness of treatment you received	☐	☐	☐	☐	☐
The **DOCTOR'S/PROVIDER'S** personal interest in you and your medical problems	☐	☐	☐	☐	☐
Advice you received about the ways to avoid illness and stay healthy	☐	☐	☐	☐	☐
The amount of time you had with the **DOCTOR/PROVIDER** during the visit	☐	☐	☐	☐	☐

	Definitely Yes	Probably Yes	Probably No	Definitely No
Would you recommend the **DOCTOR/PROVIDER** to your family or friends?	☐	☐	☐	☐

Source: The Camden Group

In addition to mailing surveys to patients separately, there are several other acceptable methods for distributing survey instruments to patients. These include mailing surveys with billing statements to random selected patients, targeting patients (i.e., by age, sex, zip code, etc.), directly handing the survey to patients as they check out from their physician appointment, or conducting telephone surveys. As part of MGMA's review of better-performing medical groups, they have tabulated the method of patient satisfaction survey distribution for these medical groups as well as the full set of medical groups participating in their annual cost survey. Figure 8-2 compares patient satisfaction distribution methods.

Figure 8-2
Survey Distribution Methods

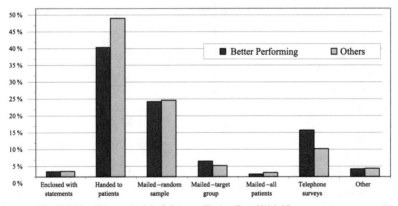

Source: Medical Group Management Association. *Performance and Practices of Successful Medical Groups,*
1999 Report Based on 1998 Data. Englewood, CO, 1999, Figure 1-16.

Data used with permission from the Medical Group Management Association, 104 Inverness Terrace East, Englewood, Colorado 80112-5306;
303-799-1111. www.mgma.com. Copyright 1999.

The Internet and other types of technology have also brought about dramatic changes in obtaining patient satisfaction data. Companies such as ProviderWeb.Net will develop a patient satisfaction survey for a medical practice. Completed surveys are scanned locally with the data being analyzed and reported back within a matter of weeks.

Some medical groups have also gone to the use of touch pads in the office as the data-entry vehicle to surveying patients. Some hotel chains use this method to measure satisfaction.

Consider Non-traditional Approaches to Patient Satisfaction

You may also wish to think proactively of other non-traditional areas of interest that would increase patient satisfaction. Convenience and the use of technology can be a major driver with patients. Originally it was thought this would be of interest to younger patients. But as more and more people have access to the Internet, there is a broader base for the use of the technology in the physician's office.

Think of new and creative ways to use the Internet or other technologies to support patient care activities. The following are a few ideas that can be easily pursued based on cost and the current state of technology:

- Diabetes: report glucose and/or HbA1c levels to the physician
- Weight management: report measurements, weight, etc.
- Blood pressure: report blood pressure readings
- E-mail health questions to providers
- Automate the process of providing laboratory test results to patients via a dial-in process
- Automate the prescription refill process
- Allow patients to scheduling appointments online
- Hold patient education programs—focus on how they can best use the Internet for research
- Provide on-site Internet access for patients to research their medical questions more easily. This would be ideal for new mothers, patients diagnosed with cancer, or those who have chronic illnesses. Rather than having patients surfing the Internet on their own, nursing staff could be available to instruct patients about the types of data available and the

addresses for recommended Websites. However, a physician knowledgeable in that subject area should review and sign off before recommending any Website for information.

MEASURING AND MONITORING QUALITY OF CARE

Measuring the quality of health care is not a new idea. For more than 30 years, organizations have been formally measuring quality in health care organizations. As payers, consumers, and regulatory agencies are demanding more accountability, the need to have a formal quality improvement process in place is becoming more and more critical for successful medical group practices.

In late 1999, the Institute of Medicine (IOM) published a report *To Err is Human*.[4] As a result of this report, the IOM brought patient safety issues to the forefront. The report estimated that medical errors (medication errors, surgical errors, poor judgment, etc.) cost approximately $1 to $2 billion annually basis, not to mention the pain and suffering that result from these errors.

This report came out of the growing recognition that safety in health care is more a problem of systems than of individuals. It also recognizes there is a need not to place blame, but rather to find out what happened and fix it. While not a totally new concept to health care, this is just beginning to emerge as an important methodology.

The measurement of the quality of care provided by a physician or mid-level provider can be as simple or as complex as an organization desires. However, there are several reasonable approaches that a medical group can take to begin to review and determine its level of quality.

---

[4] Kohn, Linda T., Janet M. Corrigan, and Molla S. Donaldson. *To Err is Human: Building a Safer Health System*. Institute of Medicine, National Academy Press, Washington, D.C., 1999.

The Joint Commission on the Accreditation of Healthcare Organizations (JCAHO) and the Accreditation Association for Ambulatory Health Care (AAAHC) are two national organizations that review and accredit ambulatory health care entities. Each of these non-profit groups has developed and published a set of standards used to measure compliance. Organizations that have gone through this process and have successfully met these standards receive a formal accreditation decision that is valid for up to three years.

While it would be ideal for every ambulatory health care organization to become accredited, there is a benefit for organizations not particularly interested in going through the accreditation process to use the standards published by both of these organizations as a measurement tool.

As an example, the standards published by AAAHC include the following broad areas of review:[5]

Core Standards (apply to all organizations)
1. Rights of patients
2. Governance
3. Administration
4. Quality of care provided
5. Quality management and improvement
    I. Peer review
    II. Quality improvement
    III. Risk management
6. Clinical records
7. Professional improvement
8. Facilities and environment

Adjunct Standards (apply only if the service is provided)
9. Anesthesia services
10. Surgical services
11. Overnight care and services
12. Dental services
13. Emergency services
14. Immediate/urgent care services

[5] Accreditation Association for Ambulatory Health Care. *Accreditation Handbook for Ambulatory Health Care 2000.* Wilmette, IL.

15. Pharmaceutical services
16. Pathology and medical laboratory services
17. Diagnostic imaging services
18. Radiation oncology treatment services
19. Occupational health services
20. Other professional and technical services
21. Teaching and publications
22. Research activities
23. Managed care professional services
24. Health education and wellness services

Within each of these standards are detailed characteristics believed to be indicative of an organization's quality. Using these standards as a starting place for your practice—making adjustments for practice size and complexity—is an excellent way to approach the measurement of quality of care.

From a more traditional definition of quality, peer review, quality improvement, and risk management are key elements. They are discussed in more detail below.

Peer Review

Peer review is a formal method of evaluating the performance of a physician or other health care provider. It may take the form of reviewing medical records, clinical outcomes, or professional competency. Peer review is a mechanism conducted by providers for determining another provider's ability to continue to render services in their specialty to patients. The granting of privileges is a direct outcome of this review process.

Quality Improvement

Quality improvement (QI) programs can focus on a range of activity in a medical group, from administrative and cost-of-care issues to clinical and actual patient outcomes. At a minimum, formal QI programs include five steps (see Figure 8-3):

Figure 8-3. Steps in QI Process

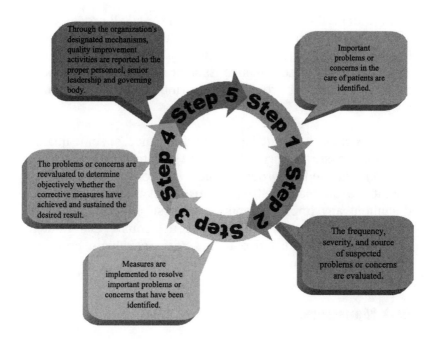

Examples of important problems or concerns that a QI program may address are listed below:

- Unacceptable (or unexpected) results in patient outcomes (e.g., complications, hospitalization, prescription errors)
- Clinical performance of providers
- Medical record review
- Quality controls
- Patient satisfaction
- Direct observation

- Employee issues/concerns
- Accessibility to patient care
- Medical/legal issues
- Over- or under-utilization
- Compliance with practice guidelines.

A critical component for a successful QI program is that the activities and resolutions are incorporated into training and ongoing education program for employees and providers.

Confidential records are maintained for all QI processes and actions taken. Not only can documentation of issues, actions taken, and results achieved potentially help protect the organization if a legal or compliance issue arises, but the documentation will assist your group in measuring performance to industry standards.

To benchmark medical group performance, specific quantifiable and measurable criteria must be selected for industry comparison. The medical group should track performance and compare it to available industry data on a regular basis. Measure and document any improvements or adverse changes that occur. This process is an iteration or a continuous cycle. Take the information learned and educate staff, reevaluate processes, and monitor improvement.

Risk Management

The ultimate goal of a risk management program is to protect the organization, its employees, and the patients it serves. Risk management can cover a myriad of issues, ranging from incident reports (whether reported by employees, patients, or visitors) to patient complaints, to allegations of improper care by a provider, to methods of handling inquiries from attorneys or governmental agencies.

The trend today is to merge risk management, quality improvement, and continuing education into one functional and coordinated department. By integrating these functions, an organization would gain maximum benefit from the investment in these processes.

It is clear that in today's consumer-focused world, medical practices are woefully behind. Basic tenets of service are often lacking in most medical offices and yet are critical components to building patient volume, which is paramount to improving financial performance. When trying to improve financial performance, cutting costs can become an excuse for poor service—one sure way to destroy the group. To ensure that a financial improvement opportunity is seized for the long-term, resources must be committed to improving patient service and quality even at a time when the organization's focus is on reducing expenses. Remember, increasing revenue through satisfied patients is often the key to a strong medical practice.

9

EFFECTIVE STAFFING: WHAT DOES IT TAKE?

Karen E. Dunbar, MBA, MHS
Benjamin S. Snyder, MPA, FACMPE

Because staffing is the largest non-physician operating expense of a medical group practice, medical practices must determine the most cost-effective means of staffing the office appropriately to meet both patient and physician expectations. This is often the primary focus of attention when trying to improve operational and financial performance.

To accomplish this overall objective, one of several basic methodologies and approaches should be taken. One relates to the general area of personnel management strategies, and another uses benchmarking.

PERSONNEL MANAGEMENT STRATEGIES

Managing employees and employee costs is critical for operational and financial success in a service business. Philosophically, the medical group must establish a formal wage and salary program for employees that places each employee in a specific job category that would be assigned a classification level. Similar-level jobs would be placed in the same classification. Associated with each classification level would be a set salary range. At one end of the range would be the beginning salary rate and at the other end would be the top of the salary range. Table 9-1 gives an example of how this position classification system would lay out for a medical group practice for selected positions.

Table 9-1. Pay Structure

Job Title	Grade	Beginning Zone 1	Beginning Zone 2	Beginning Zone 3	End of Zone 4
Accountant II	I	14.64	16.47	18.30	21.96
Accounts Payable Tech II	E	9.44	10.62	11.80	14.16
Application/System	J	16.40	18.45	20.50	24.60
Biller I	D	8.48	9.54	10.60	12.72
Biller II	E	9.44	10.62	11.80	14.16
Collector II	F	10.48	11.79	13.10	15.72
Director Business Office	O	30.72	34.56	38.40	47.26
Financial Analyst II	K	18.48	20.79	23.10	27.72
Registered Dietitian	J	16.40	18.45	20.50	24.60
Medical Assistant I	C	7.76	8.73	9.70	11.64
Medical Assistant II	E	9.44	10.62	11.80	14.16
Medical Information	F	10.48	11.79	13.10	15.72
Medical Receptionist I	D	8.48	9.54	10.60	12.72
Medical Records Clerk	C	7.76	8.73	9.70	11.64
Registered Nurse I	I	14.64	16.47	18.30	21.96

	Zone 1	Zone 2	Zone 3	Zone 4
	Employee with less than 1 year in current job	Employee with 1 to 2.9 years in current job	Employee with 3 years and above in current job	

In establishing a wage and salary program, a practice must commit to compensation and benefits that are competitive in the marketplace. If an organization expends significant money to recruit and train a new employee, it makes sense to offer competitive compensation and benefits to retain that employee. It is clearly not desirable to encourage employee turnover because an organization's compensation does not remain competitive.

Medical groups must understand with whom they are competing for new employees. If the competition is other physician offices, compensation levels will likely be less than a similar hospital-based position. In some markets there may be as much as a 10 to 12 percent difference in compensation between multi-specialty medical groups and hospitals. In other markets there may be virtually no difference.

There also may be a significant difference in benefit levels. Hospitals tend to have richer benefits compared to medical group practices. In a similar vein, multi-specialty medical groups tend to have better benefits than small, single-specialty physician offices. However, compensation levels may offset this difference.

In most markets, salary surveys of physician offices are conducted periodically. These are valuable tools in understanding compensation and benefits in your area. If such a survey does not exist in your area, there is no federal or state prohibition against physician offices sharing general employee compensation and benefits information. Often this process is overlooked because of the prohibition of comparing fees for rate-setting purposes, which is a violation of antitrust laws. One source is the management compensation data published by MGMA based on an annual national survey.

The skill mix of employees is also a key factor in staffing a physician office. Some offices feel a compelling need for virtually every nurse to be a registered nurse (RN) rather than using medical assistants (certified or non-certified) or licensed vocational (or practical) nurses (LVNs/LPNs). The cost difference between a registered nurse and medical assistant may be as much as 60 to 70 percent per hour.

If the care being provided does not require a specific level of licensure, it would make economic sense to fill the position with someone possessing the appropriate skills. Many medical groups that have de-emphasized the use of registered nurses have taken the approach to increase medical assistant compensation to be above market on the theory that they can recruit and retain the best qualified medical assistants in the area and still have lower costs than before.

Different geographic regions of the country use a variety of skill mixes. For example, in Southern California, staffing ratios (employees per FTE provider) tend to be higher, but the staff tends to have a lower skill mix. In Northern California, the opposite tends to be true. There they tend to staff with a higher skill-level employee and have fewer employees per FTE physician. In this region, physician offices also tend to de-emphasize RNs and use a higher ratio of medical assistants. They also tend to pay higher salaries to recruit and retain employees. However, while average cost per employee is higher than one would expect primarily due to cost of living, employee cost as a percentage of total expenses is identical to medical groups around the country.

The other key to a successful wage and salary administration program is to utilize a formal pay-for-performance system. While it may sound complex, this program merely provides for a formal annual evaluation process for all employees, which should tie performance to increases in salary rates or annual compensation. Performance is objectively compared to stated goals and performance criteria. Based on actual performance, a formal score is calculated that translates into a percentage salary increase.

The use of formal incentive programs can also work in medical group practices. Office management, accounts receivable management and collections, and transcription are excellent areas to implement such a program.

Most medical groups have found that the average transcriptionist transcribes about 950 lines per day. With a formal incentive program in place, many medical groups have increased the average to 1,250 lines transcribed per day. This 31 percent increase in productivity clearly reduces cost. Sharing this cost savings with transcriptionists makes business sense because it saves the organization money and rewards an individual for above-average performance.

The other area where tangible results are often felt is in collections. Setting specific collection targets each month allows employees working the accounts to see a tangible result for their efforts. When these efforts exceed average or expected performance, it would be reasonable to recognize that effort with bonus compensation. However, before establishing such a system, an analysis of collection activities must be made to ensure that the new program does not encourage the collection of the "easier" accounts. The goal should be to have the entire aged trial balance worked each month.

Table 9-2 details some measurements that could be used to establish an incentive program for a patient business office.

Table 9-2
Measurements for Establishing an Incentive Program

	Annualized FYE 6/30/99	Benchmark
Cost as a % of collections	14.5%	8 - 10%
FTEs per provider FTE [1]	0.53	0.75
Salary per FTE	30,336	27,000
Benefits as % of salaries [2]	20.1%	25.0%
Collection Percent	39.8%	50 - 51%
Days in A/R	106	60
% of A/R over 90 days	53.0%	25.0%
Accounts worked/collector/month [3]	1,050	1,248

(1) Equivalent providers were calculated based on total FFS charges divided by expected charges per provider of $400,000

(2) Excludes temporary and contract labor

(3) Department performance target

JOB DESCRIPTIONS AND PERFORMANCE STANDARDS

It is important to have clearly defined job descriptions with corresponding performance standards. Proper job descriptions are a basic tool for practice management. Figure 9-1 shows their importance and associated uses and functions.

Figure 9-1
Importance of Job Descriptions

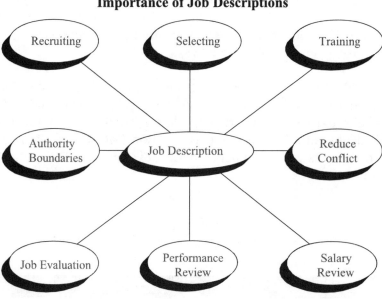

Exhibit 9-1 (at the end of the chapter) presents sample job descriptions with corresponding performance standards. We have included sample job descriptions for an office manager, check-in and check-out receptionist, and medical assistant.

In addition to having job descriptions in place, it is important to document and follow personnel and compliance policies.

BENCHMARKING EMPLOYEE STAFFING

One of the best and most effective ways to answer the staffing question is to determine how a medical group's staffing compares to others in the industry. This process is commonly referred to as benchmarking. Chapter 4 provides a thorough description of the benchmarking process. Benchmarking comparisons provide a meaningful starting point to complete an operational assessment, whether it be for financial improvement or for changing operations. Based on data available, the comparison can be made on a specialty-by-specialty basis or by comparing groups of similar sizes.

Table 9-3 compares basic staffing ratios (full-time equivalent employees per full-time equivalent physician) and salary and benefit expenses for primary care specialties to published Medical Group Management Association (MGMA) median percentages,[1] as well as to benchmarks developed by The Camden Group.

Table 9-3
Staffing Ratios vs. Salary and Benefits Expenses

Benchmark	Family Practice MGMA[4]	Family Practice Camden	Internal Medicine MGMA[4]	Internal Medicine Camden	OB/Gyn MGMA[4]	OB/Gyn Camden	Pediatrics MGMA[4]	Pediatrics Camden
Non-provider staffing								
Expense as a percentage of net revenue	31.8%	33.0%	28.7%	33.0%	25.2%	30.0%	30.1%	34.0%
FTEs per full-time provider	3.92	4.20	3.62	4.20	3.38	3.65	3.44	4.20
Front office staffing [1]								
FTEs per full-time provider	1.30	1.50	0.62	1.50	1.04	1.00	0.90	1.50
Back office staffing [2]								
FTEs per full-time provider	1.44	1.60	0.78	1.60	1.39	1.30	1.25	1.60
Billing staff								
FTEs per full-time provider	0.58	0.50	0.51	0.50	0.43	0.50	0.49	0.50
Management/other staffing [3]								
FTEs per full-time provider	1.12	0.60	0.45	0.60	1.08	0.85	0.16	0.60

Notes: Staffing numbers do not include managed care people (i.e., claims processing, etc.)

[1] Includes medical receptionist, medical records, other secretarial support, contract/temp support

[2] Includes registered nurses, licensed practical nurses, medical assistants, nurse aides, authorizations/referrals, other medical support services

[3] Management/other staffing includes general administrative, IS, housekeeping/maint/security, medical secretaries/transcription, clinical lab, radiology/imaging

[4] Numbers are medians by category; therefore they might not foot to total FTEs for MGMA

Sources:
MGMA Cost Survey: 1999 Report Based on 1998 Data. Staffing data per provider was utilized for each of the specialties. Family Practice data represents FP without OB for non-hospital owned groups.
The Camden Group proprietary database

Data used with permission from the Medical Group Management Association, 104 Inverness Terrace East, Englewood, CO 80112-5306; 303-799-1111. www.mgma.com. Copyright 1999.

[1] Medical Group Management Association. *MGMA Cost Survey, 1999 Report Based on 1998 Data.* Englewood, CO, 1999.

Using these benchmarks, performance can be compared to analyze staffing relationships at a medical group level as well as for major operational areas (front office, back office, business office, managed care functions, and administration). Depending on the area where there is a variance, focus can be initiated on processes and costs to determine the cause. If staff salaries and benefits as a percentage of net revenue are higher than expected, it may be due to either lower-than-expected revenues or higher-than-expected expenses. It could also be a result of the combination of these two factors. Variances may also be the result of allocating expenses to the wrong cost center.

Other types of benchmark comparisons are also very useful. One comparison that is an extremely sensitive measure is productive employee hours per patient visit. Because this measure is volume-dependent, employee activity in clinical areas where physicians do not visit is clearly flagged. While work in these areas—even though a physician is not present—can often be justified, monitoring the activity to ensure that there is value for the costs being expended is nevertheless worthwhile. Figure 9-2 illustrates how this calculation can assist management in understanding employee costs being incurred.

In this example, the organization established a benchmark goal of 2.85 productive employee hours per patient visit. When looking at the organization in total, there appears to be an opportunity to reduce the cost by meeting the 2.85 hours per patient visit benchmark. While this difference of .35 hours per patient visit (3.2 hours minus 2.85 hours) may appear small, it translates to one full-time employee for every 115 patient visits conducted by this medical practice. With average employee compensation and benefits being in the $30,000 to $32,000 range per FTE employee, substantial savings could result from a restructuring of work flows and employee activity.

Figure 9-2
ABC Medical Group
Productive Employee Hours per Patient Visit by Location
Pay Period Ending Sept. 25, 2000

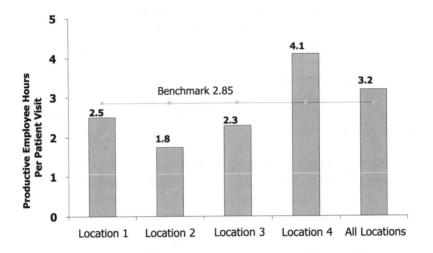

What management also saw from the information in this chart was the opportunity to understand better how Location 2 could operate with fewer employee hours than other locations. Because Location 4 was the main facility with significant support services for the entire practice, it was more understandable why that site was in excess of the target. However, Locations 1 and 3 were of similar size and full-time physician equivalency as Location 2. If Location 2, therefore, was able to operate on that staffing basis, why were the other two locations unable to operate at that level? It was that initial question that was asked, and as a result, staffing changes where made that reduced nearly 10 FTE employees between the two sites. While the average compensation for these positions was below the average for the medical group, the savings from implementing a best practice for staffing exceeded $250,000.

As organizations begin looking at staffing and relating it to physician full-time equivalency, they may need to adjust the full-time equivalency calculation for physicians if the medical group employs mid-level providers and certain licensed ancillary personnel. When using the ratio of full-time equivalent employees to full-time equivalent physicians, this ratio should be adjusted to reflect mid-level providers such as nurse practitioners, physician assistants, dieticians and other similar practitioners who utilize front office and back office personnel. While the ratio concept would be the same, there should be an adjustment in full-time equivalency to reflect the difference in patient care activity/volumes by these types of mid-level providers. The Camden Group defines most full-time mid-level practitioners as equal to 75 percent of a full-time physician. In comparison, physician practice management companies such as PhyCor have used a 50-percent equivalency for these types of mid-level practitioners. Whichever approach is taken, the aggregation of the full-time equivalency of all physicians and mid-level practitioners would give a more realistic provider staffing count for benchmarking purposes. This "new" aggregated full-time equivalent measure could be more appropriately referred to as a "full-time equivalent provider."

Using these types of specific benchmark comparisons is a relatively easy way to review the appropriateness of employee staffing levels. Other components include skill mix of personnel hired (i.e., medical assistants as opposed to registered nurses), level of experience and training, and competitive salaries in the area. The goal of any staffing plan is to be able to recruit and retain qualified personnel.

OTHER SUGGESTIONS FOR REDUCING STAFFING COSTS

One way to reduce staffing expense is to identify inefficiencies and streamline existing systems. Look for tasks that are duplicative in nature or potentially unnecessary. As much as physicians dislike implementing standardized procedures and forms, doing so minimizes exceptions that staff need to deal with every day. By streamlining the work processes, staff will become more productive and efficient, thus reducing the need to add FTEs.

As an example, many physicians have established complex rules regarding appointment scheduling. If the defined appointment types can be kept to a minimum, it is much easier for employees to schedule patients correctly, and training float personnel to cover for employees off for illness or vacation is also much easier. It is not uncommon to see as many appointment-type definitions as there are physicians in the practice. Ensuring accuracy is virtually impossible with such a degree of variability.

Evaluate staffing for front- and back-office functions. Perhaps processes can be streamlined by shifting FTEs to different job categories. If front-office staff have a difficult time answering the phones in a timely manner, then it may make sense to shift the function to back-office personnel. When patients call back two and three times because their initial phone calls have not been returned, the result is rework and duplication. Instead of adding an FTE in the front office, it may make sense to have an additional medical assistant assigned to the back office to help handle this call volume. This addition would make the department more efficient, and overtime staff could be reduced or additional capacity handled. In either case, patient and employee satisfaction should be increased.

Perhaps the practice needs to evaluate using technology instead of increasing staffing. Centralized scheduling can be of tremendous benefit to reduce hold times for patients. A refill desk for patients and pharmacists to call with requests and a nurse triage function to assist patients who require same-day appointments are other ways to maximize the efficiency of key functions.

By establishing basic personnel management processes, using benchmarks, and constantly reviewing operating procedures, a more effective and satisfied employee staff results, which will ultimately affect physician morale and satisfaction.

EXHIBIT 9-1
SAMPLE JOB DESCRIPTIONS

Position: Practice Manager   **Reports To**: Medical Group
President or Board of
Directors

Position Summary

Manages specific administrative function related to the operations of the clinic site as assigned.

Job Responsibilities

- Establishes and maintains an operating environment ensuring effective, efficient, and safe operation of the office practice that responds to patient, physician, and staff needs
- Establishes and implements policies, procedures, and systems for the assigned administrative areas
- Participates in the development and implementation of long-range plans and budgets for the medical practice
- Selects, trains, and ensures development of component personnel. Apprises employees of and adheres to the policies and procedures stipulated in the employee handbook. Schedules staff to meet the needs of the practice. Reviews and approves employee time sheets/payroll cards. Generates and completes employee performance reviews in conjunction with the physicians
- Schedules and performs OSHA training. Ensures compliance of exposure control program and establishes and maintains employee medical records in compliance with OSHA regulations
- Ensures a positive working relationship with physicians
- Coordinates the purchase of medical and office supplies and equipment. Establishes and maintains an inventory system to ensure adequate levels of office supplies

- Monitors and controls clinic expenditures within budget
- Establishes and maintains an evaluation program to ensure timely repairs and proper functioning of office and medical equipment
- Monitors and analyzes patient schedules and practice operations to determine opportunity for improvement in patient services
- Ensures the submission of timely, accurate, and complete information for billing and insurance claims processing
- Ensures patient accounts receivable are worked in a timely and efficient manner
- Reviews each physician's accounts receivable at month-end to track collection percentages and aging of account balances
- Reviews and approves all invoices for payment
- Reviews practice expenses compared to budget and implements action when appropriate
- Implements reporting system as requested by physicians
- Assists with the expansion of the office practice, as necessary
- Works with the board of directors, president, medical director, and practice physicians to ensure that quality patient care and services are provided
- Participates in professional development activities to keep current with health care trends and practices
- Maintains strictest confidentiality regarding medical group information, including patient information
- Maintains appropriate inventory control and approves all purchase orders made by clinic staff
- Performs other duties as requested
- Ensures that OSHA, federal, and state regulatory guidelines are met.

Qualifications

Experience and Education

Bachelor's degree preferred, or an equivalent of five years of management experience, including three years managing a clinic; certificate/license not required.

Knowledge

Knowledge of organization policies and systems, health care administration practices, computer systems and applications, and government and reimbursement regulations and requirements.

Abilities

Ability to take initiative, exercise independent judgment, and problem-solve; ability to work effectively with staff, patients, public, and external agencies; skill in planning, organizing, delegating, and supervising; skill in gathering and interpreting data; skill in verbal and written communication; skill in researching, preparing, and presenting comprehensive reports.

Note: This description indicates in general terms the type and level of work performed and responsibilities held by the employee(s). Duties described are not to be interpreted as being all-inclusive.

I acknowledge receipt of this job and can fulfill all the requirements of this position.

Signature: _____ Date: _____

Job Description/Summary

Manages specific administrative functions related to the operations of the clinic site as assigned.

Performance Standards[1]	Performance Tracking[2]
• 90% or greater overall patient satisfaction	• Patient surveys
• 100% physician satisfaction	• Physician feedback
• Meets or positive variance of medical practice budget	• Actual vs. budget variance report
• Meets budget guidelines	• Budget
• Maintains appropriate inventory of supplies	• Performs inventory audits
• Attends two seminars for professional development	• Attend meetings, seminars, and conferences
• Less than 5% staff turnover rate	• Tracks staffing patterns
• 100% accuracy of demographic information	• Number of accounts missing data for billing and insurance claim processing
• Fewer than 70 days of revenue in accounts receivable	• Accounts receivable ageing

Definitions

[1] Performance standards: expected measures of individual performance.

[2] Performance tracking: process activities to track achievement of performance standards.

Position: Check-In Receptionist   **Reports To:** Office Manager

Position Summary

Promotes a professional practice image by efficiently performing a variety of business and clerical tasks designed to facilitate the smooth flow of patients and work throughout the organization. Receives and registers patients, manages the telephone, schedules appointments, prepares charts, and collects payments and co-payments.

Job Responsibilities

- Cheerfully greets and registers incoming patients and visitors in a prompt and pleasant manner, determines their needs, and responds accordingly
- Presents, reviews, and processes patient registration forms; submits, orders, receives, and monitors clerical office supplies
- Collects and copies financial information (insurance cards, driver's licenses, etc.) and attaches to all new patient charts
- Verifies medical insurance coverage and documents benefit information prior to patient leaving office
- Collects co-pays from insured patients and provides receipts when warranted
- Acts as patient relations representative by answering patient inquiries either in person or on the telephone within the limits of his/her knowledge and medical practice policies
- Answers telephone, screens and direct calls and messages to the appropriate department, physician, or staff member in compliance with office policy
- Schedules patient appointments according to office policy and assists with maintaining physician on-call schedule
- Accurately maintains cash posting sheet
- Retrieves charts to accompany messages taken, when appropriate

- Maintains an accurate file system for insurance eligibility lists and office forms (e.g., return to work, release of medical records, informed consents, prescription pads)
- Follows up on patient no-shows; sends reminder notices when appropriate
- Follows security rules when providing information to outside sources
- Accepts and signs for mail and other deliveries according to office policy
- Retrieves messages from answering service each morning at [specify time] and transfer telephones each evening at [specify time]
- Prepares charts and superbills for the following day and ensures that all documents are properly filed and present in chart, as required
- Practices sterile techniques and universal precautions when accepting specimens from patients over the counter
- Maintains an orderly, neat, and clean front desk and waiting room
- Ensures adequate postage is available in the office at all times.

Qualifications

Experience and Education

One year of experience in a medical office, clinic, or other health care setting. High school graduate or equivalent; completion of a recognized medical secretarial program preferred.

Knowledge

Knowledge of modern office methods, clerical equipment, operations, and processes; familiarity with medical terms and abbreviations; knowledge of mechanics of HMOs, IPAs, and PPOs; familiarity with various medical forms, reports, and processing methods; fundamental knowledge of basic billing procedures; clear understanding of the confidentiality laws that govern the patient/physician relationship.

Abilities:

Ability to type at least 50 WPM and operate a 10-key adding machine by touch; operate or learn to operate automated systems and other office equipment; employ tact, diplomacy, and compassion with all types of people. Must possess strong written, verbal, and interpersonal skills; maintain cooperative relationships with staff members, patients, and physicians; communicate clearly and concisely; process a variety of medical reports and correspondence; follow set routines, be alert to variations, and make decisions accordingly; maintain organized and accurate records; exercise team coordination skills; serve as a patient advocate; understand and enforce the financial policy of the practice; and recognize and correct costly errors.

Note: This description indicates in general terms the type and level of work performed and responsibilities held by the employee(s). Duties described are not to be interpreted as being all-inclusive.

I acknowledge receipt of this job and can fulfill all the requirements of this position.

Signature: _____ Date: _____

Job Description

Promotes a professional practice image by efficiently performing a variety of business and clerical tasks designed to facilitate the smooth flow of patients and work throughout the organization. Receives and registers patients, manages the telephone, schedules appointments, prepares charts, and collects payments and co-payments.

Performance Standards[1]	Performance Tracking[2]
• 100% accurate verification of insurance coverage for all patients	• EOB denials
• Able to process 20-25 patients in office per day	• Office visits
• 100% co-pay collection	• Co-pays
• 100% accuracy in scheduling appointments	• Patient appointments, patient and physician feedback
• 100% accuracy in cash petty sheet	• Cash posting sheet
• 100% accuracy in messages sent to physicians	• Physician feedback
• 15 minutes average time to check-in new patients	• Patient process time
• 100% completion and turnover of mailed pre-registration packets to new patients	• Track missing demographic data

Definitions

[1] Performance Standards: expected measures of individual performance

[2] Performance Tracking: process activities to track achievement of performance standards.

Position: Check-Out Receptionist   **Reports To:** Office Manager

Position Summary

Assists in coordinating, monitoring, and directing all front-office activities. Greets and checks out patients; schedules follow-up appointments; informs patients of financial policy and accepts over-the-counter payments; posts charges for medical services rendered. (Note: This position will be the lead worker in absence of the office manager.)

Job Responsibilities

Supervisory
- Prioritizes and organizes workflow of the front office
- Responsible for maintaining good patient/staff relations
- Responsible for on-site employee training in accordance with office policies and procedures
- Responsible for supervising staff schedules relative to maintaining prompt front office coverage in conjunction with the office manager
- Responsible for informing staff of all changes or updates issued by the physician
- Coordinates and maintains physician schedule in conjunction with the office manager
- Enforces personnel policies according to the employee handbook.

Administrative
- Serves as back-up for position check-in and scheduling positions as required
- Assists in confirming next-day patient appointments by 5:00 p.m. each day
- Makes address corrections in system as warranted
- Verifies medical insurance coverage and documents benefit information appropriately
- Collects deductibles and confirms that co-payments have been made
- Checks out patients

- Reviews fee tickets for completeness
- Inquires if physician provided instructions and if additional tests were performed
- Schedules ancillary tests as directed (checks insurance type, determines if authorization is required)
- Collects patient balance
- Schedules return appointment for patient (provide appointment card)
- Checks patient off on appointment log
- Posts charges
- Reviews chart references to Rx, lab, x-rays, EKGs, or physician order and compares with superbill listed services
- Indicates completion by signing off on the physician's order once task is completed
- Inputs charges into system and stamps fee ticket with billed date upon completion
- Notifies patients of action taken on authorization and referral requests
- Reconciles superbills with appointment log and sign-in sheet at the end of each day to ensure all patients and their correlating charges have been accounted for
- Batches fee tickets at the end of the day, attaches appropriate day-end documents, and forwards copy to MSO for review and filing
- Assists in preparing patient charts and superbills for new and established patients
- Reconciles charts with appointment schedule to ensure that all charts have been pulled for next day
- Photocopies medical records when required
- Performs all other related tasks as assigned by the physician or office supervisor
- Monitors and analyzes patient schedule and practice operations to determine opportunities for improvement in patient services
- Ensures the submission of timely, accurate, and complete data to the billing office according to the established procedure
- Monitors petty cash balances at month-end and forwards disbursement record to office manager.

Qualifications

Experience and Education

High school graduate or equivalent education required. Completion of a recognized medical secretarial program preferred. One year of experience in a physician's office, clinic, or other health care setting.

Knowledge

Knowledge of modern office methods, clerical equipment operation, and processes; familiarity with medical technology and abbreviations; ICD-9-CM and CPT coding regulations; knowledge of mechanics of HMOs, IPAs, and PPOs; familiarity with various medical forms, reports, and processing methods and a basic understanding of billing procedures; clear understanding of the confidentiality laws governing the physician/patient relationship.

Abilities

Ability to type at least 50 WPM and operate a 10-key adding machine by touch. Operate or learn to operate automated systems, a calculator, a copier, and other office equipment; employ tact, diplomacy, and compassion with all types of people; possess strong written, verbal, and interpersonal skills; maintain cooperative relationships with staff members, patients, and physicians; communicate clearly and concisely; follow set routines, be alert to variations and make decisions accordingly; maintain organized and accurate records; exercise team coordination skills; serve as a patient advocate; understand and enforce the financial policy of the practice; and recognize and correct costly errors.

Note: This description indicates in general terms the type and level of work performed and responsibilities held by the employee(s). Duties described are not to be interpreted as being all-inclusive.

I acknowledge receipt of this job and can fulfill all the requirements of this position.

Signature: _____ Date: _____

Job Description/Summary

Assists in coordinating, monitoring, and directing all front-office activities. Greets and checks out patients; schedules follow-up appointments; informs patients of financial policy and accepts over-the-counter payments; posts charges for medical services rendered.

Performance Standards[1]	Performance Tracking[2]
• 100% collection of patient balance	• Charge tickets
• 100% schedule return appointments	• Appointment and schedule log
• 100% notification of patients on authorization and referral requests	• Authorization and referral log
• 100% accuracy in the end-of-day cash reconciliation of superbills	• Batch fee tickets
• 100% accuracy in posting charges	• Charge posting
• 100% balance of petty cash disbursements	• Petty cash log
• 100% completion and turnover of mailed pre-registration packets to new patients	• Track missing demographic data

Definitions

[1] Performance Standards: expected measures of individual performance.

[2] Performance Tracking: process activities to track achievement of performance standards.

Position: Medical Assistant/ Nursing Support

Reports To: Back Office Supervisor

Position Summary

Assists the physicians with the examination and treatment of patients and performs routine tasks needed to keep the clinical office training running smoothly.

Job Responsibilities

- Greets patients and escorts them to the examination or procedure room
- Takes vital signs (pulse, blood pressure, temperature) as well as weight and height; accurately transcribes results in patient's chart
- Assists in completing forms required by physician prior to examination (e.g., health questionnaires, medical histories)
- Collects and labels all specimens immediately upon receipt
- Prepares patients for examination, tests, or procedures (hands gown and instructs patient on how to put gown on, assists patient in undressing when necessary)
- Provides instruction when appropriate; obtains signed consent forms when required
- Sets up procedure trays
- Notifies physician when patient is ready for examination
- Assists physician with examinations and procedures as needed. Prepares and administers medication as prescribed by the physician
- Labels and color codes blood samples, including packaging of specimens for shipment to appropriate outside labs
- Maintains and restocks clinical supplies for back office (e.g., examination and procedure rooms) in addition to controlling inventory and generating monthly inventory list

- Organizes and keeps a running inventory of medications in medications rooms and refrigerator (routinely disposing of expired medications as warranted)
- Cleans counters per clinic policy.

Qualifications

Experience and Education
High school diploma or equivalent or completion of certificated medical assistant program preferred. A multi-tasked professional with at least 3 years of experience in performing back office activities in a medical environment.

Knowledge
Basic medical back office procedures and medical terminology; first aid measures; equipment, supplies, and instruments used in a medical office; simple, routine clinical laboratory methods; universal blood and body fluid precautions; OSHA rules and regulations; established protocol for storing poisons, narcotics, acids, caustics, and flammable items, restrictions imposed by various managed care carriers, various forms inherent to profession; patient confidentiality regulations.

Abilities
Establish and maintain cooperative relationships with staff members and; create a responsive, caring environment for patients; respond promptly to physician's direction(s); maintain medical records in a concise and accurate manner; employ correct aseptic techniques in preparation of instruments and equipment; react quickly in emergency situations and maintain current CPR card; recognize and prevent possible safety hazards; ensure proper maintenance of equipment; communicate clearly and facilitate patient education when warranted; act as advocate and assist physician in meeting the physical and mental needs of patient; exercise independent judgment; perform functions that consistently fall within the legal boundaries of profession.

Note:This description indicates in general terms the type and level of work performed and responsibilities held by the employee(s). Duties described are not to be interpreted as being all-inclusive.

I acknowledge receipt of this job description and can fulfill all of the requirements of this position.

Signature: _____ Date: _____

Job Description/Summary

Assists the physicians with the examination and treatment of patients and performs routine tasks needed to keep the clinical office running smoothly.

Definitions

Performance Standards[1]	Performance Tracking[2]
• 10-15 minute average waiting time in exam room	• Patient log and feedback
• 5 minutes average exam room turnaround for the next patient	• Patient time log
• 100% accuracy in clinical forms documentation	• Chart audit
• 100% compliance in inventory control and standardization	• Inventory control log
• 100% compliance to clinical operational protocols	• Physician and peer feedback
• 100% physician satisfaction	• Physician feedback

[1] Performance Standards: expected measures of individual performance.
[2] Performance Tracking: process activities to track achievement of performance standards.

10

ACCOUNTS RECEIVABLE MANAGEMENT

Robin G. Wallace
Karen E. Dunbar, MBA, MHS

Times have changed, and so must a medical group's approach to billing and collections. This area becomes a particular focus when the group is faced with a financial challenge and operational performance needs to be improved. Third-party payers and the government have waged a battle with providers for health care dollars, which means that business office practices must be increasingly sophisticated. Payers have imposed a series of payment obstacles in the form of coding screens, contractual mandates, eligibility checks, fee schedules, authorization/referral requirements, and filing limits, which if not adhered to could result in delayed or denied payment. All of this has occurred while unsuspecting medical groups and health care systems have continued doing business as usual.

Many medical groups have made adjustments along the way but have resisted the notion that they need to adopt stronger front-end business practices. Their concerns stemmed from the desire to prevent the business of medicine from interfering with the practice of medicine. However, with shrinking cash flow, the rising number of errors in claim submissions, and increasing payment denials, it is clear that inefficient business practices do affect the practice of medicine. Those organizations that have been slow to comprehend the signals of change now find themselves behind the curve and often struggling to keep the practice going.

BUSINESS AS USUAL DOESN'T WORK

Complex reimbursement arrangements have increased the number of transactions occurring between health care providers and health plans. Nevertheless, many organizations have not armed their workforce with basic knowledge about how the payment system works. Nor have they set up the mechanisms to ensure that the myriad of data sources that must come together to produce a claim actually converge in the appropriate places.

No longer can the approach to medical billing be treated as a totally separate function relegated to account representatives working in the basement of the medical building or residing in some off-site location across town. Instead, it must be brought to the forefront and embraced as an important part of practice operations. Coordinating the melange of systems, processes, and people that directly or indirectly contribute to the bottom line could involve a major retooling of systems. When fighting for financial survival, however, the idea is to get as many soldiers as possible in the field collecting money. By banding together to develop structured systems for sharing data with all the individuals who participate in the delivery of patient care, the necessary information pipelines can be built.

MEDICARE PULLED THE TRIGGER

Medicare triggered this reimbursement decline by changing its calculation methodology from one based on historical charges and introducing the use of the resource-based relative value system (RBRVS) in 1992. RBRVS was designed as a mechanism to measure the value of a physician's clinical cognitive work. Years later, the pressure escalated by passage of the Balanced Budget Acts of 1997 and 1999. The BBA of 1997 was the first of a one-two punch that issued mandates for billing compliance to health care entities and gave credence to the fear factor associated with the term "fraud and abuse." The second hit came through the 1999 Balanced Budget Refinement Act (BBRA), which expanded the scope of the Office of the Inspector General's (OIG) search for fraud, waste, and abuse to include individual or small medical groups and third-party billing agencies. The hefty fines attached to noncompliance were designed to provide an incentive to physicians to begin taking proper code selection and chart documentation more seriously for patients covered by government-funded insurance plans. The potential for monetary gain relative to adverse findings also improved the solvency prospects of Medicare's trust fund for another 20 years or more. Figure 10-1 indicates the amount of money Medicare is collecting as a result of billing errors.

The advent of managed care and the proliferation of discounted fee-for-service arrangements, as well as the introduction of capitated structures, further eroded the traditional reliance on charge-based fee structures. Because third party payers are also adopting Medicare's RBRVS methodology and assimilating the characteristics of managed care, collection percentages are dropping dramatically. Figure 10-2 illustrates the dramatic decrease in gross collection percentages over the past two decades, as documented by MGMA's Cost Survey.[1]

---

[1] Medical Group Management Association. *MGMA Cost Survey: 1999 Report Based on 1998 Data.* Englewood, CO, 1999.

Figure 10-1
Estimated Improper Payments by Type of Error
(Dollar in Billions)

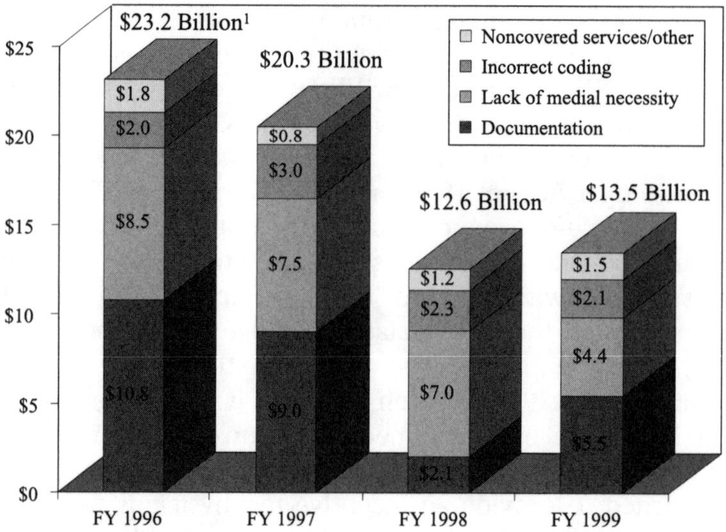

☐	Noncovered services/other
▨	Incorrect coding
▨	Lack of medial necessity
■	Documentation

$23.2 Billion[1]

$20.3 Billion

$12.6 Billion

$13.5 Billion

FY 1996 — $1.8, $2.0, $8.5, $10.8
FY 1997 — $0.8, $3.0, $7.5, $9.0
FY 1998 — $1.2, $2.3, $7.0, $2.1
FY 1999 — $1.5, $2.1, $4.4, $5.5

[1]Does not add to total due to rounding

Source: Department of Health and Human Services OIG Improper Fiscal Year 1999 Medicare Fee-For-Service Payments, Feburary 2000
A-17-99-01999

THE IMPACT OF MANAGED CARE

As managed care strengthened its foothold on reimbursement, it reshaped the way that the health care industry conducts business. Administrative duties linked to patient scheduling, registration, treatment, and billing and collections became more labor-intensive, bringing with them a whole new set of rules and regulations that affected physician decision making regarding the amount and type of medical care to be provided to patients as well as the payments to be received.

The administrative effects of managed care were so subtle that initially, the subsequent erosion of staff time and reimbursement dollars went virtually unnoticed. What were once considered to be relatively straightforward relationships quickly become convoluted. Keeping track of who the contracting

Figure 10-2
Mean Gross and Adjusted Fee-for-Service Collection Percentages
1980-1998

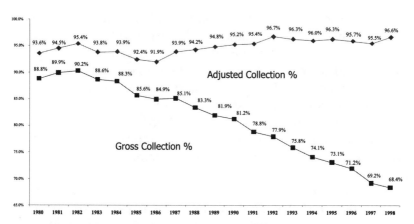

Source: *MGMA Cost Survey: 1999 Report Based on 1998 Data*
Data used with permission from the Medical Group Management Association, 104 Inverness Terrace East, Englewood, CO 80112-5306; 303-799-1111.
www.mgma.com. Copyright 1999.

entity was, and with whom the contracts resided (e.g., with the HMO, IPA , TPA, or PHO), began to get confusing for providers, let alone their support staff.

Concurrently, the capture of accurate patient demographic and insurance information has taken on monumental impor- tance. It also has become more difficult. To accommodate con- sumer demand for flexibility of choice, health plans expanded available coverage options, and frontline employees often strug- gle to navigate the myriad of plan provisions. Over time, it has become apparent that the lack of knowledge and understanding of government and payer requirements has resulted in unwar- ranted write-offs that have led to the poor financial perform- ance of many practices. Therefore, it is vital to invest time and energy in educating and developing the skills and understand- ing of staff members throughout the practice.

CONNECTING THE CORE ELEMENTS THROUGH COMMUNICATION

Key to the success of accounts receivable management is assuring that all stakeholders in the organization understand their connection to the overall billing process. Depending on the size and structure of the medical group or entity, the stakeholders can consist of the physician recruiter, the managed care department, clinic and business office managers, and support staff. Therefore, how effectively an organization manages the communication and dissemination of information critical to producing a clean claim will often determine its financial health.

Specific areas that tend to break down as a result of poor communication or no communication are provider recruitment, credentialing, patient registration, and billing. All these data elements must be plugged into a global system that supports the organization's business goals.

BUILDING A SOLID FOUNDATION

Whether starting from scratch or rebuilding billing operations, a medical practice should develop a detailed plan that will enable the organization to achieve its strategic and financial objectives. Figure 10-3 demonstrates the various steps required to build a stable and sustainable business office. This is often one of the most critical activities when trying to improve performance. A solid foundation consists of strong leadership, and identifying the organizational and staffing structures that will best meet the needs of your specific situation is an important first step. It also includes developing employee skills, implementing performance-based job descriptions, creating standardized policies and procedures, and setting performance goals for individuals as well as the organization.

Figure 10-3

Steps to Building a Stable Business Office Foundation

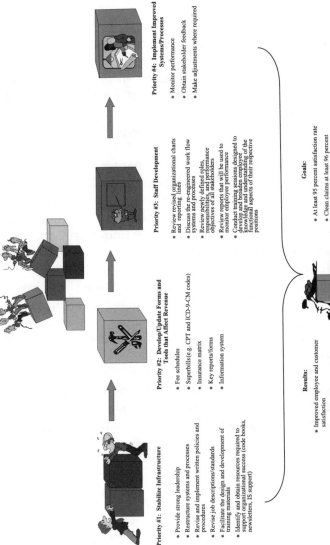

Priority #1: Stabilize Infrastructure

- Provide strong leadership
- Restructure systems and processes
- Revise and implement written policies and procedures
- Revise job descriptions/standards
- Facilitate the design and development of training materials
- Identify and obtain resources required to support organizational success (code books, newsletters, IS support)

Priority #2: Develop/Update Forms and Tools that Affect Revenue

- Fee schedules
- Superbills(e.g. CPT and ICD-9-CM codes)
- Insurance matrix
- Key reports/forms
- Information system

Priority #3: Staff Development

- Review revised organizational charts and reporting lines
- Discuss the re-engineered work flow systems and processes
- Review newly defined roles, responsibilities, and performance objectives of all stakeholders
- Review reports that will be used to monitor employee performance
- Conduct training sessions designed to develop and broaden employee knowledge and understanding of the functional aspects of their respective positions

Priority #4: Implement Improved Systems/Processes

- Monitor performance
- Obtain stakeholder feedback
- Make adjustments where required

Results:

- Improved employee and customer satisfaction
- Improved employee performance
- Reduced percentage of A/R over 90 days
- Increased cash flow
- Reduced days in A/R

Goals:

- At least 95 percent satisfaction rate
- Clean claims at least 96 percent
- 25–30 percent over 90 days
- 65–70 days in A/R depending on specialty

Business Office Structures

The accounts receivable (A/R) function can be set up in a variety of structures. The three most common billing structures are:

- **Decentralized billing** refers to the entire billing and collection process (from entering patient demographic and insurance information, charge entry through follow-up) being performed at the individual practice clinic locations.
- **Centralized billing** offices typically control the entire billing process. They receive charge batches from multiple individual practice sites. The clinical sites prepare and reconcile the batches, either by charges or hash marks, and forward them to the business office for entering patient demographic and insurance information. The central location is then responsible for the billing process, beginning with charge entry through collection. There are instances however, when the centralized business office can resemble that of a hybrid arrangement.
- **Hybrid billing** offices may have varying structures. A typical hybrid office would be set up such that entering patient demographics, insurance information, and charge entry are performed on-site at the practice location, with claim submission and collection occurring at a central location.

These three structures can be offered irrespective of whether the billing entity is an independent billing agency, a management services organization (MSO), or part of an independent group practice.

Staffing

Once a decision is reached on how the organization will be structured, the next step is building the staffing framework to make it happen. Deciding how the information will flow through the organization or how the work units will be organized are early steps in the construction process. Figure 10-4 identifies critical functions associated with billing and collections and illustrates the allocation of duties according to core work function.

The chart reflects the seven core functions that are directly linked to producing an invoice for payment. Also note the heavy reliance on the data provided by frontline personnel. The data should flow as needed from one resource to another without interruption. Collection of accurate and timely information by all employees should be the goal of every professional and non-professional health care employee. Insurance verification should be considered a standard function of the front office or a designated person within the clinic. Data entry errors and omissions should be routinely recorded, tracked, and communicated to individual staff members by the manager on at least a weekly basis at the inception of implementation, and on a monthly basis once the process is well established.

Calculating Staffing Levels

Calculating appropriate staffing will entail obtaining the productivity of providers according to specialty. This information is used to calculate a "normalized" value of a full-time equivalent (FTE) provider that is volume-based. An example of this methodology is illustrated in Table 10-1. By using MGMA median results or other preferred benchmarks as a baseline, an initial employee staffing number can be determined.

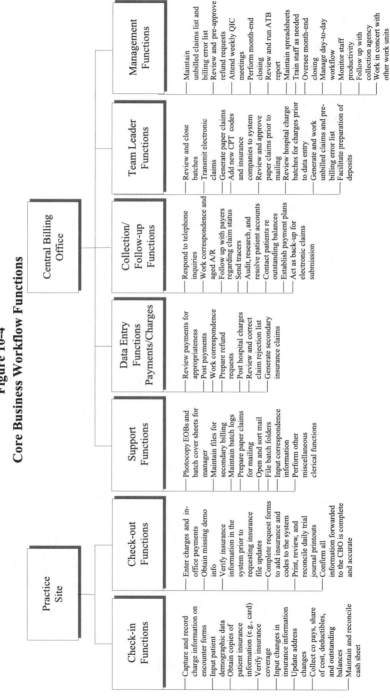

Figure 10-4
Core Business Workflow Functions

Table 10-1
Staffing Benchmarks

Benchmark	Family Practice		Internal Medicine		OB/Gyn		Pediatrics	
	MGMA[2]	Camden	MGMA[2]	Camden	MGMA[2]	Camden	MGMA[2]	Camden
Charges per FTE physician per year	338,554	484,380	296,718	478,170	746,510	760,725	401,209	465,750
Visits per FTE physician per year[1]	4,382	6,210	2,998	4,554	3,201	3,381	5,067	6,210
Billing staff								
FTEs per full-time provider	0.58	0.50	n/a	0.50	0.43	0.50	0.49	0.50

(1) *MGMA Physician Compensation and Production Survey: 1999 Report Based on 1998 Data* - for charge and visit data
(2) *MGMA Cost Survey: 1999 Report Based on 1998 Data* - for staffing data

Data used with permission from the Medical Group Management Association, 104 Inverness Terrace East, Englewood, Colorado 80112-5306; 303-799-1111. www.mgma.com. Copyright 1999.

Functional Workteams

The reporting capabilities of the practice's information system and the pool of talent available in the business office or market are important factors to consider when deciding how to organize or reconfigure billing office work teams. Several configuration options are detailed below:

- **Account or provider teams:** organized to include all the functional components of a work team that could include a team leader, a data entry representative, an account representative, and a collector. In this setting, the team is generally assigned a specific client or number of clients for whom they take complete responsibility (see Figures 10-5 and 10-6).

Figure 10-5
Billing Operation Staffing Model

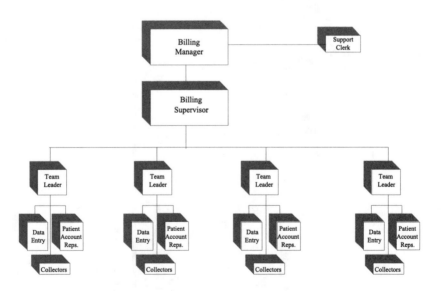

Figure 10-6
Organizational Chart for the Billing Department

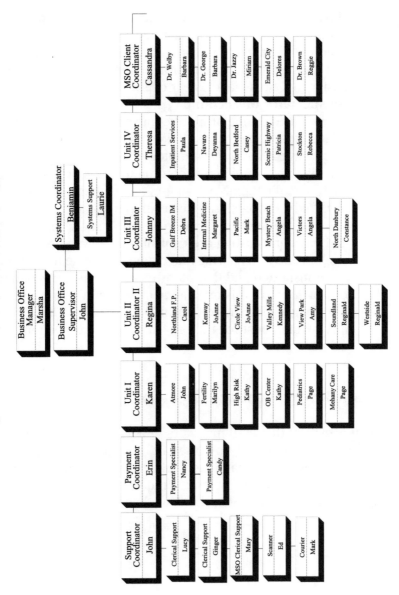

- **By financial classification:** Each biller is assigned a specific payer category or a number of payer categories, depending on the volume associated with the categories chosen (e.g., Medicare, Medicaid, workers' compensation, commercial, self pay). Data entry, which can include both charge and payment posting, can be centralized, or billers can assume responsibility for posting payments for their designated financial class or classes.
- **By specialty or account types:** Account representatives are assigned to one or more clinic site or specialty. Certain related specialties can be linked together, such as orthopedics/physical therapy, cardiology/pulmonology, etc. Teams can also be formulated according to areas of functionality, such as collections by aging category (e.g., A/R over 120 days old). Problematic payers may be assigned a special team of workers to tackle payment issues. Charge entry and payment posting are centralized. A systems analyst is responsible for ensuring that claims and patient statements are transmitted and that month-end reports are generated.
- **By patient:** In this arrangement, account representatives are assigned by the letters of the alphabet. This arrangement works best for the self- or private-pay section of the accounts.

Staff Development and Education

It is critical that staff members understand where the organization is heading and how they fit into the big picture. Once staff members understand their role in the process, they need to be provided with the tools and requisite training to perform their jobs at the standards that have been established.

If asked, the majority of employees will tell you those areas in which they believe they lack knowledge and would like assistance in developing. Another revealing source of information are remittance advices (R/As), EOBs, and EOMBs to identify areas where staff may require additional education. These documents reveal the challenges the staff may be encountering relative to coding or financial class selection, whether provider relationships with health plans are appropriately established, or even if insurance verifications are getting done. Electronic edit reports also harbor a wealth of information because they reveal the input errors made during patient registration.

Once staff have the appropriate tools and training, it is important to empower them to perform the tasks—within the scope of their knowledge and responsibilities—to function effectively. It is also important that staff understand the department or organization's chain of command and direct reporting lines.

Management

Given that performance improvement situations may call for dramatic change, the business office manager must be competent, credible, and capable of making sound business decisions. Recognizing that morale may be low and employee turnover high during this time, it will be imperative to build rapport quickly, communicate the objectives, and provide clear direction. To jump start the process, establishing employee quality and productivity expectations could provide needed structure. This may include setting goals for the number of accounts worked per day and ensuring that staff understand and participate in the push to meet the customer service targets established within the context of the organization's financial objectives. It could also encompass areas such as customer service issues that will include such items as cycle times in relation to data entry, claim generation, and payment receipt, as well as acceptable response times to customer phone inquiries or complaints. These standards are not only important during times of crisis, but they will also be an important management tool for the long haul. Exhibit 10-1 (at the end of this chapter) provides a job description with performance measures for a business office manager.

INFORMATION SYSTEMS

A variety of information systems is available in today's marketplace. Whether it's a system you own and operate or access through the Internet (ASP), it is important that the information system you select can perform the functions critical to the billing process (see Chapter 13). These key attributes are described below.

Month-End Reporting

The system must be able to create basic month-end A/R reports. The primary purpose of these reports is to determine how effectively the organization is achieving its financial and business goals. Their secondary function is to measure organizational performance and processes. They can be among the most powerful instruments for change because they play such a fundamental role in helping to map out a recovery plan. Because of this, stakeholders should become familiar with their own system's reporting capabilities (e.g., format, mnemonics, and symbols used) and educated on the type of information these various documents contain. Seven reports are critical to assessing the financial performance of any business office operation and medical practice:

- Transaction journals by CPT code, by provider/site, month-to-date, and year-to-date
- Charges, payments, and adjustments month-to-date and year-to-date

- Aging summary by major financial class
- Charges, payments, and adjustments by major payers
- Credit balance report
- Unbilled report
- Bad debt write-offs and adjustments.

Payments

Payment posting is an important function within the billing department, requiring a cadre of knowledgeable employees who have a fundamental understanding of how to interpret explanations of benefits (EOBs) and explanations of Medicare benefits (EOMB). For this reason it is important to have a system that allows fee schedules to be loaded and enables staff to review an account concurrent with the posting of payments. This function allows staff to identify payment amounts that are lower than expected so they can "flag" the account. It also allows the collector to identify the accounts requiring follow-up in a more timely manner. In a managed care market it may be worthwhile to invest in the managed care module, particularly if capitation is involved. The system should have the capability to allow various fee schedules and RBRVS/RVU values to be loaded, as well as to adjust capitation payments automatically.

System Set-Up

In an outpatient environment, it is preferable to have a system in place that is account-based rather than encounter-based. Always initiate the set-up knowing which reports you would like to receive and in what format. For instance, if the group has six locations and Dr. Brown sees patients at three offices, the following questions must be addressed:

1. Are you interested in the capability of seeing Dr. Brown's activity at each individual practice location, or are you only interested in his overall productivity for the group?

2. Will you want to track referrals?
3. What kind of security levels are available?
4. Can you set up varying degrees of access depending on the user functions and position?
5. Will you track entries made by each user?
6. Will you age your patient accounts by date of service, date of posting, or bill date?
7. How will your month-end closing be handled?
8. What must happen to enable demand statements to be printed at the business office?
9. Will the entire system need to be shut down at month-end, or will you do concurrent posting?
10. Can it produce clean claims?
11. Does it have easy-to-read screens?
12. Is it capable of linking the diagnosis to the procedure performed?
13. Does it separate workers' compensation and industrial cases or corporate accounts from routine medical accounts?

Other key functions that must be considered today include the system's capabilities to meet the Health Insurance Portability Accountability Act (HIPAA) requirements. HIPAA has redefined the way medical practices, government, and commercial payers are conducting business with regard to information exchange and access to patient information.

According to Cyber Dialogue, an Internet-based data management company, 78 percent of U.S. Internet users with health insurance are interested in managing benefits through their insurance company's website.[2] Basic online community services such as e-mail, home pages, and medical news discussion groups are just the beginning. Health care organizations can benefit by the potential replacement of paper-ridden processes that have historically bogged down their systems. By automating some of the mundane tasks, such as appointment scheduling, test result reporting, and medical records, patients will be given immediate access along with the ability to transact busi-

---

[2] http://www.nua.ie/surveys/index.cgi.

ness and obtain information instantly. Business offices of the future will be able to track and profile patients and their calling patterns, create electronic financial folders, and post payments and denials with minimal effort, as well as streamline access to eligibility information.

PERFORMANCE MEASURES

There is an old adage that says you can't manage what you don't measure, and if the goal is to promote organization-wide quality, there must be mechanisms in place to ensure that the key processes are consistently monitored and communicated on an ongoing basis.

When assessing business office operations, the most valuable data can be that derived from the organization's month-end reports. The critical performance indicators for a business office include:

- Monthly charge volume
- Payer mix trends
- A/R aging summary by major financial class

- Gross collection rate = $\dfrac{\text{Total Payments}}{\text{Total Charges}}$
- Net collection rate = $\dfrac{\text{Payments}}{\text{Charges - Adjustments}}$
- Monthly cash collections.

Some measurements, when compared to industry benchmarks, enable an organization to determine how well it fares when compared to its peers. As illustrated in Table 10-2, this information can be compared to industry standards (e.g., MGMA, other local providers) for a specific discipline of providers.

Table 10-2
Accounts Receivable Performance Standards

Accounts Receivable[1]	Family Practice	Internal Medicine	OB/ GYN	Pediatrics
Gross FFS Collection %[2]	75%	70%	68%	81%
Net FFS Collection %	98%	97%	97%	98%
Discount %[3]	25%	30%	32%	19%
Days in A/R	53.1	57.0	59.7	57.0
% A/R Over 90 Days	25%	25%	24%	22%

(1) MGMA accounts receivable data found in Tables 9.2, 10.2, 11.2, 12.2, 13.2
(2) Collections expressed as a percent of total charges
(3) Adjustments expressed as a percentage of (payments) + (adjustments)

Source: *MGMA 1999 Cost Survey, 1999 Report Based on 1998 Data* and *Physician Compensation and Production Survey, 1999 Report Based on 1998 Data.* MGMA medians are based on single specialty data.

Data used with permission from the Medical Group Management Association, 104 Inverness Terrace East, Englewood, Colorado 80112-5306; 303-799-1111. www.mgma.com. Copyright 1999.

However, the practice must adopt its own standards to guide the organization toward achieving its financial objectives. Every person in the organization should be aware of the relevant indicators for his or her specific area of performance. They should also understand the overall goals of the group. Table 10-3 lists indicators that are key to managing the collection process.

As with any improvement process, this is not a one-time occurrence. It is important to monitor these measures on a regular basis to detect trends and catch problems before they are out of control. The sample dashboard reports provided in Chapter 4 will facilitate the monitoring activities.

Table 10-3
Staff and Operating Performance Indicators

Pended claims	Verified and corrected in 24 hours
Claims: elec/paper reject rate	Less than 5%
Claims: payer submission	48 hours of visit
Payment posting	24 hours upon receipt
Payment posting	98% accuracy
Batch balance/audit report	Match 100%
Credit balance	90% resolve monthly
Clean claims spool	100% daily
Employee turnover	Less than 5% per year
Opens/dates/sorts mail	100% in 2.5 hours
Sorts/distributes mail	95% accuracy

Accountability

Setting clear measurable performance standards establishes accountability. However, if standards are to be effective, performance must be tracked and the outcome communicated to each employee. The feedback demonstrates commitment to enforcing the established standard and ensures there is no confusion about the expectations. Conduct in-services to educate staff about the benchmarks and service targets required of them. The following reports, functions, and tasks, if used consistently, can help promote the desired level of accountability and performance:

- Pre-edit or rejection reports
- Unbilled reports
- Insurance correspondence
- Random note checks
- Patient inquiries/complaints
- Dollar value by major payer.

System and Process Improvement

As noted, the data derived from month-end reports can be instrumental in identifying problem areas and promoting conformance to the established standard of zero error tolerance. Use flowcharting techniques to identify bottlenecks. Sit with staff members to record the sequence of activities comprising the core functions. You are looking for potential breakdowns, unnecessary repetitions, or task duplication. You are also looking for functions that may branch into other departments to ensure that the full cycle of events is captured. Once flowcharts are completed for each area, have a knowledgeable staff member review them to ensure that they accurately reflect the task identified. Use these findings to initiate the re-engineering process. To continue improving the systems and processes in place, they will need to be reviewed and refined on an ongoing basis. Figure 10-7 provides a sample flow chart.

Policies and Procedures

Having documented policies and procedures in place (and following them) is another critical component. A key issue that should be addressed at the onset is the organization's approach to collections. This decision should be addressed in the group or health system's financial policy. The collection of co-payments and portions of outstanding deductibles at the time of service, coverage and non-coverage issues, and discounts to be offered and under what circumstances should be covered. Another item that should be agreed upon is how small balance write-offs and bad debt accounts will be administered. Table 10-4 illustrates how more successful medical groups (as identified by the Medical Group Management Association) have clearly defined policies and procedures, especially as they relate to these important financial issues.[3]

---

[3] Medical Group Management Association. *MGMA Performance and Practices of Successful Medical Groups*. Englewood, CO, 1999.

**Figure 10-7
CBO Payment Batch Preparation and Posting
Sample Workflow Diagram**

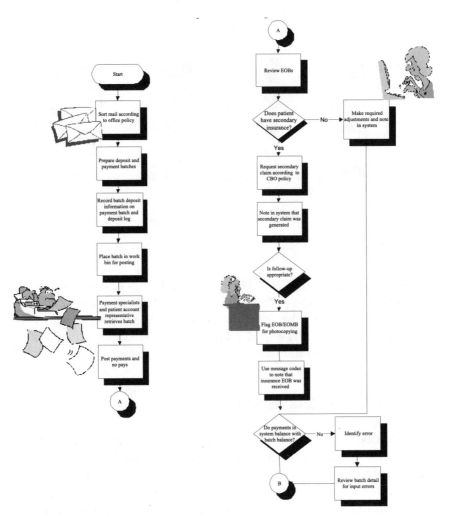

Table 10-4
Documentation of Financial Policies and Procedures for Successful Groups

■ Better-performing Medical Groups		□ Others	

Collection of co-payment at the time of service: 96.30% / 75.30%
Insurance verification prior to service: 85.19% / 62.63%
Small balance write-offs: 85.19% / 70.98%
Bad debt write-offs: 85.19% / 72.02%

Source: MGMA Performance & Practices of Successful Medical Groups, 1999

Data used with permission from the Medical Group Management Association, 104 Inverness Terrace East, Englewood, Colorado 80112-5306; 303-799-1111. www.mgma.com. Copyright 1999.

Included in Exhibit 10-2 (at the end of this chapter) is a sample policy for patient account follow-up. The policy is a step-by-step delineation of the tasks associated with this function, the responsible party, the expected tasks associated with the function, and the expected outcome.

Contractual Relationships

Because contractual relationships are critical to obtaining payment, formal systems must be established to review key aspects of contractual arrangements with new and established employees. Establish an information repository on the company's intranet or manual systems to enable employees to access organizational policies, procedures, and protocols and view updated versions of the company's contract matrix. When new agreements are signed, route them to the appropriate parties. Frequent (quarterly) information sessions should be scheduled to enable employees to stay abreast of contractual or provider changes. Establish a library of information that is specific to the organization. The library could contain coding books such as the *Physicians' Current Procedural Terminology (CPT), International Classification of Diseases 9th Revision Clinical Modification* (ICD-9-CM), Medicare, Medicaid/ Medi-Cal newsletters and manual updates, and an insurance directory.

Billing Service Arrangements

In instances where a third party billing relationship exists, it is a good idea to review the language of the billing agreement to ensure it meets Medicare guidelines with respect to the extent of the type of services offered. Also check whether there are security levels in place to protect patient confidentiality, appropriate use of provider numbers, and other relevant information. According to Medicare, "it is the provider who is ultimately responsible for the verification of the identity of each patient receiving services from them. If services are rendered to a beneficiary impersonator, providers may be liable for an overpayment."[4]

KEY FUNCTIONS AND THEIR INTERRELATIONSHIPS

Many administrative functions are tightly linked to the effectiveness of the business office. However, their importance to the process can often be forgotten or minimized, and as a result the necessary processes and links are not always put in place. The following areas require special attention:

- Physician recruitment and credentialing
- Patient registration/data collection
- Insurance verification
- Coding.

[4] Health Care Financing Administration. *Medicare Fraud and Abuse: A Practical Guide of Proactive Measures to Avoid Becoming a Victim, Second Edition.* Baltimore, Maryland, 1999.

Physician Recruitment and Credentialing

Provider recruitment and credentialing are generally performed in the background of a health care organization. Either the lead physician or recruiter is responsible for attracting new providers to grow their medical group. Poor communication or no communication of this information can result in most organizations adopting "band-aid" approaches. Consequently, these fragmented strategies have contributed to reduced collections, and they could cause further problems in the event a Medicare or carrier audit is performed.

Submitting claim forms to third party payers, specifically Medicare, using an established provider's provider number or the number of a physician who has left the practice is not an appropriate fix. Billing for these medical services as if the physicians are locum tenens is also not acceptable. There may be some instances when health plans provide temporary privileges or allow the physician to render services under a generic number because the application has been received and is pending review. In general, however, the appropriate health plan representative should be contacted to determine the policy and what specific steps should be taken to speed up the credentialing process.

A clear understanding of the timeframe required for proper credentialing will enable all parties involved to prepare better for the implications. Inquire about available in-services that the payer may host to learn about their protocols and what omissions could cause an application to be delayed or denied. Obtain actual samples of completed applications when possible and review them with the area representative to gain an understanding of correct procedures. Use this information to construct an action plan. The process of introducing new physicians and providers into the system should be organized and tightly managed.

A formalized communication methodology must be established that immediately notifies the appropriate parties (i.e., the practice manager, the person or department responsible for initiating the submission of payer applications to the various health plans, the business office, and information services) before a new provider is hired.

Establish a policy regarding the desired lead time the practice or health system requires to ensure the organization's contracted health plans recognize providers as members of the group by the first day they are scheduled to see patients. The lead time can be anywhere from three to six months, depending on the plan and the responsible party's familiarity with the application process. The arrival of a new physician or mid-level provider should never be a surprise. Failure to synchronize this process could result in lost revenue generated by the new recruit.

Make sure to use the suspend or pending bills report to track the dollar amount of claims that are pending due to the assignment of a provider number or approval of a health plan. When possible, use the payer's Internet website to obtain information on how to complete the provider application process. For larger health care systems, credentialing software may be an option.

Patient Registration/Data Collection

Of all the tasks to be performed, patient registration, which generally falls under the purview of the front office in a practice or clinic setting, is one of the most visible and critical roles relative to the A/R management function. Depending on the size of a medical practice or clinic, front-line personnel can be responsible for performing a variety of tasks associated with handling patient flow. They schedule appointments, check patients in and out, collect co-pays and outstanding balances, answer the telephones, locate charts, and calm irritated or irate patients. In short, they are the gatekeepers or control towers of the practice. They are also the people relied upon to gather, enter, and forward the all-important data required to produce a clean claim. Failures in this area will begin to unravel the effectiveness of the entire A/R process. Lack of knowledge regarding contractual arrangements or relationships, inadequate training, a high turnover rate, and department or clinic managers who don't fully understand the importance of their respective roles are just a few factors that contribute to this breakdown in service.

Insurance Verification

Pressures to get patients checked in, answer telephones, and respond to physician requests make front-office staff less inclined to perform a function they perceive as having no immediate value. Insurance verification is clearly perceived as a billing function and consequently often goes either completely undone or half-done. Incorporating this single task into the "must do" priorities for a front-office position would significantly reduce the number of denials received on the back end of the billing process.

The disconnect among the stakeholders related to the poor communication of payer requirements and the timeliness in which providers are recruited and accepted as contracted providers—in addition to the aforementioned staffing, educational, and training issues—are commonly observed in a large majority of health care organizations that are struggling financially.

Sloppy data collection, exchange processes, and posting errors have also been identified as a major reason for the proliferation of denials and subsequent write-offs that are now negatively affecting reimbursement. This creates a situation where claims are routinely transmitted with inaccurate patient demographic and insurance information, wrong financial classes, or erroneous guarantor information.

Coding

Coding and documentation are critical areas in today's focus on compliance, not to mention their importance in ensuring that physicians get paid for what they do. Physicians are at risk for ensuring that documentation supports CPT and ICD-9-CM codes reflected on the insurance claims submitted on their behalf. Like it or not, physicians are financially tied to ensuring that this function is performed correctly. This likely requires frequent education and training regarding CPT/ICD-9 coding and documentation. The group's compliance program should include the performance of regular audits of physician coding practices and trends. Physicians should be informed when claims are denied because of inaccurate coding or incomplete documentation.

While coding and documenting are primarily the physician's responsibilities, coding "experts" must be employed as part of the business office, preferably certified professional coders in larger practices. All staff should be aware of the importance of the completion of encounter forms. This includes accurate coding of CPT (procedure) as well as ICD-9 (diagnosis) codes. Accurate completion of this information at the front end will assure that claims can be submitted in a timely manner, thus ensuring that collections are maximized.

The effectiveness and efficiency of the A/R process is an essential component of a financially stable medical group. This encompasses not only the capabilities of the billing staff but also the awareness throughout the practice that many actions affect cash collections. Everyone, including physicians, needs to be aware of all the key ingredients to successful A/R management, including:

- Coding
- Health plan types and benefit structures
- Federal and state regulations
- Compliance requirements
- Information system capabilities
- The billing cycle
- Performance standards.

A well-informed and appropriately trained staff will be more alert to actions that will affect cash flow. There is almost nothing more vital to the success of a performance improvement effort.

EXHBIT 10-1
JOB DESCRIPTIONS AND STANDARDS

Position: Central Billing   **Reports To:** MSO Director
Office (Billing Manager)

Position Summary

Establishes, organizes, and orchestrates the work flow of the business office staff; coordinates office resources to ensure quality service is provided to the patients and that the financial objectives of the Central Billing Office (CBO) are consistently met; promotes patient and physician satisfaction at all times.

Job Responsibilities

Supervisory
- Establishes and maintains an effective and operating environment that ensures the effective, efficient, and safe operation of a business office that is responsive to the needs of its customers and clients, namely the patients, the physicians, co-workers, and staff
- Ensures development of competent billing personnel and the timely collection and management of the clients' accounts receivable (A/R)
- Prepares, analyzes, and verifies the organization's A/R reports to assess the present and future financial status of the client
- Oversees all aspects of personnel administration within the business office
- Reviews and approves employee time sheets/payroll cards; generates and completes employee performance reviews in conjunction with office policy
- Schedules and provides OSHA training; ensures compliance of exposure control program and establishes and maintains employee medical records in compliance with the OSHA regulations
- Establishes and maintains a positive working relationship

with the physician members and their respective office managers

- Facilitates the completion of month-end processes and provides the required financial reports to the finance department
- Coordinates the purchase of office supplies and equipment; establishes and maintains an inventory system to ensure the office maintains adequate supply levels
- Establishes a maintenance evaluation program to ensure the timely repair and proper functioning of business office equipment
- Collaborates with medical office managers to monitor and review the charge batches and to determine opportunities for improvement in current systems
- Reviews all batches for compliance to office standards prior to entering into daily work bin; facilitates a consistent flow of work from all practice sites/departments
- Establishes system to maintain statistical data as required by the position and to ensure monies collected are accurately recorded and reconciled at the end of each month (e.g., number of batches received, dollar value, percentage of charges, payments and adjustments entered on a daily basis, deposit log)
- Investigates patient and employee complaints; interprets and explains office policies and procedures; identifies, corrects, and monitors irregularities noted
- Works in conjunction with supervisor to stay abreast of changes in policy affecting physician reimbursement; establishes clear lines of communication to keep various departments and the physicians informed of the new requirements

Billing
- Coordinates and captures data required to bill the client's office, hospital, and SNF charges to third party payers; performs other miscellaneous billing functions that fall outside of the general scope of services performed in the office

- Acts as gatekeeper for all accounts forwarded to collection agency and monitors their performance monthly

Qualifications

Experience and Education

A multi-task professional with at least 5 years of supervisory experience and 4 years of hands-on related business office experience, preferably in a medical office setting. Bachelor's degree or equivalent.

Knowledge

Principles and techniques of personnel management and supervision; total knowledge and understanding of billing office procedures and medical terminology; CPT and ICD-9-CM coding regulations; Medicare/Medicaid regulations; equipment, supplies, and instruments used in a business; simple, routine clinical and laboratory methods; OSHA rules and regulations; various forms, books, and reports inherent to profession; patient confidentiality regulations.

Abilities

To organize, direct, and positively motivate staff; analyze situations accurately and adopt an effective course of action; understand and accept the inevitability of change; confer with physicians to communicate the needs of the office; accept responsibility for the overall running of the business office; create a warm, caring environment for patients and staff; facilitate a consistent stream of revenue into the organization; maintain billing records in a concise and accurate manner; act as an advocate and assist physicians in meeting business objectives; demonstrate the ability to pay attention to detail and ensure errors made by subordinates are caught and corrected early in the process; exercise independent judgment; be decisive and perform functions that consistently fall within the legal boundaries of profession.

Note: This description indicates in general terms the type and level of work performed and responsibilities held by the employee(s). Duties described are not to be interpreted as being all-inclusive.

I acknowledge receipt of this job description and can fulfill all the requirements of this position.

Signature: _____ Date: _____

Job Description/Summary

Establishes, organizes, and orchestrates the work flow of the business office staff; coordinates office resources to ensure quality service is provided to the patients and that the financial objectives of the Central Billing Office (CBO) are consistently met; promotes patient and physician satisfaction at all times.

Performance Standards[1]	Performance Tracking[2]
• Averages 67% of gross collection rate on fee-for-service accounts (comparing charges and payments to those specific charges)[3]	• Collection percentage
• Achieves 20 percent or less of A/R over 120 days	• Aged A/R reports
• Has no greater than 5 percent denial of claims	• Number of denied claims
• Has less than 2.5 months in A/R	• Aged A/R reports
• Ensures 90 percent of issues raised in monthly physician/site meetings resolved within 30 days	• Physician satisfaction
• Ensures 100 percent of issues raised in monthly physician/site meetings resolved within 60 days	• Physician satisfaction
• Ensures that sites are informed of changes/ updates for payer data of receipt	• Audits
• Achieves 90 percent patient satisfaction with billing office	• Patient satisfaction
• Has less than 5 percent electronic/paper claims rejections	• Claims rejections

Definitions

[1] Performance standards: expected measures of individual performance.

[2] Performance tracking: process activities to track achievement of performance standards.

[3] Will vary based on medical client's payer mix.

EXHIBIT 10-2
POLICIES AND PROCEDURES

Insurance Follow-Up

Purpose

To ensure that any claim that has not been paid within 28 days of electronic submission and 45 days of paper claim submission will be reviewed and appropriate follow-up completed.

Procedure	*Responsible Position*

Account Audit

1. Use "aging report" as your guidepost to determine which accounts require attention.	Patient Account Representative
2. Locate patient in the computer a. In conjunction with using the patient's account number, perform a patient search by name or social security number to check for possible multiple accounts on the same patient.	Patient Account Representative

3. Review the patient's account activity and reconcile payments and charges to achieve the balance indicated on the screen prior to contacting the carrier.
    a. Identify claims that have open balances.
    b. Pinpoint claims that may have been underpaid.
    c. Check patient notes for information that may assist in the collection process.
	Patient Account Representative

Procedure	*Responsible Position*

Tracer — Used to track unpaid claim

1. Contact the carrier to inquire whether the claim was received or paid.

Patient Account Representative/ Unit Coordinator

2. Always note the date, the name of the person contacted, and the telephone number dialed.

Patient Account Representative/ Unit Coordinator

3. Be prepared to provide the insurer with the following information:
    a. Name of the patient
    b. Name of the insured
    c. Insured's certificate or social security number
    d. Insured's group number or the name of the employer
    e. Date or dates of service in question
    f. Dollar value of the service you are inquiring about
    g. Authorization number and approval dates when warranted
    h. Name of the physician that rendered medical care to the patient and the tax ID number or provider number under which services were billed.

Patient Account Representative

4. If the carrier has no record of claim receipt, perform the following steps:
    a. Verify the name of the person to whom you are speaking, the mailing address for claims submission, and the type of plan when necessary (e.g. commercial, PPO, HMO)

Patient Account Representative/ Unit Coordinator

Procedure	*Responsible Position*

b. Inquire if it would be possible to fax the information in question. If yes, obtain the fax number.

5. Compare the information obtained with the information indicated in the system.

    a. Check system to ensure the charges are attached to the correct insurance plan

    b. Update information according to office policy

    c. Request an HIC form for the services requiring re-filing

    d. Complete the required tracer form and attach a copy to the HIC form delineating the charges in question.

Responsible Position: Patient Account Representative/ Unit Coordinator

6. Once information is faxed or mailed:

    a. Document activity in the comments field as directed. Flag account in automated tickler for follow-up and place copy of information sent to carrier in the manual tickler folder for follow-up in ten days (e.g., if you mailed the claim as a tracer and today's date is September 10, 200x, insert the copy of the forwarded request in the slot of the numerical tickler folder marked 20)

    b. Follow up with the carrier at the designated time to confirm receipt of claim and secure a payment date

    c. Place reference copy of document in the tickler folder for follow-up three days after payment is expected.

Responsible Position: Patient Account Representative/ Unit Coordinator

Procedure	*Responsible Position*
NOTE: If your inquiry regarding the non-payment of a claim was initiated by a patient, it is your responsibility to keep the patient informed of all actions taken to resolve his or her unpaid claims. For instance, when you contact the insurance carrier to follow up on an unpaid claim, you should also inform the patient of what transpired. When you follow up in ten days to verify receipt of the medical claim, call the patient and provide a verbal update. Keep the patient involved in the process by keeping him informed, and when necessary, ask him to assist you in expediting payment.	Patient Account Representative/ Unit Coordinator

Underpayments

1. All payments will be reviewed to confirm that payment is equal to the expected payment and to determine adjustment percentage. If a payment is less than expected, contact the payer to clarify why there is a discrepancy. Document the person contacted, her position, phone number, and the conversation in the note section of the patient file.	Patient Account Representative/
2. If an error was made, resubmit the claim as directed by the payer.	Patient Account Representative/
3. If the payer insists payment was correct, give the EOB to the Unit Coordinator for assignment to the collections team.	Patient Account Representative/

Procedure	*Responsible Position*
4. If the adjustment was more than 35% of the charge, forward to the Unit Coordinator for approval to make the adjustment or to determine whether the claim should be appealed.	Patient Account Representative

Denials

1. If a charge is denied because of non-coverage or termination of benefits, contact the payer to find out the reason why. The name of the person contacted, her position, phone number, and the conversation should be documented in the appropriate note or comment section of the patient's account or collection file.	Patient Account Representative
2. If the reason provided is considered unacceptable, initiate the appeal process.	Patient Account Representative
3. If the termination of the patient's benefits is confirmed, obtain the termination date and transfer the charge to patient responsibility. Contact the patient to inform him of findings and action taken. Note findings in the system and notify the site that the patient is no longer covered by this plan.	Patient Account Representative
4. If the charge is not a covered service, move it to patient responsibility. Notify the office that the service is not covered by the patient's health plan.	Patient Account Representative

Procedure	*Responsible Position*

Lack of Medical Necessity

1. Review the superbill to ensure the accuracy of data submitted to payer, especially the links between CPT code and diagnosis.

Patient Account Representative

2. If a claim is pending despite the fact that both the superbill and the information submitted to the payer are correct, but supporting documentation (physician notes, pathology reports, etc.) to justify treatment is requested, ask the physician to review the patient chart to confirm medical necessity.

Patient Account Representative

3. Initiate the appeal process, include detail on the necessity of the service (e.g., reports)

Patient Account Representative/ Unit Coordinator

4. A listing of codes that are being denied for medical necessity will be maintained and circulated to offices and billing staff on a quarterly basis.

Billing Supervisior

Denied as Workers' Compensation Injury

1. If denied because service was not authorized, review insurance coverage to confirm authorization was required (may include contacting payer).

Patient Account Representative

2. If it is not work related, determine if a first report has been sent. If not, contact the employer for name of workers' compensation carrier, then submit the first report or office notes with a claim for payment.

Patient Account Representative

Procedure	*Responsible Position*

Unauthorized Service

1. If denied because service was not authorized, review insurance coverage to confirm authorization was required (may include contacting payer).

Patient Account Representative

2. If payer made error, refile claim

Patient Account Representative

3. If authorization is required, contact the office to determine if there are extenuating circumstances to explain the lack of authorization.

Patient Account Representative

4. If there are extenuating circumstances, document the situation and file an appeal.

Patient Account Representative

Request for Additional Information

1. Provide payers with the information requested and place a copy of data sent in tickler file for follow-up.

Patient Account Representative

2. Upon receipt of flagged batch, remove liens document and review for completeness

Patient Account Representative

3. Forward to patient account representative to place in tickler for follow-up

Patient Account Representative

Procedure	*Responsible Position*
4. Place lien in a tickler file for purpose of following up with attorney each week to verify whether the lien was received, signed, and returned. If the response is yes, obtain date of mailing and verify the address where it was mailed.	Patient Account Representative
5. Upon receipt of signed lien, follow up with attorney on a monthly basis to monitor the progress of case.	Patient Account Representative
6. If lien time frame expires, contact regional practice manager to discuss whether extending the time stipulation is warranted.	Patient Account Representative
7. If approval for extension of the lien is obtained, complete a second lien and type the words "amended" under the words "Workers' Compensation," if appropriate.	Patient Account Representative
8. If approval for extension of the lien is denied, transfer responsibility for payment to the patient and note actions in the appropriate message fields.	Patient Account Representative

11

MANAGED CARE AND CAPITATION: STRATEGIES FOR SUCCESS

Michael E. Harris, MS
Laura P. Jacobs, MPH

In working to improve operational and financial performance, medical group management can focus on several managed care contracting strategies. Specifically, this chapter
examines managed care contracts and capitation reimbursement as key factors in increasing revenues, decreasing risk, and
improving financial performance. The medical group performance improvement effort should examine the group's involvement in managed care as a means to improving its financial performance. As part of this effort, the medical group may find it
necessary to cancel or renegotiate its managed care contracts
to achieve the desired results. In this process, the medical group
must review those areas of the relationship that represent the
greatest financial deficit and risk to the organization. This will
require a thorough review of operational costs as well as internal capabilities.

As a key component of the performance improvement effort,
it would be wise to assess the revenue and expense implications
related to the contracting strategy. Some medical groups have

come to the conclusion that the risks, costs, and resource requirements are simply too high in capitated arrangements and are moving back to fee-for-service structures. This chapter will provide a process to follow, enabling medical groups to assess these risks, as well as take a closer look at critical requirements for success.

CRITICAL SUCCESS FACTORS

For a medical group to succeed in capitated arrangements, the following factors must be inherent in the organization:

1. The organization must recognize that the marketplace sets price and that cost must be managed to a desired profit margin.
2. An efficient and effective administrative infrastructure must be available, either internal to the organization or through cost-effective outsourcing.
3. Accurate and timely information must be available to the physicians and management, including medical costs and utilization by service and specialty.
4. Strong medical leadership must be capable of managing an effective utilization and case management function, as well as educating physicians about the dynamics of managed care.
5. Strategies must be responsiveness to market trends: Are HMOs (and capitated arrangements) increasing, decreasing, or remaining stable in the local market?

An assessment of the organization's position with respect to these success factors will provide a template for determining appropriate action.

MANAGED CARE ASSESSMENT

A comprehensive managed care assessment will focus on the following key areas:

- Contract analysis
- Internal administrative capabilities
- Medical leadership.

Contract Analysis

In analyzing its contracts, the medical group will need to focus on revenues and expenses.

Revenues

Today's medical groups find that payer reimbursement continues to fall behind the costs of providing the care. Even as payers receive double-digit increases in some cases, provider organizations often receive small increases in contract rates—if any. This fact highlights the necessity for medical groups and other provider organizations to improve their ability to negotiate favorable contracts to retain as much of the available payer dollar as possible. It is also a reminder that medical groups must understand their internal cost structure as one key factor in being successful in managed care and capitation.

Faced with poor financial performance, many medical groups have targeted payer reimbursement as a significant contributing factor. Specifically, with capitation reimbursement mechanisms, many medical groups have begun to question whether the potential rewards will ever materialize. In many cases the real question is whether the dollars received are adequate reimbursement for the cost of the services provided. Often, however, these analyses are performed on an emotional basis, devoid of real facts. The "hassle factor" and perceived lower reimbursement of HMO patients may cause the organization to refuse capitated contracts without any real analysis of each contract's financial performance. That is why a critical analysis of each contract is the most critical step in determining the next steps in the organization's managed care strategy. The following actions comprise a thorough analysis of existing contracts:

- *Conduct an inventory of current contracts.* It is surprising that many medical groups do not have a current inventory of their contracts. This not only makes contract management and timing of renegotiation difficult, but it also can mean that the information system does not have accurate data with which to process claims accurately. Table 11-1 provides a guide for developing a contracting matrix. The most critical elements of most contracts have been listed, but there may be others that apply to particular arrangements. This will provide a guide for initiating renegotiation and will point out key differences in contractual terms, which could also help in strategizing for renegotiation.
- *Identify major payers and products.* What health plans and health plan products (e.g., Medicaid, Medicare, commercial) generate the majority of the group's enrollment? Focusing on the major payers and health plan products will make it easier to prioritize the effort to be expended for contract analysis and potential renegotiation.
- *Evaluate contract rates.* Review the rates of all contracts to determine whether they appear to be at competitive levels. There may be significant variances among the payers. Low-paying, low-volume contracts should probably be canceled so that the group can concentrate on more profitable and sizable arrangements. Review the last time the rates were renegotiated. Re-negotiating may represent a significant source of revenue for the medical group. Determine if contracts require renegotiation and begin that process. Be assertive with payers. Be prepared to request a retroactive rate increase if you feel it is justified. While "evergreen" (automatically renewing) contracts are easiest to administer, they can also lead to missed opportunities for renegotiating rates. The master matrix of contract terms and

Table 11-1
Key Contract Terms

Key contract component	Payer		
	A	B	C
Covered Services			
Non-covered and excluded services			
Enrollment projections and guarantees			
Capitation rates			
Carve-outs			
Stop loss provisions			
Utilization targets			
Payment withhold and distribution			
Data reporting requirements			
Termination clause			
Contract amendment notices			
Term of contract by service			
Authorization responsibility			
Administrative policy manual compliance			
Quality improvement activities			
Member billing			
Marketing activities			
Payer financial responsibility			

renewal dates (see Table 11-1) will be helpful in avoiding missed anniversary dates. Evaluate whether the group can afford to continue in capitated relationships, particularly in an environment in which the medical costs are increasing and the premiums are low.

- *Evaluate profit/loss for each contract.* It's not enough that capitation rates may be higher for a particular payer—this may not necessarily translate into profits. The age/sex mix and demographic or adverse selection by enrollees may be affecting the contract's profitability. Therefore, depending on the data available, a review of at least the major payers should include the elements outlined in Table 11-2.

Table 11-2
Review of Major Payers

	Payer				
	A	B	C	D	E
Revenue					
Capitation					
Co-pays					
Other Revenue					
Risk Pool					
Total Revenue					
Medical Expenses					
Internal Medical Expenses[1]					
Contracted Medical Expenses					
Out-of-Network Costs					
Other Medical Expenses					
Total Medical Expenses					
Operating Expense[2]					
Net Income					

[1]May be estimated based on percentage of total group (employed) physician compensation

[2]May be estimated based on percentage of revenue

- *Review stop loss provisions.* Many groups fail to collect revenues for clinical services rendered and covered by stop loss insurance. An immediate investigation of this area should be conducted.
- Verify risk pool distribution and advances. Verify that the medical group's risk pool distribution revenues are correct. The group may also seek an advance distribution on future risk pool distributions to improve its cash flow.

Expenses

The medical group will need to evaluate payer contracts to identify extraordinary expenses, and develop a strategy to reduce the medical expenses. The group will also need to identify ways to minimize or transfer risk back to the health plan, particularly out-of-control costs such as pharmacy expenditures.

The profit/loss analysis will provide an indication of the need for further exploration of major medical costs. The matrix illustrated in Table 11-3 will allow management to pinpoint the specific areas of excessive risk. In addition to matching current costs to contract rates, comparing them against industry benchmarks is also valuable. This is often difficult to do, given variations in specialty definitions, carve-outs, etc. Local surveys, consultants, and publications (e.g., *Capitation Report*) are resources for benchmark data. The assessment of this data will provide clear focus on what areas require attention. Several common problem areas may include:

• **Outside medical costs.** This may include contracted providers as well as out-of-network costs. If the group has contracted with providers for services it does not provide internally, there may be opportunities to renegotiate these provider rates. Many groups have found that moving contracted physicians from fee-for-service arrangements to sub-capitated arrangements makes a significant impact on reducing risk and medical costs. Alternatively, it may be advantageous to bring these services in-house. That is, it may be feasible to hire additional physician staff to serve this population. It may be that employing part-time or even full-time physicians can reduce and control the outside medical expenses.

Table 11-3
Areas of Excessive Risk

Key Service Areas	Current Cost PMPM	Benchmark Cost PMPM
Primary Care		
Medical Specialty		
Allergy		
Acupuncture		
Cardiology		
Chiropractic		
Dermatology		
Emergency Medicine		
Other Medical Specialty		
Surgical Specialty		
Anesthesiology		
Cardiac Surgery		
General Surgery		
Neurosurgery		
Etc.		
Total Medical Costs		

Experience suggests that out-of-network (OON) costs may be a major source of loss. This may be due to long-standing physician relationships, consumer demand, or lack of knowledge that these referrals are costing the group real money. This is where medical leadership is often required to intervene to control the "leakage" to outside, non-contracted providers. The contracting staff may be helpful by reducing negotiated rates.

- **Hospital utilization.** While it gets a lot of press, many medical groups still do not have institutional utilization, including acute and sub-acute care, under control. Will the implementation of a hospitalist program assist in this effort? Some groups have used hospitalists effectively to manage inpatient activity, from emergency room admits to skilled nursing stays, thereby reducing unnecessary hospitalization. However, some groups have not found success with this model. Some reasons for failure of hospitalist programs include:
  - *Use of residents* or other medical faculty as hospitalists. While these physicians are conveniently located in the hospital and may be a cost-effective option on the surface, they are not traditionally the most efficient users of resources.
  - *Optional use of hospitalists.* Many groups have moved to this model out of lack of internal support. Medical group physicians are given an option to use hospitalists rather than being mandated to do so. However, it is often not efficient because it may be difficult to generate enough of a patient load for the hospitalists to affect utilization.
  - *Lack of protocols* to guide hospital patient management. The most effective hospitalists use evidence-based guidelines as protocols for inpatient management. While variations may occur, a protocol will provide uniform guidelines, based on scientific research, that all hospitalists can follow.

• **Pharmacy risk.** Probably the most risky element of full professional capitation is taking on risk for pharmacy costs. With costs escalating close to 20 percent annually, most groups do not have the resources to manage this cost effectively. Even the groups with many years of experience in managed care are giving pharmacy risk back to the payers. In fact, several payers are equipping medical group providers with information technology (e.g., handheld palm computers) to assist with improving the management of pharmacy utilization. These devices typically provide the physician with up-to-date information relating to the health plan formulary.

• **Major vendor costs** for which the group has financial responsibility, such as lab, home health, imaging, and outpatient service expense. Can these be renegotiated?

• **Contracts with specialty and primary care providers.** These should be reviewed to ensure that they are well within the industry benchmarks. Also, pay close attention to service carveouts, which transfer financial responsibility back to the medical group.

• **Revenue not being captured.** There are many opportunities for lost revenue in capitated arrangements. These may include the following:

  • *Co-pays not collected.* Unless co-pays are religiously collected prior to the patient visit, they can represent lost revenue. Attempting to collect co-pays after services have been provided is often futile. While it seems small, multiplying $5 to $10 or more per visit can yield valuable dollars, particularly during an effort to improve performance, when every penny counts.

  • *Carveouts or exclusions not appropriately billed* by the medical group. If certain services are excluded or "carved out" of the capitated rate, be sure that billing systems exist to capture the charges and appropriately bill the payer. This is another reason to scrupulously maintain the division of responsibility matrix. Further, many payers have multiple products, with a confusing array of benefits. This often causes inaccurate or missed billing.

  • *Claims not paid correctly* by the medical group. Too often, groups pay outside claims inaccurately because either the contract terms are too confusing or because information systems are not maintained with current terms. This can result in duplicate claims being paid, claims being paid at inaccurate rates, and, as a result, unnecessary dollars leaving the group.

By conducting a comprehensive review of these factors, management will have a clear idea of where to focus attention. It may also pinpoint weaknesses in managed care operations that require attention.

Internal Administrative Capabilities

A review of managed care operating costs is likely to be included in the organization's review of its financial performance, as outlined in Chapters 4 and 7. But there are some key functions that should be critically evaluated, not just for their cost, but with a focus on their effectiveness.

Referral Management and Authorizations
The referral and authorization systems, as an aspect of utilization management (UM), are crucial in managing medical costs. Examine whether the systems are in place to monitor and control referrals for which the group is financially responsible. Gaining control in this area has the potential to yield significant financial rewards. Often this area is the "leaky valve" for out-of-network costs, where referrals that could have been handled by the group are being referred outside. The referral and authorization function should be catching these referrals before they happen. The staff may also be aware of high-volume, non-contracted providers, which could be targeted to establish contractual relationships.

Assuming that protocols, policies, and procedures have been established for this function, it is just as important that they are adhered to. A review should be conducted to ensure that adequate processes are in place and dedicated, knowledgeable staff exist to review, monitor, and implement corrective actions regarding patient authorizations and referrals. Remember that the authorization department is a "cash disbursing" entity within the medical group. Every hour, they are giving away money. For this reason, this area should receive strong support and oversight by the medical director.

Case Management
Another critical aspect of UM is the management of high-cost and chronic cases. Experienced nursing staff must be available to work closely with the medical director to ensure that these cases are proactively managed. Many medical groups who have succeeded under capitated arrangements are focusing increasing attention on identifying and managing patients with chronic disorders. This includes the frail elderly, as well as patients with hypertension, diabetes, asthma, and congestive heart failure. An effective case management function will require the physicians to identify and agree on protocols for effective disease management. The medical group should investigate through its utilization management process the use of published clinical pathways, which will assist the group in establishing consistent protocols for patient management.

Eligibility
Obtaining accurate eligibility information is the bane of many managed care organizations. Not only is the information often inaccurate from the payers, but it is often submitted in cumbersome paper format. By the time it is entered into the medical group's system, it is already out of date. For this reason, even given the weaknesses in the data, groups should seek to obtain eligibility data electronically to the extent possible. Regular audits should then be performed to match the capita-

tion received with the eligibility list.

Contracting and Claims Management

One of the greatest sources of mismanagement, most often inadvertent, is a lack of communication between the contracting department and the claims department. Unless clear procedures are in place, with clear lines of responsibility for translating negotiated contracts into accurate claims payment, there are many opportunities for inaccurate claims payment, which will lead to unnecessary costs. As noted previously, this requires diligent maintenance of benefit and division of financial responsibility (DOFR) tables, which are included in the provider agreements between the group and the health plan. This often requires the involvement of the information systems (IS) department to ensure that the system is capable of managing the contract terms negotiated. The same sort of communication must also occur with the business office to ensure that carved-out services are appropriately billed.

Information Systems

Chapter 13 identifies ways to assess IS capabilities. The weaknesses in IS capabilities are never more apparent than when trying to compile data for analysis of managed care contracts. Before entering into capitated arrangements, the organization must be confident that it has the ability to capture a reasonable amount of data, not to mention the ability to process claims and manage eligibility efficiently.

Medical Leadership

The cornerstone of successful medical groups is strong medical leadership. Nowhere is this more apparent than in groups that take on managed care risk. The medical director (see Chapter 3, Exhibit 3-1 for job description) must be willing to stand up to physicians both within and outside the group to manage utilization effectively. In addition, and even more important, is the knack for educating physicians and explaining the intricacies of managed care economics. Information must be shared with all physicians concerning medical costs, referrals, and utilization rates if there is to be improvement in managing costs.

In addition to providing internal leadership, the medical director can also be an effective liaison with the payers. During contract negotiations, this person is often a key player. The medical director should establish relationships with the payers' medical directors to ensure that when problems arise there is a platform to address concerns and reach resolution. The medical director's communication skills are as important as his or her knowledge of managed care.

IMPLEMENTING CHANGE

Once you have pinpointed the root causes of losses related to managed care, you should incorporate the action plan into the performance improvement plan, as outlined in Chapter 2. Some of the key actions will likely include:

- Renegotiating contracts
- Redesigning internal processes
- Reviewing outsourcing options
- Strengthening medical leadership.

Renegotiating Contracts

Based on the profit/loss analysis, market assessment, and enrollment by payer, priorities for renegotiating contracts will be clear. These will also prepare the contracting team with facts as they approach payers in negotiations. In addition to simple increases in capitation rates, other factors should be considered, such as:

- Carving out or excluding high-risk areas, including pharmacy, transplants, and other tertiary/quartenary services
- Stop-loss provisions and coverage
- Low enrollment guarantees
- Limitations on retroactive additions and deletions to eligibility
- Converting to fee-for-service rates.

In addition to payer contracts, another key factor in reducing costs may be renegotiating outside provider agreements. This is another area where the medical director will play a key role, both in identifying providers with whom to contract as well as being an active participant in the negotiation process itself. As noted earlier, many groups have successfully reduced costs by moving to sub-capitating specialists, which is generally only possible when exclusive arrangements can be developed with specialty groups or IPAs.

Redesigning Internal Processes

Key managed care functions, including claims management, utilization and quality management, eligibility, IS, and contracting, must be operating at optimal performance. Depending on the outcome of the assessment, actions may include staff reductions, additions, and enhancements to IS. Redesigning or clarifying processes, communication tools, and reporting tools may also be necessary.

Reviewing Outsourcing Options

Another option many groups have considered is the out-sourcing of many managed care functions. Depending on the market, management services organizations (MSOs) may be capable of taking on these tasks. This may be the most cost-effective option, particularly if managed care enrollment is low. On the other hand, careful investigation of MSO capabilities and track records should be evaluated before making a commitment.

With today's Internet capabilities, another avenue to consider may be the use of application service providers (ASPs), particularly for claims processing and other IS resources. The Trizetto Group is one such provider that has focused on managed care applications. In time, payers may also develop consolidated resources to allow providers to access their claims management capabilities. While there are shortcomings to this alternative, including reliance on payers as well as the sheer volatility of the HMO industry, it may be a consideration in certain markets.

Strengthening Medical Leadership

Weak medical leadership will be the Achilles heel of a managed care organization. Resources must be dedicated to guaranteeing that the most capable person is in place and that he or she is given the authority to carry out his or her responsibilities. This may require recruiting from outside the organization, which is often contrary to popular wishes in many medical groups. An effective leader will also require adequate information, which brings us back to the IS capabilities addressed.

As with all aspects of medical group operations, an effective managed care strategy is dependent on the organization's commitment to this line of business. Because it does require an extra measure of effort and resources, entering into capitated arrangements must not be taken lightly. Even in single-specialty and primary care groups, capitation must be carefully evaluated and constantly monitored. With solvency standards being implemented in many states, the necessity for groups to achieve financial stability under managed care is even more significant. In many markets, HMOs and capitation payment for physicians are a fact of life and comprise an undeniable share of the market. As a result, a thorough review of contract performance and a detailed action plan for improvement will be an integral part of the performance improvement process for many medical groups.

12

ENHANCING AND FINDING NEW SOURCES OF REVENUE

Benjamin S. Snyder, MPA, FACMPE

With declining reimbursements for both fee-for-service and managed care business, virtually every medical group has found it necessary to constantly evaluate and tighten the reigns on operating expenses. After years of this kind of management focus, many practices now find themselves at a point where they can no longer afford to cut expenses and continue to operate in a reasonably effective manner. Having spent so much time and effort on cost-cutting measures, many medical group practices have lost sight of the opportunities on the revenue side of their operation. This chapter details suggestions and ideas of where to look for revenue enhancement and new revenue sources, which are key components to enhancing performance improvement.

MAXIMIZING PAYMENTS FROM PAYERS

As contracted payment rates have become more and more common during the past five years, most medical group practices have not effectively managed the terms and conditions of their payer contracts. It is not uncommon to find that payments for services billed are often not at the amount stated in the contract. Either the insurance carrier has made a unilateral change in payment rates, or it is simply paying the claims in error.

Many carriers have a disconnect between their contracting department and their claims department. Rates are not always correctly entered for each provider, the wrong conversion factors are used, the wrong year of the Medicare RBRVS system is being used, and payments are based on the wrong definition of "units" used to determine payments.

Medical groups must establish a process to create expected payment rates by payer contract for all procedures provided to patients. This process would result in an expected payment table by payer. This expected payment table could then be used to quickly compare a payment amount received to contract terms without a significant manual look-up effort. For larger operations, payment postings and explanation of benefit reviews should be segregated by payer. By taking this approach to processing payment information received, personnel become literal experts in how payments are being made by payer. Many information systems will allow automated auditing of actual against expected payments from payers.

One additional benefit of this approach to payment posting reviews is that the profitability for each payer contract could evolve without a tremendous amount of extra effort. Those individuals charged with this review process could aggregate this payment information manually if the practice management system being used does not provide reports detailing charges, payments, and adjustments by payer.

The review of this payment information should also be used to provide feedback to physicians and other providers. Often there is a gap in a provider's understanding of how a service is reimbursed based on medical record documentation. While more and more providers are complying with the medical record documentation requirements associated with evaluation and management CPT codes promulgated by the Health Care Financing Administration (HCFA) for Medicare and Medicaid beneficiary payments, most medical group providers do not actually see the payment results of their coding efforts.

Because physician compensation is ultimately tied to actual payments received, most providers are receptive to gaining a better understanding of the financial impact of their coding efforts. While HCFA assumed physicians were "over-coding" prior to guidelines being released several years ago, many now believe that providers are more likely to be "under-coding" for their patient care efforts. Rather than view all this coding documentation as being another barrier to being paid, it should be looked at as a mechanism to be properly paid for services rendered.

Another benefit to this medical record documentation process is a more complete medical record supporting the care rendered to patients. From a pure risk management perspective, this would suggest a lower risk factor that might translate into fewer malpractice claims. Fewer claims could result in lower malpractice premiums.

There may also be opportunities for revenue enhancement for services provided that have not been billed on a separate basis. Because every dollar billed translates into a net dollar collected, it is important to update charges and to bill for all appropriate services provided. Injections and supplies are some of the items that should be reviewed. Even though HCFA now limits what kind of supplies can be billed under a physician provider number, there are still opportunities with other payers. For example, while HCFA prohibits an orthopedic surgeon from billing for crutches or a walker given to a Medicare or Medicaid patient, that same prohibition does not apply to other payers.

In addition, because reimbursements have been relatively flat for a number of years, many providers have not formally increased their fees, as the handful of best-paying patients would feel the impact. While this approach has generally made sense, some payers now are covering 100 percent of a fee billed. What this may be indicating is that fees may now be below the maximum payment threshold. As payment reimbursements are monitored, this may be one more opportunity for increased net revenue.

For medical groups receiving a full capitation payment for physician services or a sub-capitation payment for either primary care or selected specialty services, a similar approach should be taken. The terms and conditions of each managed care contract should be reviewed. Questions that need to be asked include:

- *Is the correct capitation or sub-capitation amount being paid?* Many of these programs pay on an age- and sex-adjusted basis. Auditing these payments may uncover discrepancies. Also, occasionally the patient is not in the correct category for payment. Patients on dialysis and those classified as being totally disabled are usually paid at a higher monthly rate. However, it is not uncommon for these chronic conditions not to be incorporated or noted when payments are calculated for providers.
- *Are co-payments being consistently collected?* As an accommodation to existing patients, many medical groups bill patients the $5 or $15 office visit co-payment amount. This is an expensive proposition. Medical groups need to enact processes that ensure the collection of all co-payments at the time of service. While billing maybe a convenience for patients, the cost to bill and process the payment is probably greater than the amount collected. Changing this practice would reduce billing and collection costs, but

more important, every co-payment dollar due would be collected. It is also possible that many of these co-payment dollars are being unknowingly written off based on small balance write-off programs common in large medical group practice billing systems.

• *Are there "carveout" services that can be billed separately from the capitation payment?* Injectible drugs, immunizations, and other services are commonly excluded from a primary care physician sub-capitation. Often other ancillary services are reimbursed on fee-for-service basis separate from any capitation payment. This trend is becoming common to full physician capitation payments.

• *Is there stop loss coverage?* Once a certain value of services is provided, many managed care plans provide a stop loss limit, where services in excess of this amount are paid on a fee basis. This can provide an important revenue source for high-cost patients but could easily be missed if the appropriate systems are not in place.

• *Do capitation payments match the eligibility information provided?* Many managed care organizations have different computer systems for eligibility and capitation payments. As a result, auditing capitated payments to eligibility lists is key.

• *Is there retroactive eligibility activity?* Many managed care organizations process tremendous amounts of retroactive additions, deletions, and changes to enrollee eligibility. Some of these are beyond the time frames detailed in the contract. Retroactivity audits may translate into significant found revenue dollars for a provider.

• *Are the benefit tables set up properly to support claims payments to outside providers?* Many medical groups have not either fully or properly set up benefit tables for claims payment. Improperly set-up benefit tables create a tremendous amount of additional labor costs associated with outside claims payments. In addition, manual efforts associated with the payment of outside claims tend to also incorrectly pay claims.

Unfortunately, most of these claims payment errors are in favor of the provider being paid. A number of medical groups who have successfully automated this claims adjudication process have found that they were overpaying outside contracted providers by an average of 12 percent.

EXPANDING CURRENT SERVICE LINES

When looking to increase revenue, administrators often overlook the potential for increasing their core business or service lines. Extending hours, making walk-in appointments more available, or possibly sharing an additional office with another medical practice in a different location may draw additional business without a significant increase in overhead. In each of these instances, a relatively straightforward proforma could be prepared as part of the evaluation process.

New service lines such as occupational medicine (pre-placement and work injury treatment) and the expansion of ancillary services, such as laboratory and x-ray services, are traditional sources of new business. In the occupational medicine area, a natural extension would be physical therapy and the dispensing of prepackaged pharmaceuticals. Gastroenterologists may want to consider bringing endoscopy and other GI procedures back into the office.

Opportunities may also exist for the addition of a mid-level provider or another physician in the same specialty or in a specialty that accounts for a significant number of the referrals made. While this latter initiative may be fraught with political and on-call coverage issues, it is nevertheless one worth pursuing before making a go or no-go decision.

Other opportunities also exist that would further expand the current definition of current core services. This may require a more formal business planning process, as illustrated in Figure 12-1.

Figure 12-1. Developing New Sources of Revenue

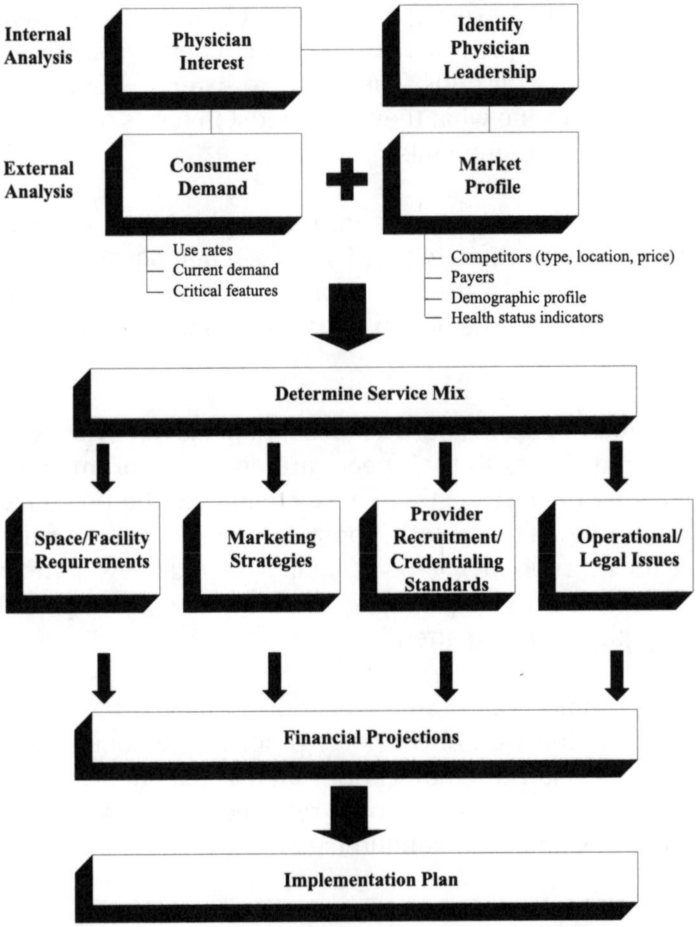

MARKETING

While often discounted as a costly luxury, marketing describes a broad array of activities that can successfully increase volume. Many of these activities do not have to be costly.

Conduct Market Research

Feedback from patients, physicians, and other referral sources is essential in laying the groundwork for your marketing plan. It will identify the strengths and weaknesses of the group from your "customer's" eyes. From individual interviews, surveys, and focus groups, market research can take many forms. Chapter 8 provides sample patient surveys and ideas for conducting focus groups. The key is to listen to your key audiences to determine what they value most in terms of service and other practice components.

Do not underestimate the influence physicians have in recommending and referring patients to other physicians. Every communication the medical group has with other physicians should emphasize the quality of care the medical practice provides.

Presentations and educational seminars given by the medical group's physicians to their peers are effective forums for communicating their strengths. These events can be publicized by coordinating efforts with their hospital's public relations department, announcing the event in a hospital newsletter, mailing letters directly to physicians, or contacting and personally inviting physicians to attend.

Establishing good communication among referral sources should be a function of everyday practice. Personalized physician-to-physician communication, such as telephone calls or letters to inform a physician of a referred patient's progress, is required to establish and build trust.

Depending on the available budget, a monthly or quarterly newsletter should be considered an effective tool in communicating the capabilities of the practice. The newsletter should contain information about continuing education courses completed, interesting articles on new techniques or procedures, or details of the other attributes that differentiate your physicians and demonstrate quality. In addition to distributing the newsletter to potential referring physicians, distribute it to patients, senior groups, or other community organizations.

Improve Communication with Patients

Frequent communication with patients will also help build loyalty and keep the group and its services foremost in their minds.

Communication activities that could improve patient satisfaction and build loyalty include sending birthday cards to patients with milestone birthdays (i.e., first, fifth, fiftieth, sixty-fifth), informing patients of relevant health fairs and educational events, sending thank-you notes to patients who refer family or friends, or providing information on other newsworthy events where your organization will be present (e.g., charitable events, new procedures or techniques, success stories).

Improving communication with patients can also be accomplished by re-examining your reception area to identify ways to communicate quality. Rather than hanging physicians' diplomas, awards, and honors in the back office where patients rarely see them, proudly display these credentials in the reception area where patients have the time to read about and gain confidence in their physicians. Consider displaying patient testimonials, success stories, and other materials that demonstrate and give patients a perception of quality.

In addition, friendly, good-natured, and patient office personnel can do much to enhance the practice and improve communication and patient satisfaction.

Develop a Presence on the Web

In this technological age, establishing a presence on the Internet can be an effective tool for physicians and medical groups to gain visibility and exposure to a more educated and informed audience. A Web page will not only serve as an information dissemination vehicle but also as a valuable communication tool among physicians and patients. Physicians can cost-effectively send birthday cards, follow-up or reminder notes, or other information about new products, services, staff, office hours, or medical procedures to existing patients via e-mail. The Internet gives physicians a powerful tool for reaching patients and colleagues and providing positive communication that will improve loyalty and trust.

Partner for Public Relations Success

Public relations can be a low-cost marketing tool and is often underutilized. The media is constantly looking for newsworthy events and often welcomes leads for good stories. Consider partnering with a hospital's public relations department to identify and publish patient success stories (being sensitive to patients' desires) that may be of interest to the community. People want to read about their physician in the newspaper or see their physician on television. These media activities reassure your patients that they are also receiving quality care.

Other public relations partnership opportunities may exist with the local medical society. Consider collectively sponsoring a weekly or monthly medical column in the local newspaper, providing interesting articles on consumer health and medical education to the community. This column may also be a vehicle for communicating patient success stories.

Participate in Promotional and Sponsorship Opportunities

Actively participating in community events will help increase exposure and overall awareness of your organization. Promotional activities may include participating in health fairs, offering free screenings or discounted immunizations, presenting health education seminars at public schools or community events, or volunteering as team physicians for local school sports teams. As you develop promotional activities, remember that women make 64 to 80 percent of the health care decisions in their households.[1] Promotions and advertisements focusing on or featuring women are often more successful in reaching the family decision-makers.

For most organizations, whether in the health care industry or not, offering free products and services is often the least expensive marketing tool. It provides a benefit to patients, allows them to develop a relationship with the physician, and encourages future participation.

Implementing these cost-effective marketing strategies will help increase patient satisfaction, build patient loyalty, and attract patients with choice. Although marketing budgets are often small, physicians and medical groups can still achieve powerful results.[2]

[1] Ngeo, Christine. The First Gatekeeper. *Modern Healthcare* 1998; 28(27):34.
[2] Herrod, Kimball. Cost-Effective Marketing Strategies: Achieving Powerful Results with a Small Budget. *Group Practice Journal* March 2000:49-51.

INTRODUCING NEW SERVICE LINES

New revenue sources may also come from adding new services to the practice. Some services are more innovative, creative, and contemporary than others, and not all of these suggested services lines may be right for every medical group. Whatever additional service lines you add, it is imperative that they fit into your organization's mission, vision, and overall strategy. Otherwise, the foundation for the medical practice itself may be negatively affected.

As with any new program, financial projections must be developed and reviewed in conjunction with the basic objectives of the service line.

Complementary and Alternative Medicine

In 1993, consumers in the United States spent approximately $11 billion on complementary and alternative medicine (CAM) treatments. Spending has increased dramatically and is expected to continue to increase for the foreseeable future. While many payers are expanding coverage to include some CAM services, a significant portion of the dollars spent remains out-of-pocket. Figure 12-2 illustrates the increase in spending by consumers in the U.S. alone.

A study conducted in 1998 reported that patients visited CAM providers three times as often as their primary care physicians. In addition, more often than not, these patients did not inform their primary care physician about these CAM treatments or all of the products they were using.

Given both the potential revenue and quality of care issues relating to existing patients who seek CAM services, many medical groups have been inspired to begin incorporating these services into their practices. This includes services such as acupuncture, biofeedback, chiropractic,

Figure 12-2
Out-of-Pocket Dollars Spent on CAM Services[3] (in Billions)

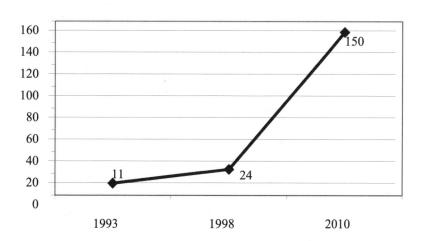

massage therapy, naturopathy, nutritional counseling, podiatry, and yoga/body works. Another common and often essential CAM service to offer is a natural products dispensary selling herbs, nutritional supplements, books, or other self-care materials.[4] Patients want these services and are now seeking them elsewhere. By incorporating the services within the medical practice, patients for the first time would have a single organization to look to for their health care needs.

While many physicians do not believe in CAM services, they all have patients who are taking herbs, vitamins, and other over-the-counter products, which may or may not be beneficial. In addition, many of these patients may actually be taking these over-the-counter items in the wrong dosages or in the wrong combination. It is interesting that Medical Economics Company, the publisher of the Physicians' Desk Reference for Pharmaceuticals (PDR), is now publishing similar information about herbs and vitamins.

[3] James Orlikoff. Health Forum Summit 2000: Mastering 21st Century Healthcare Governance Issues, May 2000.
[4] Villanueva, Karen. Building a Successful Integrative Medicine Center. *Hooper, Lundy, Bookman, Inc. Healthcare Law Monitor*. Special Report Issue, August 16, 1999.

Over-the-Counter Products

Many practices are also beginning to sell a variety of over-the-counter products, which could range from skin care products (creams, sunscreen, products containing Retin-A®, and soaps) to aromatherapy or relaxation products (candles, bath salts, soaps, or oils). These over-the-counter products appear to do especially well when associated with a specific specialty such as dermatology. Expanding on this concept, a dermatology practice may want to consider selling sunscreen products, sun protective clothing, and other similar products.

If the practice were interested in creating or expanding CAM services, it might want to focus more on products such as vitamins, herbs, aromatherapy items, books, or self-care materials. The group could create an Internet area for patients' use with a recommended list of Websites dealing with questions and answers about alternative therapies and CAM-type services.

There is one point, however, that is critical in evaluating these services. If a medical group is interested in providing over-the-counter products to patients, the organization will want to have agreement from the physician staff. Disagreements will only contribute to internal strife and mixed messages to patients. Patients are looking for answers and a unified approach to their medical care. If the physicians don't believe in the concept or products, patients will very quickly pick that up.

When first beginning to sell these products, the medical group should test market the items. Just as commercial business do, start small and see what sells and keep track of what items patients are asking for. Also, create formal inventory controls.

Ancillary Services

Although fraud and abuse may be of concern, ancillary services are still a key focus area for increasing physician revenue. Some of the typical ancillaries include mammograms, ultrasounds, laboratory work, treadmill tests, and bone density scans. When analyzing these ancillary services as potential new service lines, future changes in reimbursement should be considered. For example, if reimbursement for specific, high-volume tests is anticipated to decline in the near future, how will that affect the financial viability of continuing to provide that service? The probability of reimbursement changes should be incorporated into all financial projections.

Sources of ancillary revenue may also come from a different focus of a related service. For example, the Marshfield Clinic several years ago discovered the need for quality pathology services to support veterinary medicine. With minimal capital investment, the Marshfield Clinic has become one of the leading laboratories in the country for veterinary medicine, with tissue-reading facilities in Detroit, Michigan and Marshfield, Wisconsin. The major challenge was to train medical transcriptionists to become familiar with the hundreds of different species with which veterinary medicine deals.

OFFERING CONTRACT SERVICES FOR CORPORATE CLIENTS

Many medical groups have turned to the corporate world to increase their revenue. They market to larger corporations, county and governmental agencies, and small companies for business. Services may include performing executive physicals, immunizations for overseas travel, vaccinations for certain exposures (e.g., hepatitis B series, annual influenza shots), hearing tests, pre-placement examinations, and work injury treatment.

Another possible source of corporate revenue may relate to providing medical director services for nursing homes or technical consulting services for medically related Internet companies.

Other services that could be marketed to individual and corporate clients could include:

- Back-to-school physicals
- Sports physicals
- Wellness and screening services
- Mammography
- Hearing tests
- EKGs
- Blood pressure monitoring
- Diabetes and blood sugar testing
- Cholesterol screening
- Glaucoma testing
- Bone density testing
- PSA testing
- Patient education
- Smoking
- Diet
- Exercise prescriptions.

CONDUCTING CLINICAL RESEARCH

Many medical groups and single-physician practices have targeted clinical research studies as a way to increase revenue. Pharmaceutical companies are continually looking for physicians to participate in clinical trials required for either pre- or post-FDA review and approval of new treatments. These firms are willing to cover 100 percent of physician office fees, including ancillary services, to pay the physician a research investigator stipend, and to pay the participating patient a stipend at certain milestones in the study. With the cost of drug research so high, pharmaceutical companies are eager to work with physicians who can deliver patients for their research studies. Without these patients, a drug will never move through the FDA approval process. With 17-year patents tied to the original date of filing as compared to the date approved by the FDA, the pressure is on to move this process along as quickly as possible. Every day of delay can mean $1.3 million of lost revenue.[5]

Patients are also making an impact on the clinical trials industry. "Patients want not only safety and effectiveness from the drugs they use, but also therapeutic outcomes that improve the quality of their life....Some patients—AIDS and HIV-positive patients are a prime example—(they) see participation in a clinical trial as a 'right' to promising treatment and demandaccess."[6]

Currently, most clinical research studies appear to be focusing on allergy and immunology, cardiology, endocrinology (diabetes), neurology, cancer, rheumatology (arthritis), infectious diseases, and HIV. However, the number of candidate drugs and treatments is expected to increase dramatically during the next decade. This prediction is based on the human genome project and the new genome mapping that will occur. Some estimates predict that every new genome map will yield 10 to 20 new potential drugs.[7]

This indicates that the demand for investigators will continue to increase. It will be critical for pharmaceutical companies to be creative in helping to design better, more efficient trials and to support physicians in recruiting study participants.[8]

[5] ARCP White Paper on Future Trends: Their Impact on Sponsors, CROs and Investigative Sites. Washington, D.C., 1997.
[6] ACRP White Paper on Future Trends: Part I; ACRP. *The Monitor,* Spring 1999.
[7] CenterWatch. Pharmacogenomics: Reshaping the Future of Drug Development. May 1, 1998:1.
[8] ACRP White Paper on Future Trends: Part I; ACRP. *The Monitor,* Spring 1999.

The qualifications necessary for a physician to participate in clinical research trials are met relatively easily. Physicians should be board-certified in the particular specialty on which the clinical trial is focused, have the ability to attract the required number of qualified patients to enroll in the study within a specified time period, and either employ or contract with a qualified clinical research coordinator to help facilitate the clinical trial process. Companies who supply clinical coordinators are also good sources for clinical research studies based on their many industry contacts. In major cities today, it is not uncommon to hear radio ads seeking patients for enrollment in a clinical research trial. The Internet has also become an effective tool to recruit clinical study patients.

EXPLORING OTHER NEW REVENUE SOURCES

Historically, many primary care physicians have referred procedures to specialists rather than perform the procedures themselves. It may make sense for a medical group to review its history and volume of procedure referrals to determine if a medical group physician can provide these services and if doing so makes sense. It is also not uncommon to find medical group physicians referring to physicians outside their group even though well qualified physicians are members of the practice.

Some medical groups are very strong in their practice management expertise, billing and collections processes, and managed care contracting. If there are strengths in these areas, why not consider selling these services to other providers? Doing so would provide a new source of revenue while helping offset fixed overhead expenses.

During a performance improvement process, the focus is often on expense management and reduction. While important, it is just as important to identify opportunities to increase the medical practice's revenue base. In many medical practices today, expenses have been reduced as much as possible, but there is still insufficient revenue to support the required infrastructure.

The opportunities are there. It is a matter of trying to identify them, developing plans to support the ideas, and then executing those plans that are approved. Every idea has the potential to translate into additional net revenue.

13

CHOOSING THE RIGHT INFORMATION SYSTEMS

Timothy C. Henderson, MBA
Richard Friedland, MBA, FHIMSS

The use of more advanced computer technology is rapidly becoming one of the cornerstone management tools for medical group practices. While physician practices have traditionally not been at the forefront of using computers to support their business, times are finally beginning to change. Physicians for the first time are thinking beyond billing, accounts receivable management, and scheduling applications. The use of the Internet for accessing medical information, e-mails to and from patients, electronic medical records, and continuing medication lists are all now on their way to being incorporated into operations.

There are several barriers to moving this process forward: one is when medical group employees and more senior physicians within the practice do not embrace change, while another relates to a medical group's current economic status. With so many medical groups struggling to maintain current physician compensation levels, they tend to postpone funding for technology initiatives.

Compounding this situation is the fact that the poor financial performance experienced by many medical groups is due in many ways to the lack of investment in computer systems and in knowledgeable staff. This is evidenced by poor performance in the area of accounts receivable management and the failure to fully utilize the computer applications purchased. This situation applies to both small and large medical groups. Small medical practices tend to have issues with accounts receivable management and patient collections. Larger medical groups tend to have the same issues with patient collections and with capitation payments in managed care.

Medical group practices are complex business operations. While the public now perceives that minimal paperwork is associated with patient billing and the collection process, the reality is that this process is still very paper-intensive and is a major challenge to manage because of the great variations in the type of data that must be submitted to payers. Managing the business successfully requires a high level of employee sophistication and technology to support the process.

Beyond the billing and collection process, medical groups also have a critical need to be able to extract data regarding the financial performance of payer contracts. Besides knowing monthly collections, the medical group needs to know if it is making money on its managed care and preferred provider organization (PPO) contracts. These two questions become extremely important in trying to improve a medical group's economic performance.

Medical practices are filled with data, but capturing it in a useful way can be difficult. The key is to capture and transform the data into useful information. This process may be complex, but it will enable the organization to accomplish its business goals.

When the organization is facing financial and operational challenges, it is essential to perform an in-depth examination of the current information system (IS) applications. Even in difficult financial times, it is imperative to think about solving key problems with the existing information systems or what is expected of a replacement. Without first going through an organized evaluation process, switching information systems is doomed to failure. Regardless of the quality or price of the new system versus the old, unless underlying problems are addressed, the dysfunction will not be solved simply by changing the IS capabilities.

Making the decision to select and purchase a new information system is an expensive, time-consuming undertaking and should be approached in an organized manner. The medical group should perform a comprehensive needs assessment to determine information requirements, identify management reporting formats and content, and help set information system priorities. Once the need for a new system has been validated, the information gathered creates the foundation for developing the request for information and proposal.

The next step involves following an accepted methodology to analyze vendor responses and evaluate the alternative systems. This is critical to ensuring that system features will meet the organization's needs and expectations. Contract negotiations with the identified vendors of choice represent the final phase of the selection process.

Because of the broad scope and complexity of tasks, line managers seldom have the time or expertise to run such a project and are tempted to take shortcuts or eliminate critical steps. The potential pitfalls are enormous and may well jeopardize a successful process. The organization may want to consider involving an outside consultant who is experienced in performing information systems assessments and system selection projects.

The process described in this chapter is illustrated in Figure 13-1.

Figure 13-1
Critical Steps for Effective Information System Development

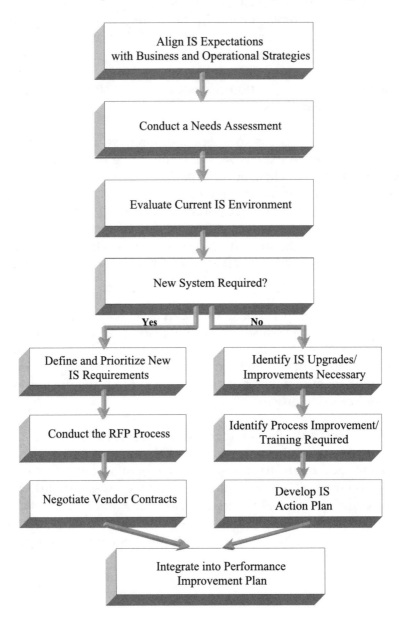

ALIGN IS EXPECTATIONS WITH BUSINESS AND OPERATIONAL STRATEGIES

Aligning expectations for an information system with the medical group's business and operational strategies involves two key steps:

1. Build assumptions based on strategic business plans
2. Appoint an information systems steering or management committee.

Build Assumptions Based on Strategic Business Plans

Assumptions must be based on current strategic business plans that specifically outline the parameters of the business medical group's goals and direction. That is, the organization's immediate needs must be distinguished from those that are more long-term in nature. Given the limited resources of most medical groups, the organization cannot afford any missteps in pursuing information systems solutions. Therefore, the operational and strategic priorities addressed in the strategic business plan must drive the information systems plans and selection process. Figure 13-2 illustrates the impact that various strategic goals have on information system profiles.

Appoint an Information Systems Steering or Management Committee

An organizational structure should be put in place to review and approve the various steps and tasks to be performed. Normally, a steering or selection committee is created that is responsible for reviewing system evaluations and assumptions, assisting in setting priorities, monitoring progress in achieving IS goals, and overseeing any new IS selection process. The steering committee, depending upon practice size, normally consists of four to six members appointed from across user constituencies.

Figure 13-2

IS Alignment Planning Matrix

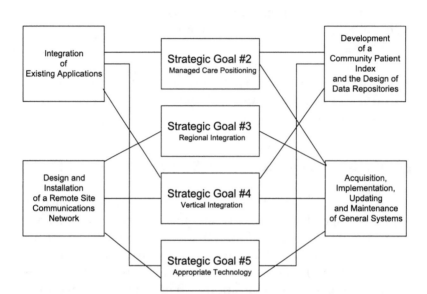

CONDUCT A USER NEEDS ASSESSMENT

Perhaps the most frequent reason for the failure of any automation attempt is that the selected systems did not fit the user's requirements. Thus, the most important step in any IS activity is to gather enough information to define those requirements through interaction with potential system users and stakeholders by questionnaire, interview, and discussion. A needs analysis report is then generated to document current systems, identify weaknesses and unsatisfactory performance, document wants and desires of users, and establish access to and level of information detail. Depending on the size of the organization and the scope of the IS needs review, this can be performed internally or by an outside, objective third party. This process is typically performed in the following sequence:

1. Interview users by functional area
2. Develop a systems requirements matrix
3. Specify management reporting format and content.

Interview Users by Functional Area

The most important source of IS needs is the potential system user. Interviewing the user helps identify critical information needs and translates them into functional requirements. The needs assessment process also provides for user education and the "molding" of expectations. This step may have been accomplished in the process of assessing the organization's performance (Chapter 2) but nevertheless may need focused attention to ensure that specific needs are addressed.

User input can be obtained most efficiently by using functional requirements checklists or user interviews. The functional requirements checklist is a list in which users rank system capabilities according to importance (i.e., required, desired, and not needed). A combination of interview and checklist methods is recommended. Table 13-1 identifies the various functional areas to review.

A needs assessment normally proceeds as follows:

- Meet with users to determine the level of user satisfaction with current applications.
- Identify user issues and problems.
- Identify user concerns.
- Educate users on how a different system can help them.

Table 13-1
Functional Areas to Review
Work Breakdown Structure

Information Systems	Patient Billing	Patient Care	Ancillary Services	Administration
Operations	Registration	Appointment Scheduling	Laboratory	Top Executives
Networks & Connectivity	Data Entry	Records Management	X-ray	Finance
Communications	Coding	Transcription	Pharmacy	Accounting
Training & Education	Third-Party Billing	Nursing	Physical Therapy	Human Resources
PC Support	Patient Accounting	Order Entry	Occupational Medicine	Materials Management
User Support/ Help Desk	Credit & Collections	Results Reporting	Optical Dispensing	Facilities Management
	Managed Care	Electronic Patient Record	Behavioral Health	

Develop a System Requirements Matrix

Once the checklists have been drafted and the interviews conducted, a system requirements matrix must be developed that combines all "critical," "necessary," and "hoped for" functional requirements; restates them in a logical order; and ranks them for later system evaluation use. The steering committee will review and approve this matrix prior to moving ahead.

Specify Management Reporting Format and Content

Insufficient management reporting is often a critical system weakness. Identifying the group's management reporting needs begins with the organization's business objectives. Because these objectives define what the group wants to accomplish, management report content must reflect measurements of how well they are meeting the objectives. Management reports become performance index tools that regularly inform staff whether group objectives are being achieved (see Chapter 4).

There appears to be a vast range of creative possibilities in developing reporting format and content, and no single set provides optimal organizational performance measurement. The most frequently encountered reports seem to fall into several broad categories:

- Reports for physician compensation calculations (encounter summary, RVU analysis, revenue and production, practice analysis)
- Financial reports to manage revenue (aged trial balance, payment analysis, service code analysis, credit balances, payer mix, collection ratio, and days in accounts receivable)
- Patient management reports to access provider utilization (daily patient appointment lists, face sheets, no-show lists, appointment availability, resource schedules, and utilization)
- Managed care reports to monitor risk contracts (eligibility/enrollment census, referral analysis, authorization status, claims activity, stop loss limit checking, and service limit checking).

EVALUATE THE CURRENT IS ENVIRONMENT

The information systems environment must be evaluated to determine its level of dysfunction. Once you have identified and assessed user information needs, you can conduct an evaluation of the data processing organization and systems by using the same types of survey tools. Lack of user training or incomplete understanding of existing system capabilities may be the issues to address rather than acquiring a new system. Further, the system may have been designed around ineffective processes. If procedures are improved through the performance improvement effort, problems attributed to IS functionality may be eliminated.

Develop an Inventory of Current Systems

To set information systems initiatives appropriately, it is necessary to identify all systems and modules currently in place on mainframe, mid-range, and personal computers located throughout the organization. The interfaces connecting these systems also must be identified to determine connector and linkage requirements.

Develop a High-Level Information Systems Problem List

To identify current system problems, a high-level evaluation should include a review of the following items:

- Capacity remaining on the current/existing hardware
- Percentage of system capacity during peak usage
- System downtime
- Types of service and level of support provided by IS and current system vendor
- Status of projects currently in process
- User knowledge of the existing system
- Capability of the IS staff to install a new system.

Table 13-2 shows a sample problem diagnosis grid to highlight current system issues.

Review Benchmarks

Benchmarks are another way to determine dysfunction in information systems. Benchmarks are measures that indicate system or task functioning and are frequently used to evaluate performance levels. Some commonly used benchmarks might be average terminal response time, downtime, system capacity, days in accounts receivable, and staffing ratios.

Table 13-2
Problem Diagnosis Grid

Symptoms	Problems					
	Insufficient Hardware Capacity or Upgradability	Limited Software Capabilities	Poor Software Design	Lack of Integrated Systems	Poor Vendor Support	Inadequate Data Communications
Poor Response Time	X		X			x
Frequent System Downtime	X		X		X	X
Manually Intensive Operations	X	X		X		
Management Lacks Critical Information		X	X	X		
IS Always Fighting "Fires"	X	X	X	X	X	X

Medical practices can use various sources of benchmarking data. As noted in Chapter 4, the Medical Group Management Association publishes an annual cost report and medical group benchmarks by type and size of organization, including IS costs. Jewson Enterprises (Redwood City, California) publishes a physician-office medical information systems report that lists information systems benchmarks and medical group trends.

Examine Help Desk Call Logs

Help desk logs can assist in determining the extent and frequency of user problems with application systems and information technology infrastructure. Review of these logs also presents an opportunity to assess training and education effectiveness.

Prioritize Information Systems Initiatives

Setting information systems priorities involves three primary qualifiers: (1) how well is IS performing as a business-within-a-business in terms of strategy, process, personnel, and technology; (2) where is IS not supporting general business processes; and (3) how much is being invested, and is it being spent in the right areas?

IS priorities are then established based on management's priorities, costs, and the need for certain sequencing. For example, to satisfy the physician's highest priority of an online problem list, an interface engine and a data repository that will require at least two years to install will be necessary. Consequently, other priorities that can be met more readily can be scheduled for more immediate implementation.

DETERMINE WHETHER A NEW SYSTEM IS REQUIRED

The required system functionality as indicated by the system requirements matrix should also be compared with the capabilities of the current system. This can be done by the appropriate department managers and reviewed by the steering committee. The capabilities of the present system can be evaluated with a format similar to the information needs checklists in Table 13-3 by using columns to indicate the degree the current system meets user needs.

Table 13-3

REQUEST FOR PROPOSAL
PRACTICE MANAGEMENT SYSTEM

Automated Functions:
1 = Satisfactory
2 = Unsatisfactory
3 = Does Not Provide

Functions	Required	Desired	N/A	1	2	3	Comments
1.00 GENERAL FUNCTIONALITY							
1.01 Provide security to all employee information.							
1.02 Direct screen-to-screen navigation without returning to menu.							
1.03 Real-time interfaces between applications and systems.							
1.04 User friendly and easy to navigate around system.							
1.05 Provides both menu selection and expert mode.							
1.06 Provides multiple methods to search and select data.							
1.07 Supports quick movement between applications without losing data.							
1.08 Provides easy-to-use reporting tools, depending upon user skill level.							
1.09 Option to print immediately or queue print jobs for non—peak-time printing.							
1.10 Cross-functional area reporting.							
1.11 Support forward and backward scrolling on all multi-page screens.							
1.12 Word processing available on system.							
1.13 Context-sensitive help function.							
1.14 Table lookup during data entry without loss of previously entered data.							
1.15 Remote system access.							
1.16 User control of display sequence (e.g., reverse chronological order).							

Table 13-3 (cont'd)

REQUEST FOR PROPOSAL
PRACTICE MANAGEMENT SYSTEM

Automated Functions:
1 = Satisfactory
2 = Unsatisfactory
3 = Does Not Provide

Functions	Required	Desired	N/A	1	2	3	Comments
1.17 Produce and manage correspondence.							
1.18 Provides translations of correspondence in other languages.							
1.19 Common notepad/comments across applications.							
1.20 Provides work management support ("to do" lists, tickler files).							
1.21 Uses colors or highlights to key data entry process.							
1.22 User-definable/controlled security that supports tight access/update controls.							
1.23 Provides audit trail of all updates made to system.							
1.24 Limits amount of paper required through increased use of system.							
1.25 User-definable screens.							
1.26 Supports electronic mail.							

After reviewing the prioritized information needs, the practice should evaluate possible alternatives to the purchase of a new system. Alternatives might include:

- Negotiating with the current software vendor to provide enhancements
- Supplementing the existing hardware with other computer systems
- Activating applications or modules purchased but not utilized
- Adding applications obtained from other sources to the existing hardware
- Modifying or customizing existing systems
- Introducing process improvement initiatives
- Conducting in-service training and user skill-building.

These solutions must be embodied in a detailed action plan that can be incorporated into the performance improvement plan, which should also guide the steering committee's work. If, however, the system is totally dysfunctional, as evidenced by a low scoring on the systems requirements matrix, or if the vendor has withdrawn support of the system or will not make appropriate modifications to raise the score to an acceptable level, a new selection process must begin.

DETERMINE AND PRIORITIZE NEW IS REQUIRE-MENTS

Once the decision has been made to implement a new information system, the medical group needs to define and prioritize the new system requirements.

Define Information Systems Selection Criteria

Identifying IS selection criteria will permit a systematic comparison of the ability of various vendors to meet the organization's needs. Selection criteria should include:

- The vendor's ability to meet the functional requirements
- The vendor's ability and experience interfacing to the practice's existing systems
- System costs: capital, installation, and ongoing maintenance
- Service capabilities
- How the new system will be supported once the installation is complete
- The vendor's response time for resolving hardware and software problems
- The vendor's ability to install the system
- References to indicate how well a system functions.

Prioritize Selection Criteria

Once the selection criteria are identified, they should be weighted according to the level of importance determined by the steering committee. For example, selection criteria must be determined realistically. It is unlikely that any vendor will meet all the users' information needs. If the selection criteria are accurately defined, an appropriate comparison can be made between vendors.

Identify Potential Vendors Using a Request for Information (RFI) Process

Using the functional requirements document and selection criteria, the practice can begin to narrow the vendor list to those vendors who appear to meet its standards. Potential vendors initially can be defined as those who are marketing systems that address the functional needs of the practice.

The first source of potential vendor identification might be MGMA, which lists recommended system vendors. If additional vendors are required, trade publications, vendor marketing data, and industry system publications can be consulted. For example, the magazine *Computers in Healthcare* publishes vendor systems evaluations each year. With today's available Web-based systems, application service providers (ASPs) should also be evaluated and compared to traditional hardware solutions. *Healthcare Informatics* published monthly, regularly publishes lists of ASPs applicable to medical providers.

A request for information (RFI) allows a practice to investigate marketed systems to focus on available system functions and further narrow the list of vendors who will receive the complete request for proposal (RFP). Functional requirements are included with the RFI but are not as specific or complete as those submitted with the RFP. An RFI usually requests:

- General company information
- Company philosophy
- Financial status
- Dollars allocated to research and development
- Hardware platforms
- Experience with practices of similar size
- Client references.

The general format of the RFI includes:

- Introduction
- Practice profile
- Response guidelines
- Vendor profile
- General vendor information
- General system information (type of hardware, operating system, etc.)
- System implementation and training (conditions and duration)
- Functional requirements (developed from information needs)
- System cost summary (hardware, software, implementation, training, and miscellaneous costs).

An RFI should be sent to no more than eight or ten vendors. Allow at least 30 days for vendor responses. Once the responses have been received, the analysis of the functional capabilities of each vendor and their projected costs can begin.

CONDUCT THE RFP PROCESS

Conducting the RFP process involves preparing the RFP and evaluating vendor proposals (see Figure 13-3).

Figure 13-3. RFP Process

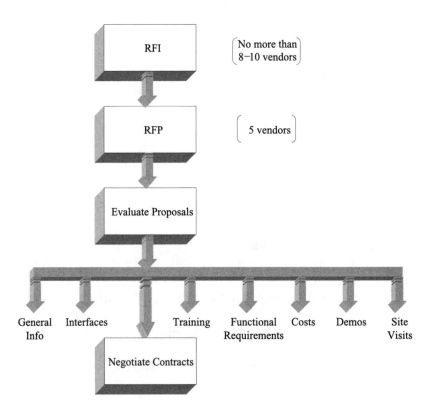

Prepare the Request For Proposal

The purpose of the request for proposal (RFP) is to select two vendor finalists with whom the group will negotiate for the purchase of a system. Vendor responses to the RFP should be considered as part of the final contract and should be so stated as a condition of response to the RFP. The RFP should be concise and all-inclusive to reduce misunderstandings and misconceptions before final contract negotiations. It should be sent to no more than five vendors, as analysis of vendor responses is comprehensive and very time-consuming. Vendors should be allowed at least four to five weeks to respond to the RFP.

The RFP usually includes the following sections, with requests for more detail than the RFI:

- Introduction
- Group profile
- Key number summary
- Response guidelines
- Hardware requirements
- Functional requirements
- Contractual items
- Site preparation requirements and responsibilities
- Interfaces
- Availability and costs of technical and user training
- General vendor information.
- References
- Personnel requirements to operate and maintain the system properly.

Evaluate Vendor Proposals

Evaluating vendor proposals is one of the most critical parts of the system selection process. This section of the chapter discusses the methodology required to analyze and compare vendor proposals.

Evaluate General Vendor Information

The location of the nearest vendor's support office is important, especially when different time zones are considered. Proposal evaluation should address how the vendor will provide support on a continuous basis.

Although the size of a vendor's organization is not indicative of quality software applications or support, size does play an important role in the number of personnel available to install and support the system. The maturity of an application, the number of years it has been marketed, and the number of installations indicate the staying power of the application. Systems that have been marketed for less than a year may not yet be stable and should be viewed with caution.

The vendor's financial stability is extremely important. Organizations experiencing financial difficulty often have system support, research and development, and system implementation problems. The financial evaluation of the vendor should involve an in-depth review of financial statements, and any notes should be scrutinized. Particularly today, with many new application software start-up companies, it is important to have confidence in the vendor's likelihood of long-term survival.

The evaluation of vendor user groups should focus on the strength of the user organization, frequency of meetings, and the availability of a local user group. A strong user group benefits all system users and provides a positive commentary on vendor customer service efforts.

Vendor references are a critical part of the system evaluation. A list of specific questions should be compiled based on the group's priorities and the vendor's response to the functional requirements section of the RFP.

Evaluate Proposed Interfaces

As the industry moves toward open system architecture, interfaces become more important. Each vendor's ability to interface with existing systems should be evaluated on the following issues:

- Cost of the interface
- Direction of interfaces
- Type of interface downtime experience
- Length of interface downtime
- Method for protecting data integrity during the interface process
- Number of similar interfaces installed
- Type of data to be transferred for each interface
- Degree of security, backup, and disaster recovery provided.

Evaluate Training Programs

During the evaluation of the vendor's training methodologies, it is important to consider how each will affect the group:

- Training provided on-site can benefit the group because employees are not required to travel. However, interruptions during training sessions must be kept to a minimum.
- Off-site training is usually more expensive because of transportation and lodging costs.
- Vendors often prefer to train at vendor training sites and often employ the "train the trainer" methodology.

If the vendor's training costs are included with the software pricing, they should be broken out so they can be analyzed on a competitive basis with other vendors.

Evaluate Response to Functional Requirements

The functional capabilities are the most important aspect of any application software. Functional requirements are developed from user input, the functional requirements checklist, and the systems requirements matrix. Functional requirements are submitted to vendors to ascertain and compare system functionality.

Vendors should indicate items currently under development and those that will be priced separately upon completion. Enhancements planned for functions that are currently operational should also be identified and explained. Vendors should be informed that any questions left unanswered will be assumed not to be included in the system.

Evaluating the vendor's ability to meet the functional requirements as specified in the RFP is critical to vendor selection and can be conducted using a weighted analysis, which is based on the number of vendor responses multiplied by the importance of the functional requirement to the group. See Table 13-4 for a sample evaluation form.

Evaluate Vendor Costs

Each portion of the application system should be priced separately whenever possible. The vendor should include all of the medical group's costs. All hardware, software, and related items should be identified as to one-time costs that occur at purchase time only; one-time extended costs that occur once at purchase time for multiple items; recurring costs; replacement costs; and other costs, such as cost per hour for holiday support, travel and expenses, and cost for overtime hours.

Table 13-4

CAPABILITIES ASSESSMENT FORM
PRACTICE MANAGEMENT SYSTEM

Need Description	Weighted Value	Level of Importance			Comments
		Required	Desired	Not Needed	
APPOINTMENT SCHEDULING					
1.00 Provide online access to the following information during appointment scheduling:					
1.01 Patient demographic					
1.02 Patient insurance					
1.03 Patient PCP					
1.04 Responsible party					
1.05 Member eligibility					
1.06 Patient/member benefit and copayment					
1.07 Patient financial (outstanding balance)					
1.08 Patient/member issues (problems/complaints)					
1.09 Referral inquiry (for appointments requiring referrals)					
2.00 Allow the lookup of a patient by the following information:					
2.01 Patient identification number					
2.02 Unique member ID number					
2.03 Patient name					
2.04 Patient name by Soundex					
2.05 Patient AKA (Also Known As)					
2.06 Patient Social Security number					
2.07 Patient medical record number					
2.08 Wildcard search on patient name					
2.09 HMO/Insurance member number					
3.00 Allow the user to select the appropriate patient from a list of patients meeting selection criteria and automatically transfer necessary information to the appointment scheduling screen					
4.00 If a patient has not previously been registered, allow the user to query eligibility files for the indicated information					
4.01 Allow automatic transfer of eligibility data to registration files during this query					
4.02 Allow automatic transfer of eligibility data to appointment scheduling screens during this inquiry					
5.00 For members/patients not included in either registration or eligibility databases, allow assignment of a temporary patient ID number					
5.01 Allow subsequent transfer of temporary information to a permanent patient number once one has been established					
6.00 Support collection of "presenting complaint" at time of appointment scheduling					
7.00 Provide for the scheduling of equipment, rooms or other resources as well as the scheduling of physicians (resource scheduling)					
8.00 Support user definition of appointment types					
8.01 Provide online lists of appointment types for selection by the user					
8.02 Provide online lists of appointment times by provider for selection by the user					
9.00 Maintain previous months' schedules for inquiry					

Table 13-4 (Cont'd)

CAPABILITIES ASSESSMENT FORM
PRACTICE MANAGEMENT SYSTEM

	Need Description	Weighted Value	Level of Importance			Comments
			Required	Desired	Not Needed	
10.00	Provide a warning to the operator during appointment scheduling for:					
10.01	Copayment requirements					
10.02	Late payment/balance owing status					
10.03	Special handling classification and/or notes					
10.04	Potential COB eligibility					
10.05	Patient HMO/Insurance carrier ineligibility					
10.06	Patient primary care site different from service site being scheduled					
10.07	Patient PCP different from provider being scheduled					
10.08	Provider being scheduled not within patient's assigned PCP team/call group					
10.09	Authorization required for the scheduled service					
11.00	Allow for the development of standard provider/resource schedules or templates					
11.01	Individualize templates by provider/resource					
11.02	Allow one physician to have more than one template					
11.03	Restrict schedules to allow certain types of appointments to be scheduled only at specified times of the day or week (e.g., no physical exams on Mondays, treadmills on Tuesdays)					
11.04	Customize standard schedules to accommodate physician meetings, vacations, and special events					
11.05	Designate "hold" times on the schedule					
12.00	Allow the classification of appointment types (e.g., physical exams, follow-up visits, immunization) with:					
12.01	Varying corresponding time increments required for each					
12.02	Personnel and resources required for each					
12.03	Prerequisites for each (e.g., blood drawn plus two days to receive result prior to physician appointment)					
12.04	Varying classifications by physician					
13.00	Allow defining treatment components associated with a specific exam or test (e.g., executive physical = blood test + chest x-ray + treadmill + audiometric exam + physician's exam)					
13.01	Schedule the specific exam with the system automatically including all individual components and required resources					
14.00	Support sequential appointment scheduling whereby all services required for a patient can be input and the system will automatically search for and schedule all necessary resources in sequential time blocks					
15.00	Support dependent scheduling whereby a service with specific user-defined prerequisites cannot be scheduled unless those prerequisites are met					
16.00	Allow for the scheduling of overlapping appointments					
16.01	Allow or disallow by physician or resource					

Because medical groups have finite resources, costs are an important focal point for system evaluation. Cost categories should be identified and compared, such as:

- Hardware costs
- Associated support and maintenance costs
- Software costs
- Interface costs
- Installation/implementation costs
- Training costs
- Other costs.

Because the analysis process is cumbersome and time-consuming, it is tempting to perform only a cursory analysis. It is important that the analysis be an objective review and that a complete analysis be performed to make realistic comparisons. Time spent in this phase can save countless dollars as well as minimize unmet expectations.

Request System Demonstrations

System demonstrations provide an opportunity for users and management staff to participate in a visual evaluation of system presentation, features, and functions. Vendors should be asked to follow a standard presentation format and include scripted scenarios indicative of high-priority medical group concerns. At the end of each demonstration, attendees should complete evaluations.

Conduct Site Visits

When properly structured, site visits provide information leading to the final ranking of vendors. Site visits are not junkets but are rather a means for the medical group to identify critical elements to include in the final contract. Be sure to select sites that are using the current versions of the software you are considering.

Weight and Evaluate Criteria

The steering committee should evaluate the vendor proposals in a carefully thought-out and objective manner. Using grids and quantitative evaluation tools will help keep the evaluation objective.

Response criteria can be weighted according to the importance of various categories to the overall ability of the system to meet the group's requirements: functional requirements, costs, service capabilities, training and installation, and references. A sample is shown in Table 13-5.

Table 13-5. Sample Response Criteria

Priority	Scores			
	Vendor 1	Vendor 2	Vendor 3	Vendor 4
1. Functional Requirements				
2. Cost				
3. References				
4. Service Capabilities				
5. Training/Installation				
6. Demos				

The purpose of this evaluation will be to force the steering committee to select no more than two vendors with which to enter negotiations.

NEGOTIATE VENDOR CONTRACTS

The purpose of vendor contract negotiations is to help the medical group obtain the best price for specific performance standards. Standard vendor contracts are usually one-sided and should be avoided.

Validate Vendor Proposals

Original vendor proposals are rarely accurate. Vendors can be expected to modify up to 15 percent of their claims regarding system capabilities. The purpose of contract negotiations is to force the vendor to state clearly what the system will do. Negotiations for performance guarantees (hardware, software, and interfaces), price guarantees, appropriate payment schedules and terms, installation guarantees, post-installation guarantees, and price reductions are conducted during this time.

Settle All Hardware Configurations and Operational Issues

Before starting negotiations, each vendor should validate all their RFP responses, addendums, and other communications. All materials provided by the vendor, including their system's ability to meet the stated functional requirements, should become part of the contract. At this point, vendors should reverify that their configurations and prices are correct and include all exhibits, attachments, and appendices that will be made part of the final contract.

Conduct Simultaneous Negotiations with the Top Two Finalists

Once site visits have been completed, the two top vendors should be identified. Simultaneous negotiations should take place with these finalists for the following reasons:

- Vendors are more likely to grant concessions if another vendor is involved in the final negotiations. Medical groups have lost a significant advantage by negotiating with only their first-choice vendor.
- When two vendors are involved, each believes they have a 50-50 chance of winning the contract, which is preferable to a one-in-four chance if four vendors are involved.
- If problems arise with the medical group's vendor of choice, the other vendor presents a viable alternative without having to start the selection process over.

Follow a Logical Sequence When Negotiating the Contract

All hardware configurations and operational issues should be settled before contract negotiations. Negotiations can then focus on costs, contract language, protective covenants, and other items. Contract negotiation time is reduced if the salesperson is bypassed at this stage and negotiations are conducted with a vendor representative who is empowered to sign a final contract.

- Review all license and support (maintenance) agreements of each vendor.
- Provide suggested language changes where the vendor is unclear or the clause only protects the vendor. (For example, most vendor support agreements describe when payment is due and what happens if the customer fails to pay, but state nothing about the vendor failing to perform his obligations or the rights of the customer to escrow, withhold, or decrease payments for vendor non-performance.)
- Recommend additional clauses/paragraphs for business

and technical items discussed during the analysis and site visit phases but not addressed in the agreements.

- Send the recommended changes to the vendor for review before negotiations.
- Meet with each vendor and negotiate all agreements.
- Review all negotiated clauses and amendments to ensure they are correct.
- Analyze business offerings in detail. Analyze implementation costs, staff, organization, hardware, and facility requirements.
- Integrate technical, business, and contractual issues and prepare a briefing package for the steering committee.
- Meet with the steering committee to evaluate business, technical, and contractual offerings.
- Prepare and perform, in conjunction with the steering committee members, presentations to the medical group.

Contract Negotiating Guidelines

- Signing the standard vendor contract will result in a one-sided arrangement with all protection for the vendor and little, if any, for the medical group.
- Most vendors attempt to maximize up-front payments. These payments should be minimized and tied to various stages of implementation. The majority should be paid after system acceptance.
- Key definitions should be included in the contract, especially when hardware is tied to configurations. For example, the definition of a "test" should be included when negotiating for a laboratory system because some vendors consider original orders while others consider the number of results. A clear definition of "system acceptance" should be included in the contract.
- Involving lawyers in the process will increase costs and the length of negotiations. Lawyers look at a contract for protection in court. A contract should be written to keep the parties from ever going to court.

Information systems are the cornerstone of successful medical group operations. Without a functional system, operations are unlikely to be maximized. Today's options for Internet-based applications and innovative technology solutions both excite and challenge medical group administrators. The possibilities are virtually endless in applying technology to enhance operational efficiency and effectiveness. However, the pursuit of technology can also lead to the medical practice's downfall if it is improperly prioritized and analyzed. Information systems are management *tools*, not an end in themselves. By carefully linking operational and strategic goals to technology capabilities, the medical practice is most likely to achieve its desired performance objectives.

When a medical group faces challenges, a successful improvement process depends on understanding the needs of users and aligning information systems initiatives with business goals. This process is not a casual commitment and has the potential to disrupt every aspect of the business for a significant period of time. However, if done properly, it becomes the basis of an information system strategic plan and lays the foundation for future growth. Ongoing success will depend on periodically repeating the process and continually realigning information systems efforts.

14

KEY SUCCESS FACTORS AND CASE STUDIES

Michael R. Manansala, MPH, MBA
Mary J. Witt, MSW

The need to improve performance is usually driven by the medical group's profitability—or lack of profitability. There are differences, however, in how health care organizations view such activities. An independent medical group that has a limited cash position to meet payroll for the next few months will require an aggressive performance improvement strategy that is time-dependent. A hospital-owned medical group might determine that changes are necessary if it perceives a significant increase in monthly losses per physician. Such a situation may not be critically time-dependent. In other cases, a hospital-owned group may wish to reduce financial losses per physician from $100,000 to $15,000 in 18 to 24 months. If the objective is to reduce the loss within six months, the performance improvement initiatives will be very different.

In all situations the remedy may be similar, but the intensity and the aggressiveness of the action plan will be quite different. Therefore, understanding organizational objectives is critical in attempting to implement an effective performance improvement plan.

his chapter concludes with two case studies that illustrate how a medical group can respond to various challenges and implement a performance improvement initiative.

ORGANIZATIONAL CHALLENGES

The development of a performance improvement action plan does not guarantee that implementation will be successful. Successful execution requires the right initiatives using appropriate management tools. Even more important, however, is how the implementation process is executed. A perfect business plan to improve performance will fail if the leadership of the organization does not have physician buy-in. Other challenges that impact success include failure to build momentum for change, inability to enact significant changes on multiple fronts at once to maintain morale, failure to address departmental turf issues, and failure to balance financial goals and the quality of care provided. Thus, it is imperative that individuals with prior experience in improving performance—along with a thorough understanding of organizational dynamics—lead the improvement effort.

Some of the most critical challenges are discussed below.

Physician Buy-In and Support

Many articles have been written about the importance of including the key physicians in the decision-making process. This was also highlighted in Chapter 2. Clearly this process is extremely important; however, in many cases, physicians tend to react with utmost skepticism and distrust of management efforts to improve performance, especially if the same management team that was viewed as creating the problems is implementing the changes. This factor is probably the most significant factor affecting how many physicians will stay in the organization through the effort.

To counter such distrust and skepticism, often changes in management must occur. The new leadership must have the authority to make the changes necessary to show improvement in the financial and operational performance of the medical group. Early success in performance improvement, such as increased collection of co-pays, improvement in billing and collections, and higher contract rates, will slowly dispel the physicians' skepticism.

Multiple Changes

Often multiple changes must occur simultaneously for performance to improve. These often include modification of physician compensation and incentives, management restructuring, staff reduction, expense control, and information system modifications. Unfortunately, the timing of these changes may not lend itself to an orderly process and this often creates difficulties for the organization. For example, physicians may not want their compensation changed until the billing and collection performance is improved or the contracting department has negotiated higher rates from insurance companies. In hospital-based practices, physicians may want continued subsidies from the hospital until the problems are fixed. Unfortunately, physicians in such medical groups tend to assign all the blame for poor performance on management and fail to examine their own behavior or responsibilities for the problem, such as low productivity.

The leadership must have a solid assessment of the organization's ability to change on multiple fronts. During this critical period, it will be necessary to drive the organization to its limits. Excellent execution by managers, staff, physicians, and other ancillary support departments will be required to effect improvement. Obviously this change process requires the support and commitment of the entire organization. Recognizing achievements as they occur is an important part of maintaining motivation.

Momentum for Change

The improvement process requires time to implement. The uncertainty and need for change might create initial resistance. Building momentum for change is very difficult, requiring everyone to understand their role in the process and what benefits they will derive from such efforts. Moreover, the direction and objectives must be delineated clearly so that performance can be measured and rewarded with appropriate incentives. Many performance improvement initiatives fail to account for the time required to make this culture shift, and timelines for completion are not met. As a result, execution becomes bogged down and objectives are not achieved.

Performance Standards

Successful efforts to improve performance require specific objectives. One tool that improves the chance of success is organizational benchmarking, as discussed in Chapter 4. For example, performance standards for the check-out person to achieve 98 percent collection of co-pays and patient financial responsibility provide individual staff with a goal and a direction. The resulting impact on group morale and passion to perform at higher levels can be surprising. If the achievement of such objectives is coupled with rewards and recognition through bonus or performance reviews, this will provide the catalyst that further improves the performance of the medical group. The improvement also builds the momentum for change in other areas, and additional enhancements in performance are gained.

CASE STUDIES

The following case studies offer real-world examples that describe the process of improving performance in a dynamic way.

CASE STUDY 1: WEST MEDICAL GROUP

The West Medical Group, composed of 19 physicians and four mid-level providers, had a family practice department that was losing $59,000 per physician. The department had six family practitioners. The group was approximately 50 percent capitated and was one of three major groups in the community, one of which was a large multi-specialty group. There were also many solo practices and small partnerships in the community. The West Group had been the first group in the community to accept capitation and was owned by one of the two hospitals in town.

Assessment, Benchmarking, and Setting Targets

By using national benchmarks, the practice was able to identify specific reasons for the loss. As a starting point, the practice compared one critical revenue indicator and one expense variable for the department to national benchmarks: visits per physician FTE and expense categories as a percentage of net revenue. Variances were identified and analyzed.

In this case, as can be seen from Figure 14-1, physician productivity was below MGMA medians and significantly below Camden benchmarks.[1,2]

---

[1] The Camden Group benchmarks are based on its proprietary database on medical group practices.

[2] Medical Group Management Association. *Physician Compensation and Production Survey: 1999 Report Based on 1998 Data*. Englewood, CO, 1999.

Figure 14-1: Family Practice Visits/Physician

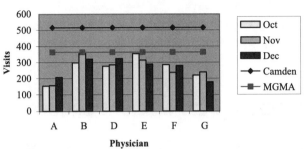

Source: The Camden Group

MGMA 1999 Physician Compensation and Production Survey Based on 1998 Data.

Data used with permission from the Medical Group Management Association, 104 Inverness Terrace East, Englewood, Colorado 8012-5306; 303-799-1111. www.mgma.com. Copyright 1999.

Table 14-1 indicates that, while expense categories varied slightly from The Camden Group's benchmarks, these variances were explained by the fact that revenue for the department was lower than expected.

The variance analysis also included identification of any unique characteristics of the practice that could affect the department's ability to achieve the benchmark. This medical group differed from many medical groups because it had been acquired by a hospital two years before. Also, they had not addressed their compensation formula for several years. While their compensation formula rewarded productivity, it was measured by charges, which the hospital had significantly raised twice since the purchase without changing the compensation formula. Thus, productivity as measured by visits actually dropped after purchase, while individual compensation rose.

To ensure that all significant variables were identified, The Camden Group performed a more detailed analysis of revenue. Charge per visit was also reviewed to determine whether coding or service mix, as well as visit volume, could be affecting revenue. In this case, the variance in charge per visit was minor for all but one physician. For that physician, further analysis of

Table 14-1. Family Practice
Annual Income/Expense Statement

Expense	Current Year $	Percent Net Revenue	Camden Benchmark $	Percent Net Revenue	Variance
Charges	1,683,000		$2,031,324		
Contractual Allowances	420,750		507,831		
Net Revenue	1,262,250		1,523,493		
OPERATING EXPENSES					
Staff Salaries/Benefits	492,278	39.0%	583,498	38.3%	-1%
Medical Supplies	56,801	4.5%	61,549	4.0%	0%
Lab/Radiology	37,868	3.0%	50,275	3.3%	0%
Facility	103,631	8.2%	102,074	6.7%	-2%
Malpractice	14,516	1.2%	22,852	1.5%	0%
Professional Services	11,486	0.9%	10,664	0.7%	-1%
Marketing	5,049	0.4%	6,094	0.4%	0%
General & Administrative	38,246	3.0%	42,048	2.8%	0%
Total Operating Expenses	759,875	60.2%	879,055	57.7%	-3%
PRACTICE GROSS INCOME	502,376	39.8%	644,438	42.3%	3%
PROVIDER EXPENSES					
Mid-level Salaries/Benefits	0		0		
Physician Salaries/Benefits	840,000		626,438		
CME	18,000		18,000		
Total Provider Expenses	858,000		644,438		
NET INCOME (LOSS) BEFORE COPORATE ALLOCATIONS	(355,625)		0		
CORPORATE ALLOCATIONS	0		0		
NET INCOME	(355,625)		0		

Source: The Camden Group

his office visit coding revealed that he consistently under-coded his office visits.

The physicians initially rejected the finding that the deficit was caused by low volume rather than high expenses. They resented being told that they needed to see more patients because they felt that they were working as hard as they could. They no longer remembered when they had been seeing more patients or how they had done it. That changed, however, when visit data from the year before purchase was reviewed and demonstrated that visit volume had dropped for all family physicians after purchase. Also, after they had carefully reviewed their expenses, they realized that they could not accomplish improved financial performance by cutting expenses.

Once they agreed that the problem was volume, they had to establish a new visit target or benchmark. While they agreed that the ultimate goal was to move visit volumes to MGMA medians, they decided to phase in this target over 12 months so that physicians and staff could experience short-term success as well as long-term achievement. The initial target was set at visit volume for the year prior to purchase, and it was to be achieved within six months.

Taking Action

As noted, behavior does not change just because benchmarks or targets are identified. Performance improvement only occurs if an action plan to achieve the targets is created and implemented. The action plan often is more complex than initially anticipated because of the interdependency of critical variables related to the target. In this case, while the initial focus was on restructuring the compensation plan, it quickly became apparent that changing the compensation formula alone would not achieve the desired performance because so many other factors affected the department's ability to see more patients. Therefore, the action plan also had to address work flow processes, scheduling, and patient flow. In other words, the entire process for seeing patients had to be re-engineered.

Given the magnitude of change required, the implementation process had to be interactive to succeed. The key constituencies (staff, physicians, and management) needed to provide input and receive feedback throughout the process to ensure that all issues affecting visit volume were resolved. To gain buy-in by all parties, they were involved in problem identification, understanding variances, finalizing practice-specific benchmarks, and developing the action plan. In addition, they received ongoing feedback on the findings of Phase I and II

(Assessment and Planning) and implementation progress in Phase III (Implementation). By involving everyone in the process, the vision, goals, and objectives were understood by all. They also possessed a sense of ownership and control, which people need when they are asked to change their behavior.

The action plan contained five major initiatives:

- Revision of the compensation plan
- Improvement in telephone response
- Increased access through schedule modification
- Better management of patient flow
- Provision of physician training in coding and techniques to increase productivity.

Accomplishments

1. The compensation plan formula was revised. The plan continued to be based on productivity. However, productivity was now defined as a combination of visits and relative value units (RVUs) as defined by Medicare RBRVS. To be eligible for any bonus, physicians needed to have, at a minimum, the number of visits required to cover their base salary plus benefits. The formula used to determine the visit base was:
   > *Base family practice salary + benefits*
   > Net revenue per visit
   > Bonuses were to be awarded based on RVUs over the minimum threshold (visit base converted into RVUs) and group citizenship.
2. The phone answering process was modified. An automated attendant was implemented to direct calls more efficiently. Staff performance standards for on-hold times (45 seconds) and call abandonment rates (3 percent) were established. These will be monitored regularly and reported to staff. Staff will receive small rewards (such as movie

tickets or certificates for fast food restaurants) for consistently exceeding standards.

3. The clinic work day had shortened almost an hour for each of the family practitioners since purchase. Therefore, the first change in the schedule was to add the hour back onto the schedule. In addition, the number of visit categories was reduced to make scheduling simpler. Also, physicians met with their nurses each morning to identify slots for same-day appointments.

4. The entire patient visit was analyzed. Time studies tracked each segment of the visit. Staff and physicians then brainstormed ways to improve the efficiency of the visit. Both the check-in and check-out processes were revised to decrease waiting time through reallocation of staff.

5. Coding training improved the coding of the outlier physician, and his charge per visit increased by 8 percent because his coding now reflected his documentation. Physicians also developed new time management and interview skills, enabling them to increase their visit volume.

As a result of these changes, the practice quickly achieved a 17 percent increase in visit volume, as can be seen from Figure 14-2. The compensation plan provided the appropriate incentive to increase productivity. However, this success could not have been achieved without re-engineering the work flow processes relating to phone calls, scheduling, and patient flow.

Figure 14-2
Visits/Physician Comparison Before and After New Compensation
Plan

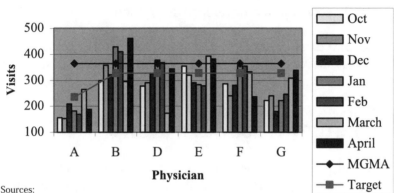

Sources:
(1) The Camden Group
(2) *MGMA 1999 Physician Compensation and Production Survey Based on 1998 Data*

Data used with permission from the Medical Group Management Association, 104 Inverness Terrace East, Englewood, Colorado 80112-5306; 303-799-1111. www.mgma.com. Copyright 1999.

Ongoing Challenges

Although there has been considerable success, a number of challenges still face the medical group:

- The first of these is to maintain the visit momentum of the physicians. All the family practitioners are in their fifties, and they have little desire to maintain the extended work schedule that was implemented. At this point, because they do not want to accept lower compensation, they are continuing to see more patients than in the past. However, it is unlikely that volume will increase much more.
- The group faces aggressive competition from two other medical groups in town, one of which is owned by the other hospital in town. Both competitors are aggressively recruiting primary care physicians.
- Because the group is located in a small town, it is difficult to find trained staff. Also, several new employers with higher salary scales have made it difficult to recruit new employees with the group's current pay ranges.

• There still is not a common vision within the family practice department, let alone the group. In fact, the group almost split apart before the purchase by the hospital, and little cohesion has developed since then.

Despite these challenges, the group has been encouraged by its initial success. Therefore, it has been energized to begin to tackle the competition as well as define a common vision.

CASE STUDY 2: SOUTHERN SYSTEM

A health system in the southern United States was faced with the need to improve the financial and operational performance of its owned medical groups as well as the MSO that provides the management services to the group and other independent medical groups in the community. The system lost about $10 million on the group, which is composed of approximately 90 physicians in 28 sites. The MSO was under-performing, with a financial deficit of $200,000 per year. Fifty percent of the MSO was owned by the system and 50 percent by independent medical groups. The initial assessment showed the hospital-owned group was struggling because of numerous factors, including:

• Production below MGMA medians
• Guaranteed salaries
• Runaway medical costs in a capitated model
• Below-market reimbursement from contracts
• Duplicative and inefficient management
• High MSO costs
• Poor performance in billing and collection
• Poor physician-management relationships.

The competitive landscape included three major hospitals, all of which were struggling with the deficits incurred in their affiliated or owned practices. Managed care had about 35-45 percent penetration, and hospital financial performance was trending downward throughout the community. The pressure to cut losses was therefore paramount for all providers in the community. Given the necessary changes in the medical groups, there was a sense of uneasiness among all the physicians.

Action Plan

The Camden Group was brought in to assess the situation and recommended a strategic redirection of the MSO and the hospital-owned medical group. The external physicians were unable to provide the capital necessary to support the MSO. As a result, the system took over the operations of the MSO and purchased the partnership interest of the independent medical groups. However, they continue to purchase services from the MSO at market rates.
Additional recommendations included:

- Changing physician compensation through an 80/20 compensation model (20 percent at risk)
- Eliminating the messenger model contracting approach and utilizing the system leverage for joint hospital/ physician contracting
- Renegotiating contracts for higher rates and converting capitated contracts to fee-for-service
- Educating and improving coding and compliance performance of the physicians
- Restructuring and instituting effective billing and collection policies and procedures to improve performance
- Establishing financial and operational benchmarks throughout the organization
- Consolidating physicians sites from 28 to 19
- Recruiting and hiring a new executive director to manage the MSO and the hospital-owned group. (The Camden Group served as interim manager while this process was underway.)

Accomplishments

Cost reduction efforts achieved savings of $2.5 million. Performance improvement in billing and collection added $3.0 million in revenues, and contracts increased an average of 5-8 percent. Physician losses were thus reduced from $110,000 to $20,000 per physician in about 24 months. Physician productivity increased by $2 million. About eight physicians left the community, and two joined the competition.

A FINAL WORD

The performance improvement process, if successful, is a very rewarding experience for any organization. It changes the culture and mindset of the organization, and those who remain remember the lessons learned. Management must view performance improvement as a continuous process to remain viable and successful in the future. The tools and processes identified in this book provide the foundation to raise the level of performance of any medical group.

Proactive planning is critical to remaining successful. It also is important that groups remember the lessons learned from past missteps. Given increased tumultuousness in the industry, reversion to financial deterioration is common. Therefore, management must continue to plan, monitor, and proactively identify opportunities for performance improvement. Physicians, management, and staff must continue to perform above expectations to prevent the potential erosion of the group's medical, operational, and financial performance.

ACRONYMS

A/R	accounts receivable
AAAHC	Accreditation Association for Ambulatory Health Care
ACMPE	American College of Medical Practice Executives
ACPE	American College of Physician Executives
AMA	American Medical Association
AMGA	American Medical Group Association
ASP	application service provider
ATB	aged trial balance
BBA	Balanced Budget Act
BBRA	Balanced Budget Refinement Act
CAM	complementary alternative medicine
CBO	central billing office
CME	continuing medical education
CPT	current procedural terminology
DIGMA	drop-in group medical appointment
DOFR	division of financial responsibility
E&M	evaluation and management
EOB	explanation of benefits
EOMB	explanation of Medicare benefits
ER	emergency room
FDA	Food and Drug Administration
FFS	fee for service
FTE	full-time equivalent
GHAA	Group Health Association of America
HCFA	Health Care Financing Administration
HEDIS	Health Plan Employer Data Information Set
HIC	health insurance claim
HIPAA	Health Insurance Portability and Accountability Act

HMO	health maintenance organization
IDS	integrated delivery system
IOM	Institute of Medicine
IPA	independent practice association
IS	information systems
JCAHO	Joint Commission of the Accreditation of Healthcare Organizations
LPN	licensed practical nurse
LVN	licensed vocational nurse
MGMA	Medical Group Management Association
MPH	master's of public health
MSO	management services organization
OIG	Office of the Inspector General
OON	out of network
OSHA	Occupational Safety and Health Administration
PCP	primary care physician
PHO	physician-hospital organization
PMPM	per member per month
POS	point of service
PPM	physician practice management
PPO	preferred provider organization
QI	quality improvement
QIC	quality improvement committee
R/A	remittance advice
RBRVS	resource-based relative value system
RFI	request for information
RFP	request for proposal
RN	registered nurse
RVU	relative value unit
SCHIP	State Children's Health Insurance Program
SNF	skilled nursing facility
SWOT	strengths, weaknesses, opportunities, and threats
TPA	third party administrator
UM	utilization management

ABOUT THE AUTHORS

Karen E. Dunbar, MBA, MHS

Ms. Dunbar, a senior consultant with The Camden Group, has seven years of health care experience with medical groups, hospitals, and integrated delivery systems. Her work includes management service organization (MSO) development and turnaround, practice management, primary care group practice development, physician compensation formulas, hospital/physician relationships, and management service agreement valuations.

Prior to joining The Camden Group, Ms. Dunbar served as Acting Operational Director of SMH Physician Services, Inc., which owned and operated practices for 28 physicians. She earned her bachelor's degree from Illinois Wesleyan University and her master's degree in business administration and health care management from the University of Florida.

Richard Friedland, MBA, FHIMSS

Mr. Friedland has worked in health care for more than 30 years and currently serves as Vice President, Hospital Services, with MC Informatics. He has performed or managed hospital operational analyses in more than 100 institutions ranging in size from 50 to more than 1,200 beds. Mr. Friedland has developed long-range strategic information systems plans for meeting current and future needs of health care institutions. He has developed formal requests for proposal for health care data processing systems and analyzed vendor proposals. Because of his knowledge of hospital operations and information technology, he frequently serves as liaison between users and providers of information technology services.

Mr. Friedland is the former chairman of the HIMSS Fellows Advisory Council and former president of the Colorado Association of Hospital Information Systems. He is a frequent speaker on the topics of planning for strategic information systems and system selection.

Michael E. Harris, MS

Mr. Harris is a manager with The Camden Group with over 24 years of health care experience in the areas of managed care contracting, IPA, MSO and medical group operations, and management of ancillary services. Mr. Harris is responsible for analyzing current contract terminology and rates and contract negotiation with payers. He recently contributed to a manual on health care capitation and risk contracting.

Prior to joining The Camden Group, Mr. Harris was president of Pacific EyeNet, Inc., which is based in Los Angeles County. His responsibilities included contract negotiations for physician services and claims administration, as well as managing the day-to-day operations of the MSO. He has also held positions with La Vida Medical Group and IPA; Axminster Medical Group; United Health Plan, The Watts Health Foundation; and Hawthorne Community Medical Group, Inc., Maxicare, all based in Los Angeles County. Mr. Harris received his bachelor's degree from the University of Southern California and his master's degree in health care management from California State University, Los Angeles.

Timothy C. Henderson, MBA

Mr. Henderson has more than 30 years of health care industry experience that includes both large and small group practice administration, information systems management, and needs analysis and information technology planning.

Mr. Henderson currently serves as Vice President, Physician Services Division, with MC Informatics, a management and technical consulting firm that specializes in the health care market. He performs business analyses and information technology assessment studies for integrated health care delivery system clients across the country. In addition, he works with the firm's sales executives and consulting staff to promote a better understanding of the complexities of current group practice environments.

Laura P. Jacobs, MPH

Ms. Jacobs is a vice president with The Camden Group and has been with the firm since 1990. She directs the firm's medical group advisory services, having more than 20 years of experience in the areas of medical group development and management, physician compensation, strategic planning, marketing, managed care strategy, and physician-hospital relationships.

Ms. Jacobs has assisted provider organizations throughout the country with physician compensation redesign, operational assessment and performance improvement, merger facilitation, and strategic planning. She has led operational improvement and turnaround engagements for MSOs and medical groups; facilitated the development of integrated medical groups, guiding the design of their structure, governance, strategy, compensation, and operations; and directed the strategic and business planning process for hospitals, medical groups, IPAs, and integrated delivery systems. Ms. Jacobs is a frequent speaker for hospital and physician groups regarding current trends in medical practice, managed care, physician compensation, and operational improvement and benchmarking.

Prior to joining The Camden Group, Ms. Jacobs held administrative positions at St. Vincent Medical Center and Orthopedic Hospital in Los Angeles and Presbyterian Intercommunity Hospital in Whittier, California. She received her bachelor's degree from Stanford University and her master's in health services management from the University of California, Berkeley.

Michael R. Manansala, MPH, MBA

Mr. Manansala is a manager with The Camden Group with more than 17 years of experience in hospital administration and medical group management. He has a proven track record in turnaround management of troubled IPA and medical group organizations. Mr. Manansala also has extensive experience in the formation of foundation and MSO models. In addition, he has consulted with medical groups regarding practice management issues, strategic market positioning, practice valuations, medical group sales and acquisitions, managed care contracting, and provider network development. Mr. Manansala has published numerous articles on current health care issues and is a contributing author for the *Capitation & Risk Contracting Manual.*

Prior to joining The Camden Group, Mr. Manansala was the CEO of a multi-site family practice group. He also was CEO of a successful IPA and Director of Business Development and Planning for a major hospital in Southern California. In addition, he has been an adjunct faculty member in several graduate health care management programs. Mr. Manansala received his bachelor's degree from the University of California, San Francisco, a master's degree in public health from the University of Hawaii, and a master's degree in business administration with a concentration in finance from the University of Hawaii, Graduate School of Business.

Benjamin S. Snyder, MPA, FACMPE

Mr. Snyder, a vice president with The Camden Group, has more than 25 years experience in the field of medical group management and ambulatory care. He has been the senior executive for large multi-specialty medical groups in a variety of settings, including those affiliated with integrated delivery systems. He has extensive experience with medical groups in highly competitive managed care markets.

Mr. Snyder has led medical groups through strategic planning as well as operational improvement. He has been responsible for daily operations for medical groups with over 200 physicians and provided technical advisory services to IPAs with over 5,000 physicians. He has facilitated the development of integrated medical groups, guiding the design of their structure, governance, business strategy, information systems, and operations.

Mr. Snyder has held executive positions at Camino Medical Group, Inc., UniHealth/UniMed Management Services Division, Sharp HealthCare, San Jose Medical Clinic, Inc., and Scripps Clinic and Research Foundation. He received his bachelor's degree from the University of Maryland and his master's in public administration with a certificate in health services administration from the University of Southern California. He is a fellow, American College of Medical Practice Executives; past president, California Medical Group Management Association (MGMA); president-elect, Western Section MGMA; treasurer, Accreditation Association for Ambulatory Health Care (AAAHC); member, Environment of Care Committee, American Medical Association's AMAP Program; and voting member, California Medical Association's Council on Legislation.

Steve T. Valentine, MPA

Mr. Valentine is president of The Camden Group. With more than 20 years of health care consulting experience, he has considerable expertise in the areas of strategic planning, business transactions, mergers, hospital-medical group relationships, and integrated delivery networks. Mr. Valentine is a nationally recognized author and speaker on health care issues and is frequently quoted in *Modern Healthcare, California Medicine, Managed Care Outlook,* and many other publications. He recently co-authored a workbook on capitation.

Mr. Valentine has directed numerous strategic planning and merger engagements for a wide variety of health care organizations. He is a recognized facilitator of hospital board, medical staff, and management retreats. He is on the editorial board of two publications and a panel expert on another. He also sits on the board and chairs the Audit Committee of HealthCare Partners, LTD, an MSO managing 300,000 patients. Prior to joining The Camden Group, he was an engagement executive in Ernst & Young's Health Care Business Advisory Group. His previous experience included senior positions at Amherst Associates, Pacific Health Resources, National Medical Enterprises, and the Health Systems Agency of San Diego and Imperial Counties. He was selected by *California Medicine* as one of California's top 100 most influential people, and he also received a similar honor for Los Angeles County from the *Los Angeles Business Journal.*

Mr. Valentine received his bachelor's degree from San Diego State University and his master's in health services administration from the University of Southern California. He also completed the Ernst & Young Management program with the Kellogg School at Northwestern University.

Robin G. Wallace

Ms. Wallace is a medical practice operations senior consultant for The Camden Group and has been with the firm since 1993. She has 15 years of hands-on experience in medical practice management and consulting. She specializes in guiding physicians and other health care professionals in the areas of practice development and administration, strategic planning, accounts receivable management, developing compliance programs, computer selection and conversion, managed care and IPA contract negotiation, and staffing allocation and development.

As part of The Camden Group's turnaround team, Ms. Wallace has assisted several health care organizations and MSO clients around the country increase their revenue by restructuring their business office operations. She is skilled at developing and implementing enhanced work flow systems, training tools, and staffing protocols that fortify the organization's infrastructure and effectively resolve performance issues. She has coordinated and provided oversight management for the creation and successful start-up of a community-based faculty practice for a major academic medical center. Her interest and knowledge of changing legislation affecting health care reimbursement has made her the Camden Group's resident reimbursement specialist on compliance issues. She has also been a speaker for the American College of Staff Development on Improving Business Office Operations.

Prior to joining The Camden Group, Ms. Wallace was the president of Wallace & Wallace Enterprises, an independent consulting firm she founded and operated for five years. She has also held administrative positions in various physician practices and medical groups. She completed her undergraduate education in nursing and also earned a certification in Health Care Administration from UCLA's School of Public Health.

Mary J. Witt, MSW

Mary Witt, a manager with The Camden Group, has over 20 years of health care experience. She has held management positions in hospitals, health systems, and MSOs. She has extensive experience in medical group, MSO, and PHO development, as well as operational improvement, practice management, managed care, health care marketing, and physician recruitment.

Ms. Witt is a frequent speaker and author on medical group and managed care issues as well as physician-hospital relationships. She speaks regularly for MGMA, the American College of Medical Practice Administration, and Voluntary Hospitals of America. She has written for the MGMA's journal and is quoted in health care magazines and newsletters, including *Modern Physician.*

As a consultant for The Camden Group, Ms. Witt facilitates medical group formation, MSO and PHO development, and managed care strategic planning. She leads medical group operational improvement and turnaround projects for integrated delivery systems throughout the country. In addition, she has led the development of medical groups and MSOs in Arizona, California, and New York. She also has assisted hospitals and medical groups in the development of their managed care strategies.

Prior to joining The Camden Group, she was vice president of operations for PrimeCare Health Services, a management services organization serving over 100 physicians through the provision of practice management and managed care services. She has also served as the director of physician services and manager of contracting for a multi-hospital system. She has a master's degree from the University of Michigan and a bachelor's degree from the University of Wisconsin, Milwaukee, where she graduated with honors.

INDEX